Teaching Heritage Language Learners: Voices from the Classroom

Co-Editors:
John B. Webb, Ed.D.
Princeton University

Barbara L. Miller, Ph.D.
Hunter College High School,
City University of New York

ACTFL Series 2000

Cover Art—*True Energy*, Oil on Wood Relief:
Carlo Thertus
(See Artist's Statement, page 255)

Production Editor:
Margaret Madigan

Book Design:
Leslie Hendrix

ISBN 0-9705798-0-2

Manufactured in the United States of America.

00 01 02 03 04 05 06 07 08 09 0 9 8 7 6 5 4 3 2 1

❋ Dedication ❋

To my nonna, Caterina Taddonio, who taught me the music of her Italian language, but not its words, because, she said, "You are an American." And to my dearest friend and husband, Terence Robert Anderson, whose love of language is a daily inspiration and support to me in my work and in my life.

Barbara L. Miller

To my mom, Mary Webb (née Semrov), whose heritage Slovenian language and culture, even in the rural hamlet of Roseboom, in upstate New York where we lived, was a subtle but wonderful and powerful part of the person I grew up to be.

John B. Webb

Contents ✄

Chapter 3. Goals and Fundamental Beliefs

PART TWO: VOICES FROM THE CLASSROOM

Chapter 4. Standards and Heritage Language Learners

Chapter 5. Inside the Heritage Language Classroom

Preface

Paul García ✳
ACTFL President

*Don't wait for strangers to remind you of your duty, you have a
conscience and a spirit for that. All the good you do must come from
your own initiative.*

Popol Vuh

P oets, and even sitcom characters, use the images of past or imagined events
to evoke feelings and convey thoughts. Recall the popular phrase of a
recent television character, Sophia, from the show, *Golden Girls.* "Picture
this," she would begin; thereupon, she would speak of her youth in Sicily or of an
immigrant experience in the United States. "Picture this ... " is a strategy we often
use to communicate both formally or informally. As language teachers, we use
first-person experiences to call classroom and cultural behaviors to students'
minds. Further, we now illustrate the implementation of our national standards
through the convention of scenarios that are real or imagined learning events.

Allow me to place a scenario backward in time, to the not-too-distant past of
Williamsburg, Brooklyn, a section where Italian, then Jewish, and after them
Puerto Rican families encountered an explicitly multicultural New York City.
Immigrants shopped on Broadway, on Flushing Avenue, and on Moore Street, in

stores and shops and markets where the owner-vendors did not "look" like them or speak with the same-accented English (if they spoke any English at all). Inter-generational and intragenerational conversations often took place, if a language barrier existed, between the monolingual customer utilizing the bilingual servic-es of a child to speak to the (oftentimes bilingual English and yet another lan-guage) vendor, or the monolingual customer speaking with a bilingual stock-room clerk acting as the third party intermediary for the vendor.

Such a scenario of the 1940s and 1950s requires only slight modification and "linguistic-ethnic-geographical" re-placement to be representative elsewhere in our country of a common immigrant history. Economically, such streets as those of Brooklyn existed —and exist—nationwide. Miami, Boston, coastal and rural areas, California, Hawaii, all have or had their ethnic and linguistic equiva-lent of "Little Havana." Newcomers to the United States naturally found them-selves as consumers or patrons of businesses whose "sales employees" did not speak as they did. As time went by, their neighbors, who often found work "in the back," began to assume posts "at the front." Economics literally changed the business face of neighborhoods. The customers' purchasing power, that is, determined the vernacular of the market streets, just as, years later, Senator Paul Simon commented when he relayed the remarks of a Japanese businessman, that the language of business is the language of the customer. Linguistic and cultural responsiveness is the thread that connects our ethnic past to our present and fore-seeable future, not through the modern technologies and advertising slogans such as "*Yo quiero* Taco Bell" and "*Fahrvergnugen*." That thread of heritage lan-guages and cultures and American economic adaptability also have influenced the educational scene, and, as we contemplate the new millennium with a view to demographic projections and geopolitical instability, they may again do so.

What role will the heritage language students play in the next twenty or so years in K-16 education, and in second (and no longer foreign) language edu-cation in particular? What can we learn from present practices and experimen-tal perspectives that will enhance the preparedness and quality of language edu-cators? Which of today's students will assume our professional roles, and thus contribute to the cultural diversity of tomorrow's teacher corps?

The present volume is a response to these and related questions, some of language-specific value and interest, and others of a more general, albeit complex, socioeconomic pattern. The editors and authors are to be commended for mak-ing "the heritage language learner" a topic of wide-ranging scholarly discussion and passion. As the first Latino president of ACTFL, as a heritage speaker of

Spanish and Italian from post-World War II Williamsburg, and as a teacher of German by vocation, I read and endorse the chapters herein as acknowledgement and commemoration of all our histories and our future, of our common movement from the "stockroom" to the "salesroom." Our writers bring to language education a topic that remains a national education priority for the twenty-first century: now picture this …

Acknowledgments

The ACTFL Series 2000, *Teaching Heritage Language Learners: Voices from the Classroom*, is based on the work of the ACTFL/Hunter College Project entitled *Collaborative Teacher Education Program: A Model for Second Language Instruction for Inner City Schools*, which was supported by the Fund for the Improvement of Postsecondary Education (FIPSE), United States Department of Education, Grant Number P116B70602.

The Editors would like to acknowledge the outstanding work of the ACTFL/Hunter College FIPSE Project Development Team, who worked for three years, from September 1997 to June 2000, to conceptualize and design a program to prepare teachers of foreign languages, in this case Spanish, Haitian Créole, and French, to work more effectively with heritage language learners. This book is the product of their insights, their sensitivity, their dedication, their know-how, and their classroom experiences.

The Project Development Team

Emma Abreu-Perez
Louis B. Brandeis High School, New York City

Jocelyne Daniel
East Ramapo Central School District, Spring Valley, New York

Jamie B. Draper, Project Co-Director
American Council on the Teaching of Foreign Languages

John Figueroa
Roslyn High School, Roslyn, New York

Maria Giacone
New York City Board of Education

Juan Mendez
High School for Enterprise, Business and Technology, New York City

Jean Mirvil
PS 116, New York City

Migdalia Romero
Hunter College of the City University of New York

Diana Scalera
High School for Environmental Studies, New York City

Dora Villani
Ardsley High School, Ardsley, New York

John B. Webb, Project Co-Director
Princeton University

Administrative Assistants:
Lillian Buckley, *Hunter College*
June H. Hicks, *ACTFL*

Consultants to the Project:
Rozevel Jean-Baptiste, *New York City Board of Education*
Isias Lerner, *Graduate Center of the City University of New York*
Barbara L. Miller, *Hunter College High School, City University of New York*
Yves Raymond, *Erasmus Hall High School, New York City*
Ana Roca, *Florida International University, Miami, Florida*
Stephanie Soper, *Council on Basic Education, Washington, D.C.*
Guadalupe Valdés, *Stanford University*

The Editors also wish to thank Michael Nugent, the Project's FIPSE Grant Officer for his valuable input, and the members of the ACTFL Executive Council for their support in the publication of this volume.

Dora Villani and Adriana L. Macera-Aloia gratefully acknowledge the students whose work enriches this volume.

PART ONE

Heritage Language Learners

Introduction ❋

A young man, an eleven-year-old, walked into the Foreign Language Office of a suburban New York junior high school where he had been enrolled by his parents four weeks earlier, shortly after his arrival from Haiti. His father, a lawyer in Haiti, had come to the United States eight years before and, after working at several jobs, finally had been able to secure more permanent employment in a small factory in the area. Three years after her husband went to the United States, the young man's mother, a nurse in Port-au-Prince, joined her husband and began working as a cleaner on the night shift in an office building in the center of town. Both of them supplemented their incomes with various additional jobs, often working eighteen hours a day, seven days a week, with their only real break coming on Sunday afternoons when they attended services at a local church, where many from the Haitian community were members. Together, they purchased a small home in the neighborhood near the school and began the long process of saving money to bring their son to the United States.

The young man was only six years old when his mother left Haiti. He went to live with his aunt and her three children in a small village a few hours drive north of the capital city. He had very few memories of his father, who had gone to the United States when the boy was only three years old. The separation from his mother was even more painful because he feared that he might never see her again. Nevertheless, he adapted himself to life with his aunt and cousins and, even if reluctantly at first, came to feel at home. He went to the village school where he began to study French, a language that puzzled him at times. It was similar to Créole, which he spoke at home and everywhere but school, yet it was a very different language, as well. He was a curious, active child and quickly became very popular with his classmates and adored by his teachers for his good behavior, his smiling personality, and his impressive intellect. He had a good voice and loved to sing. He found an old guitar, which a neighbor repaired for him, and, when he wasn't memorizing his lessons for school the next day, he spent time teaching himself to play on the guitar songs he could sing. Over time, he became very good, and played for special events in school and for family and neighborhood gatherings. He was equally talented as a painter and, whenever his mother and father sent some money from New York, his aunt would buy him paints. Soon the walls of his aunt's home were decorated with a growing collection of his work. In short, he was a talented and well-liked boy, and his aunt grew to be as proud of him as she was of her own children. In spite of the fact that he missed his mother and looked forward to the time when he would board the plane for the big trip to New York to be with his parents, he carved out a fairly happy life in a place where he felt loved and fulfilled.

When the phone call finally came telling him that he would leave Haiti to go to New York, he was both thrilled and apprehensive. He knew his father only from the pictures that came in the letters. Even his recollection of his mother had faded somewhat with time, so that she too seemed a bit of a stranger. Then, there was the little sister who had been born about a year after his mother arrived in New York. He had been his parents' only child, and like all young children might, he wondered how, after all these years, he would fit into this new family picture.

The day he left for New York, his aunt prepared some of his favorite foods to eat on the plane—the familiar *cabrit* that he loved, even though it was made from his neighbor's goats, which he liked to play with, until they were butchered. There were rice and peas that his aunt made almost every day in her large *chaudière*. His aunt wept openly when she kissed him good-bye but, feeling quite the young man that afternoon, he fought back his tears until the plane cleared the runway and was rising out over the blue of the sea.

When he arrived in New York into the arms of his eager, happy parents, not the wary looks of his new sister, the chilly wind that was blowing as they left the International Arrivals Building at Kennedy Airport, or the mad rush of the traffic as they headed north out of New York City could dampen his enthusiasm for this new adventure. He had experienced these emotions before—the tugging sadness at being separated from a loved one, the strange feelings of unreality that accompany major life changes. He remembered feeling them the day his mother left, so they were no strangers to him this time around. He would tuck them away for now as he embraced a new life. After all, he could sing, he could play the guitar, he could draw and paint, he was a good student, and he had always been well liked by everyone who knew him.

His parents told him that he would start school right away, because they did not want him to get behind in his studies. "You can't do anything without schooling," they repeated many times during those first two days at home before they accompanied him to school for the formal enrollment.

That morning, he put on the new pants and shirt that had been purchased for this special occasion, and when he walked in the front door of the very large junior high school for the first time, he carried himself tall and proud, even though he was shaking inside. He already had experienced the jumbled sounds of English all around him when he and his parents had gone shopping for his new outfit. It seemed strange to hear people speaking a language that he was completely unable to understand, so it was a relief to get back home to the familiar and comforting rhythm of his native *Créole*. When he and his parents entered the school office where he would be registered, he quickly realized that no one spoke *Créole*. He also noticed his parents were uneasy in the school setting, in the presence of teachers, after all teachers are to be revered. Even his parents' English, after several years in the country, did not measure up. There were papers to sign; there was the question of his passport; his parents had to produce documents proving that they lived in the school district. The people at the school wanted to know whether he had ever been to school! A man who introduced himself as "the French teacher" came to translate. He spoke a kind of unfamiliar French. His accent was strange, so it was really difficult for the young man to understand what he was saying. The French teacher appeared nervous and ill at ease when he spoke, and it was clear from the questions that he kept asking that he did not understand what the new student had been saying much of the time. He did, however, seemed like a friendly man, not like the stern, formal teachers the boy had known in Haiti.

When the registration process was finally over, the English teacher came to the office to escort the young man to class. There were last-minute instructions about where to get the bus home at the end of the day, a daily program to follow, special clothes for some kind of sports class, money to buy lunch, and a host of other matters that were simply too complicated to deal with at the time. Then there were the handshakes and the good-byes for now, as he left his parents to go with the English teacher who couldn't speak either French or *Créole* and the nervous French teacher with whom it was so hard to communicate. Oh yes, there was that fear, that familiar ache of sadness that always accompanied these major changes in life.

The young man entered that first classroom where there were twenty-five other students, many from Haiti, many from other countries he had never heard of, all recent arrivals learning English for the first time. There were gestures, raised voices, books, and students doing all kinds of things. The teacher was friendly and smiling, she seemed as if she was trying to act just like the students. Her manner of teaching was so completely different from that of his Haitian teachers, she did not seem like a teacher at all. After English class, there was math, then science, then history, then gym. It all seemed like a great big, totally confusing whirl. Even after several days, there was no familiar pattern to what was going on. It was very troubling. School, a place that always had been a source of inspiration and success, now was frightening. Teachers, people whose behavior always had been predictable and who had always praised and rewarded him, now were puzzling and sometimes strangely mercurial behind their smiles and good humor. Under such conditions, self-confidence and self-worth can crumble.

Some of the other newly arrived students were nice. Certainly, they always stayed together, probably for lack of knowing what else to do. The ones from other countries stared and smiled at the Haitians; the Haitians stared and smiled back. The strangeness of the whole atmosphere was compounded by the fact that other Haitians, the ones who had been in the United States for a while, were not to be trusted. Some, rather than being sensitive to the plight of the newcomers, taunted them, laughed at them, and got them into trouble. The White American students tended to steer clear of the Haitian students, and some of the Black students were not very helpful, even though their skin was the same color as his. That was particularly disappointing. How would one ever find one's place in this setting? How was this young man ever to shine here as a person and as a student as he had in his school in Haiti?

The young man felt so very alone. He loved being with his parents once again after all these years. He was even starting to get used to his little sister. But his parents were away from home, working so many hours each day that he rarely saw them. Sometimes they left the house in the morning before he woke up, and he would have to get himself ready to go to school. It was not like in Haiti. On many days, there was no one at home when he came in after school, so he would spend many hours alone. It was not like in Haiti at all. So, in spite of his joy at being with his mother and father, he felt that gnawing pain in his chest that comes with homesickness when you miss someone or some place very much. At the same time, he knew down deep inside that he was not the only one who felt that way. The English teacher decorated the walls of her classroom with maps of all the countries that were represented in her class. Students gathered by those maps every day at the beginning of class, and every day, he was one of them. Like all the others, he found himself touching the spot on the map that had been home, the dot with a Haitian name next to it where his aunt and his cousins lived, that place where, unlike now, he had been somebody.

It was so easy to get into trouble in school, even for someone like this young man whose behavior had always been exemplary. In Haiti, he knew exactly what was expected of him. He had always been told that if one listens to what teachers say, if one is obedient and respectful, then one will do well. Therefore, he was always on his best behavior and hard working. He listened to what his teacher said, he memorized his lessons dutifully so that he could stand and perform perfect recitations in class, and he always lowered his eyes and his head when speaking to his teachers to show the kind of respect that they were supposed to receive. Here in this school, it seemed as if he was always doing something wrong, even though he watched the American students very carefully so he would be sure to know how to conduct himself correctly. It never seemed to work. Sometimes, it had the opposite effect and, the young man, rather than being praised for his good behavior found himself scolded in front his classmates. It even seemed to him that the teacher's scolding would get more severe whenever he lowered his eyes in a desperate attempt to show that he really did respect his teachers. The pride with which he walked into the school on that first day was turning into a feeling of shame.

At first, he thought that French class would be one time in the day when he could escape the difficulties he was experiencing elsewhere. He spoke *Créole* fluently (after all, it was his language), and he had studied French in school in Haiti, so he certainly could understand everything that was said to him in French. He could not read or write in *Créole*, but he had made a lot of progress in his ability to read, write, and speak in French. Of course, sometimes when he was speaking French and did not know the right word, he would quickly substitute a word in *Créole* and everyone would know what he meant. That is what everyone did in school. Yes, in French class, at least, he would be able to be more himself and show his teachers and his classmates what kind of student he really was.

French class turned out to be a devastating experience for the young man. Even in the one place where he had some real knowledge to demonstrate, he found himself failing. The teacher's way of speaking French that he had noticed on the very first day in school made it difficult sometimes for him to understand the lessons and what was expected of him. When the young man spoke in class, he found that what he said was not understood either because he pronounced it differently or because he used an unfamiliar word or phrase, or because he, unknowingly, made some grammatical error. Sometimes, it even seemed to him as if the teacher enjoyed his mistakes, and he soon became aware that the other students in the class thought he was really stupid because he could not even function in his own language. That morning before he appeared in the Foreign Language office, he had been the only student in the class to fail the French test.

As the young man stepped into his office, the French teacher noticed that the brightness that had always been a part of the boy's personality seemed to have faded, the pride of his gait had faltered. He was no longer the same young man who had entered the school four weeks ago. As he stood there, the corners of his mouth began to curl down, as the tears began to streak what used to be his smiling face. His whole body began to shake with the sobs of a person on the edge of desperation. Through that cascade of emotion, his words carried this message:

Nobody in this school knows that I am a good person, a good student! Nobody knows that in my country, I was the best student in my class! Nobody knows that I can sing, that I can play the guitar, that I can paint. Nobody knows how much I miss my country and my friends. Here in this school I feel nothing but disappointment and shame. Even in my French class, the only place where I could do well, I am ashamed!

My work as co-editor of this volume, *Teaching Heritage Language Learners: Voices from the Classroom*, and my efforts as one of the directors of the project from which this volume emanated are dedicated to this young man. I was the young French teacher who met that boy years ago on his first day at school.

Just as he was not alone in his homesickness, his fear, his frustration, and his sadness in that school, he was and still is not alone in those feelings as a heritage language learner in schools across the country. The troubling part is that he was and still is not alone in those feelings in foreign language classes in the nation's schools. I do not mean this as an indictment of foreign language teachers or of the foreign language education profession. It is merely a statement of fact.

Certainly, as a young teacher of French, before this student entered my office, there had been no intention on my part to contribute in any way to his undoing. I liked him. He was a really nice, energetic, spirited young person. That he had suffered in my French class was an anathema to me; I was horrified! He had been assigned to my class, as had a number of Haitian students. To begin with, I was young and relatively inexperienced as a teacher. My confidence in my own ability to use French was still shaky. The student's accent was unfamiliar to me. At that time, I did not know much about Haiti, or Haitians, or the Haitian language issues, and I certainly did not speak *Créole* back then, as I do now. I did not know that he was adding *Créole* to the French that he spoke. I thought that our difficulties in communicating stemmed from my own inadequacies in French, and it made me feel uneasy and insecure. I was puzzled by his writing and speaking abilities and by the kinds of errors he made in class. I guess that when I had opportunities to correct his French, I felt as if I might be helping him, in spite of my inadequacies. Maybe his errors made me feel better. I do not know. All I know is that I did not know what to do with him or the other Haitian students in my classes. Nothing in my training as a foreign language teacher prepared me to work with him, and I did not know where to go to find help. In that state of mind, it would have been very easy for me to fall prey to the notion that he should be learning English—forget about his French, much less his *Créole*.

"I did not know." That is exactly the issue for the foreign language profession when it comes to the heritage language learner. Our training and our experience, unless we have spent a significant portion of our careers working in schools where there are large numbers of heritage language learners, have prepared us essentially to work with English-speaking students who are learning the languages that we teach for the first time. The textbooks and ancillary materials, and most professional development programs are geared for those students. Yet, to an increasing extent, our foreign language classes are populated with students who have, in their lives, some important connection to the language they are studying. It may be the language of their grandparents and they hear it, see it, or even use it when they are in their presence and in the presence of other family members, even though they may not use it at home. It may be the language of their parents, so they are closely connected to it as a part of their everyday lives. Many of the learners may use that language exclusively at home and turn to English only when they are out in the community. Some of the students come from homes where they are the only fluent speakers of English and, after school hours, sometimes even at a very young age, they assume responsibility for linking their parents to the outside world. They negotiate rental contracts, arrange for installations with utility companies, speak to doctors and lawyers, and even come to school to translate at parent conferences with their own teachers. Still others may have little direct contact with the language, but somewhere in their cultural memory there is a link, a desire to connect to childhood that is important in some intrinsic way. The range of heritage language learners is broad, but they are there in our classes. Many times, we do not even know it until we do or say something that causes a student to reveal that connection to the language. We do not know, and yet the heritage language learner is a significant part of our student population.

When the National Foreign Language Standards Task Force began its deliberations in 1993 to reach a national consensus on what the learners in our nation's foreign language classrooms should know and be able to do, it soon became apparent that, as a profession, we were not adequately prepared to provide meaningful and responsive instruction to heritage language learners. As a group, the members of the Task Force agreed that there was work to be done in this domain. The challenge was where to begin.

In Chapter One of this volume, Jamie B. Draper and June H. Hicks present an outline of the history and the research dealing with heritage language learners in foreign language classrooms. While it is evident that impressive work has been done by distinguished scholars and researchers, there is no coherent program or plan of action for classroom teachers at the middle/junior and senior high school levels. That reality is further complicated by the lack of teacher preparation programs that focus specifically on the teaching of heritage language learners so as to provide the badly needed preservice and inservice training. "We don't know." So the profession continues to prepare teachers in the foreign language education paradigm without addressing the teaching of heritage languages, thus perpetuating the problem for teachers and learners alike.

In 1997, ACTFL and Hunter College embarked upon a three-year project, supported by the Fund for the Improvement of Postsecondary Education (FIPSE) of the United States Department of Education, to develop a program specifically designed to prepare foreign language teachers to work more effectively with heritage language learners. Given the lack of research and information, the shortage of materials for the teaching of heritage language learners at the secondary level, and the virtual non-existence of teacher preparations programs with a focus on heritage language learners, Jamie B. Draper, the Project Co-Director, and I turned to the one reliable source of expertise that did exist—classroom teachers and school administrators in New York City public schools who had a history of success in working with those learners. We assembled a Project Development Team composed of eight such people who were then joined by college professors/researchers from the Department of Curriculum and Teaching of Hunter College.

This collaborative effort between a teacher preparation institution and school-based professionals proved to be utterly magical. The classroom teachers had much to share about what teachers in general should know and be able to do in order to teach heritage language learners successfully. The Team met regularly for one full year to conceptualize and design the program. In order to build an information base from which to work, we organized an invitational colloquium of one hundred New York City teachers experienced in working with heritage language learners to find out from them what THEY thought teachers should know and be able to do when working with this population. We brought in consultants on assessment, linguistics and origins of language varieties, standards, and a distinguished specialist in the teaching of English language arts, Barbara L. Miller, whose input was so enlightening that she became co-editor of this volume. The Team's effort was further augmented by a school-based research project designed to examine successful teaching strategies in heritage language classes through observations and interviews with teachers, supervisors, and students.

In the second year of the project, the teacher preparation program began to take real shape in the form of an Academy on Working with Heritage Language Learners. That Academy was taught by the members of the grant's Project Development Team. After evaluation and re-examination of the course content, a second Academy was held in the spring 2000 semester. Now, starting in the academic year 2001–2002, all students seeking certification as teachers of foreign languages through the Hunter College program will be required to take a methods course specifically for the teaching of heritage language learners, in addition to the regular foreign language methods course.

The fruits of the ACTFL/Hunter College project are contained in this volume. Everyone who was involved in shaping the teacher preparation program that grew out of that project has contributed to the pages of this book. We are sharing what we have learned. It is the voice of teachers combined with the voices of their students speaking to us from the classrooms of their schools, guiding us as we undertake the most human of endeavors—enabling a nation of young people to enrich their lives, and ours, by maintaining and strengthening their ties to their heritage, to their conscience, to their intelligence, to their souls.

John B. Webb, Ed.D., Co-Editor
Princeton University

Chapter 1

Teaching Heritage Languages:
The Road Traveled

Editors' Notes

Before embarking on any voyage or undertaking any project, before considering ideas or planning new initiatives, it is essential to take a good look at the road already traveled. Not only does it save us from duplicating efforts and from stumbling unnecessarily, such a look also enables us to profit from the good minds and from the wisdom that has come from the experiences of others.

Certainly, in the past thirty years, there is a wealth of material and research that has come from the work done in bilingual education and the teaching of English as a Second Language. The issues associated with children of immigrants in the schools have been a fundamental part of the literature in education since the very beginning of the country's history. Diversity was behind the founding of the Common School, and the classroom figured prominently as the melting pot where the "American" would be created. Although we have come a long distance from the melting pot, to the salad bowl, to the rainbow, to the mosaic, there is still much to be learned, a long road still to be traveled. This is particularly true in the case of the heritage language learner in the foreign language classroom. It is hoped that this volume will move us a little farther down that road.

Before we share what was learned from the ACTFL/Hunter College Project, it is important for you, the reader, to do the same thing as the Project Development Team did before it began its work. Like the Team, you will want to take a look at the road traveled to see what others have to tell us. Jamie B. Draper and June H. Hicks provide us with that overview and a bibliography that can serve as a valuable resource for anyone wishing to explore at greater depth where we've been and what we've learned.

Where We've Been; What We've Learned

Jamie B. Draper and June H. Hicks ✳

There were nearly 25 million foreign-born individuals residing in the United States in 1996, a 25 percent increase since the 1990 United States Census Report (Campbell and Peyton 1998). The majority of this population are from Spanish-speaking countries, followed by members of Asian language groups (Campbell and Peyton 1998). While the United States government views multilingualism as essential to the national interest (Peale 1991; Brecht and Ingold 1998) and recognizes the value of language skills among the nation's citizenry, the educational system historically has not given priority status to the nurturing of the linguisitic abilities of its language minority students. Instead, the emphasis has been placed on the development and maintenance of their English language skills often at the expense of their native language skills (Marcos 1999). Students are frequently assigned to classes in English as a Second Language (ESL) or enrolled in remedial English classes to supplement their regularly scheduled instruction in English. If they have any instruction in their heritage language in school, it is most often through enrollment in a foreign language class with students learning that language for the first time. The result is that teachers of foreign languages find themselves teaching classes in which an increasing percentage or even a majority of the students are not the traditional foreign language learners that teachers were trained to teach. The approaches that they have employed successfully for years with foreign language learners are no longer adequate or appropriate, and the resulting sense of frustration and inadequacy has become a part of their daily teaching experience. The heritage language learners in their classes experience a similar kind of frustration. Indeed, as the linguistic composition of the United States population continues to change, and as schools continue to experience a significant growth in the population of heritage language learners, it is becoming increasingly evident that the needs of these students are not being adequately addressed.

Language Minorities in the United States

Since the very beginning, people from around the world have immigrated to the United States in hopes of creating a better life for themselves and their families. While the dominance of the English language has never really been in question, issues of language diversity and assimilation have always been a part of the national discussion. As early as 1906, Congress passed a measure requiring anyone seeking American citizenship to be able to speak English (Crawford 1992, p.55). That same year, the House Committee on Immigration and Naturalization asserted that anyone who was unable to speak English after being in the country for five years "must be so deficient in mental capacity, or so careless of the opportunities afforded him...that he would make an undesirable citizen" (quoted in Crawford 1992, p.55).

This was not a new phenomenon. During the 1800s the relationship between the United States government and Native Americans was fraught with serious problems. The Indian Peace Commission of 1868 was charged with the responsibility of finding out why Native Americans were not adhering to policies of manifest destiny that were part of the national agenda. In its findings, the Commission concluded that the source of the difficulty was "in the difference of language" (quoted in Crawford 1992, p.43). Native American children were taken from their homes and shipped to boarding schools where instruction in Native American languages was forbidden by law (Crawford 1992, p.44). That practice was not abolished until the mid-twentieth century.

That sentiment carried on years later. During the 1920s "English only" advocates also linked the continued use of a foreign language with substandard intelligence and an answer to the cause of mental retardation in immigrant children (Portes, Hao 1998, p.270). Even President Theodore Roosevelt stated, "We have room for but one language here, and that is the English language; for we intend to see that the crucible turns people out as Americans, and not dwellers in a polyglot boarding house" (Quoted in Portes, Hao 1998 from Brumberg 1986, p.7) In the 1980s, following another wave of immigration, legal and otherwise, "English Only" measures began appearing on state ballots nationwide, with several passing by large margins (Crawford 1992, p.61). The debate on the role of non-English languages continues.

Language Maintenance among Language Minority Groups

In addressing the issue of minority language maintenance, it is also necessary to look at the roles of the individuals involved in the process of language maintenance. The maintenance of a heritage language cannot be achieved by the heritage language learners alone. The community, teachers, and parents all need to be involved to ensure that the first language is not lost. The heritage language learner's role is most important, as she or he will need to make every effort to maintain his or her first language. However, the community also plays a vital role in helping to maintain language. As a minority language speaker begins to learn English or any other new language, the community must encourage the learners to advance their linguistic skills in the heritage language. The community must also realize that it is the primary contact that a minority language speaker has with its language, and that it ultimately will be responsible for keeping the language alive through its future generations (Valdés 1995, p.310). School teachers also play an important role in a student's maintenance of a home language. They must learn to respect their students' home language and to help their students understand that they may still use their native language while learning English, emphasizing that doing so will not be detrimental to them (Zentella 1986; Soto, Smrekar, Neckovei 1999, p.1). Since students spend most of their day with a teacher, they will sense a teacher's attitude toward their home language.

A prime example of this is Maria Ramirez, named bilingual teacher of the year by NABE (National Association for Bilingual Education), and born to Mexican immigrants (Checkley 1996). Ramirez said, "At school, we were asked to always speak English. We were not encouraged to speak Spanish." She continued, "My language is part of who I am. If you take that away, you don't respect my whole person" (Checkley 1996). Her experiences confirmed for her that a teacher's lack of support communicates that the student is not important

(Checkley 1996). With this in mind, all three groups will need to work together to ensure that the heritage language is not lost.

The Teaching of Heritage Language Learners in the United States

The teaching of heritage languages is not a recent phenomenon. In 1839, many states authorized bilingual education programs in the states, specifically the teaching of German language to children of German heritage in public schools (Crawford 1992, p.46). One hundred years later the country as a whole was confronted with the urgent need to provide adequate education for its larger and more diversified immigrant population. This forced educators, as never before, to deal with issues of language and cultural differences in their schools. In spite of the mounting pressure for sensitivity to language and culture in the schools, it took nearly seven decades before the magnitude of the immigration of Spanish-speakers resulted in schools addressing the issue of teaching Spanish to heritage learners of Spanish (Teschner 1983). In the late 1970s and early 1980s, educators began to rethink their methods of teaching Spanish to their Spanish-speaking students, because it had become evident that the techniques used to teach Spanish to monolingual speakers were not effective in teaching bilingual/heritage speakers (Rodriguez Pino 1997).

Although some progress has been made in addressing the instruction of heritage language learners, a 1997 survey conducted by the Center for Applied Linguistics, showed that only 7 percent of secondary schools in the United States offer heritage/native language classes, an increase of a mere 3 percent over a preceding ten years. In colleges and universities, language courses are still designed primarily for English speakers learning a second language (Brecht and Ingold 1998).

Heritage language instruction historically has been handled in three ways. One long-standing tradition that has helped to maintain heritage languages has been for members of the heritage language community to teach the language on weekends or after school. The other is for the language to be taught in school districts by teachers either during school as a part of the regular curriculum, or after school (Valdés 1995, p.303). The community-based programs, often referred to as Saturday Schools, focus on maintaining the heritage language and culture among the youth of the community. The heritage language programs offered by school districts are open to all students with varying levels of proficiency in the language, as well as monolingual students studying the language for the first time

(Valdés 1995, p.303). In still a third program model, dual immersion, monolingual students and heritage language students are placed together in the same class and instruction is offered in both languages. This type of program allows monolingual students to learn a second language while the heritage language students are able to further develop skills in their language (Valdés 1997, p.411). Valdés further points out that some language communities have been unsuccessful in having their language added to school curriculum.

Certain language groups, such as the Chinese, the Koreans, and the Russians, have started their own language programs in both weekend and after school programs (Valdés 1995, p.303; Marcos 1999). Still others, particularly the Spanish-speaking communities have successfully persuaded schools to start courses as early as the elementary grades (Valdés 1995, p.303). The reality, of course, is that evening and weekend courses are seriously limited in what they can accomplish, because they often lack the resources necessary for success, including trained instructors, funding, and curricular materials (Brecht and Ingold 1998).

Definition of Heritage Language Learner

The term "heritage language learner," relatively new in language education research, refers to someone who has had exposure to a non-English language outside the formal education system. It most often refers to someone with a home background in the language, but may refer to anyone who has had in-depth exposure to another language. Other terms used to describe this population include "native speaker," "bilingual," and "home background." While these terms are often used interchangeably, they can have very different interpretations.

Guadalupe Valdés, professor and researcher at Stanford University, stated that "for most people, a native speaker is one who can function in all settings in which other native speakers normally function. Moreover, to be considered fully native, a speaker must be indistinguishable from other native speakers. When interacting with them, other native speakers should assume that he or she acquired the language from infancy" (Valdés 1998, p.153). Claire Kramsch notes that "originally native speakership was viewed as an uncontroversial privilege of birth. Those who were born into a language were considered its native speakers, with grammatical intuitions that non-native speakers did not have" (quoted in Valdés 1998, p.152). Heritage speakers may be classified as individuals who speak their first language, which is not English, in the home, or are foreign-born (Campbell and Peyton 1998). Heritage language learners may also be defined as individuals who have learned a language other than English somewhere other than in school (Scalera 1997).

The New York City public school system has yet another means of classifying its language minority students. "Literacy" students have no or limited English skills and are generally enrolled in courses in English as a Second Language. The "Native" track is available for heritage speakers of Spanish. These students are generally first- and second-generation speakers of Spanish with varying degrees of proficiency in the heritage language, but who are proficient in English. The Texas Framework for Languages Other Than English (Texas Education Agency, 1997) describes the range of students with "home backgrounds" in languages other than English, including:

- Students who are able to understand oral language, but unable to speak the language beyond single-word answers.
- Students who can speak the language fluently but have little to no experience with the language in its written form.
- Students who have come to the United States from non-English speaking countries. They can understand and speak the language fluently; however, their reading and writing skills may be limited due to a lack of formal education in their countries of origin.
- Fluent bilingual students who understand, speak, read, and write another language very well.

Peale describes native speakers as those who are English dominant with oral proficiency in the language and with "linguistic skills that are beyond those which are typically developed in four years of high school Spanish" (Peale 1991, p.448).

Finally, Valdés developed the following charts (see p. 21 and p. 22) using a Spanish for Native Speakers class to help illustrate the characteristics of heritage language learners, their language development needs and the different abilities brought to the classroom.

Achieving Success with Heritage Language Learners

While there appears to be widespread recognition that heritage language learners are different from the traditional foreign language student, the challenges involved in meeting their needs are also widely recognized. Instruction must serve an extraordinarily diverse group of students, even in programs specifically designed to meet their needs; instructional materials, while improving, are still not as readily available as their more traditional counterparts; teacher preparation remains an enigma; administrative support is unpredictable; assessment is an open question; and a strong research base is lacking (Roca 1997; Rodriguez Pino 1997; Brecht and Ingold 1998; Campbell and Peyton 1998; Valdés 1999). Nevertheless, there is a growing understanding of the issues that affect the success or failure of heritage language learning. This section will explore current understanding of these issues.

Teacher Attitudes and Expectations

The role of the teacher in determining the success or failure of students in heritage language classrooms cannot be understated. Despite increasing attention being paid to these issues, the average teacher of heritage language learners is

Table 1. Selected Characteristics of Students who Enroll in SNS Language Courses

Generation	Schooling	Academic Skills in English	Language Characteristics
Newly arrived	Good schooling in Spanish speaking country	English language learners	Fluent speakers of prestige variety of Spanish
	Little schooling in Spanish speaking country		Fluent speakers of colloquial/stigmatized varieties of Spanish
U.S. born and raised	Access to bilingual instruction in U.S.	Good academic skills in English	Fluent speakers of prestige variety of Spanish
		Poor academic skills in English	Fluent speakers of colloquial/stigmatized varieties of Spanish
	Educated exclusively through English	Good academic skills in English	Limited speakers of prestige variety of Spanish
	No academic skills in Spanish	Poor academic skills in English	Limited speakers of colloquial/stigmatized varieties of Spanish Receptive bilinguals

Reprinted with permission from: Valdés 1995, p.306.

either a foreign language teacher certified in the heritage language with a fairly high level of proficiency, or a native speaker of the target language who may or may not be a certified language teacher. By and large these teachers are isolated within their schools, and have no obvious means of support other than their own willingness to seek help. As Scalera (1997) notes:

> Given the lack of all other types of support, you, as a teacher of heritage language learners, are the single most important element that will determine the success of your students. Your beliefs about how to teach and about the abilities of heritage language learners will have a major impact on the decisions you make in terms of use of class time, what types of assignments you provide, and how and why students are motivated to learn.

Due to past emphasis on the teaching of the "standard" dialect to heritage

---

Table 2. Student Characteristics and Needs

Student Characteristics	Needs
Newly-arrived immigrant children	Language maintenance
	Continued development of age-appropriate language competencies
	Acquisition of prestige variety of the language
Newly-arrived immigrant adolescents/young adults	
High literacy	Language maintenance
	Continued development of age-appropriate language competencies
Low literacy	Language maintenance
	Development of literacy skills in first language
	Continued development of age appropriate language competencies
	Acquisition of prestige variety of language
Second and third generation bilinguals	Maintenance, retrieval, and/or acquisition of language competencies (e.g., oral productive abilities)
	Expansion of bilingual range
	Transfer of literacy skills developed in English to Spanish
	Acquisition of prestige variety of the language

Reprinted with permission from: Valdés 1995, p.306, 307.

language learners, many teachers have viewed, and continue to view, their role as one of correcting the language used by their students; that what students bring with them to the classroom is not valid. This, coupled with the often negative societal attitudes toward these languages and the people who speak them, leads students to see no perceived value in something that is integral to who they are as people (Villa 1996; Valdés 1999).

Lack of understanding of the nature of both societal as well as individual bilingualism has also been a factor in determining teacher attitudes toward heritage language learners (Zentella 1986; Gutierrez 1997; Clair and Adger 1999; Valdés 1999). The nature of languages in contact is such that word borrowing is a norm and leads to enrichment of the language over time. *Anglicismos* are not by nature bad. They are, instead, evidence of the richness of language. By the same token, bilinguals have an internal control over which language to use in which context, and will easily switch between the two languages depending on the topic of conversation. As Gutierrez (1997, p.35) explains:

> Teachers need to be made aware that heritage speakers are not simply imperfect speakers of Spanish who have fallen short of the monolingual norm. They are, rather, complex persons who are fundamentally different from monolinguals. Unlike monolingual speakers of Spanish from societies in which Spanish is the sole or primary language, bilingual United States Latinos and Latinas are members of speech communities in which a single language does not meet all their communicative needs.

It is extremely important to remember that the educational system is a political institution and, as such, is not immune, and more often than not reflects, the cultural, political and social struggles of the society at large (Valdés 1999). This can have a profound impact on the heritage language classroom, because those students in particular are often on the losing end of those struggles. Teachers placed in heritage language programs, particularly those who are not native speakers themselves, may feel threatened by the abilities their students do have. They will often use their authority as the teacher to maintain a semblance of an advantage over their students (Scalera 1994; Ariza 1998), creating yet another power struggle in the minds of the students. This power struggle can further erode the motivation of students and their interest in pursuing their language study.

The key to success in the heritage language classroom, then, is for the teacher to respect and value the language and cultural experiences that students bring to the classroom (Valdés 1980; Zentella 1986; Scalera 1994; Colville-Hall, et al. 1995;

Ariza 1998; Clair and Adger 1999). They must understand that there is no "standard" language (Villa 1996), and that what students bring are the building blocks for future growth in the language. Teachers also need to know their students (Ariza 1998). They need to understand not only their linguistic capabilities but also who they are as people, what their backgrounds are and what their interests are. This should be accomplished through real communication with the students, with their parents, and with others in the school community.

Teachers need to be able to reevaluate their role within the classroom (Faltis 1990; Scalera 1997; Ariza 1998). They need to back away from the notion of "teacher as leader" and begin to view themselves as facilitators. They need to be able to adapt to the needs and capabilities of their students, rather than trying to make students fit into preconceived notions of the types of students they should be.

Student Attitudes and Expectations

Student motivation has long been recognized as a determinant of success in the foreign language classroom, and, as noted above, the motivation of the heritage language students can be greatly influenced by both teacher and societal attitudes toward their home languages. Heritage language learners very often have different reasons for studying the language than their foreign language counterparts. Sometimes, they seek greater understanding of their culture or seek to connect with members of their family (Mazzocco 1996); others see language study as an "easy" way to fulfill a language requirement (Teschner 1983). Still others study it because of family pressure or at the insistence of guidance counselors.

Equally diverse are the societal attitudes that sap the motivation of students. We have already discussed how lack of respect for the language variety spoken by the student can reduce motivation. The status afforded the language within its own culture can also impact on student motivation. This is particularly true in the case of Haitian *Créole*, which is only now beginning to be recognized by Haitians as a legitimate language worthy of study in its own right. Finally, the attitude of parents toward the maintenance of the language can have a tremendous impact on the willingness of students to grow in their language capabilities.

Griego-Jones (1994) found that not only student attitudes toward language development were important, but also their understanding of what biliteracy was and what it could mean to them. It was found that, even in environments that are favorable to language development, if students did not understand the benefits of their dual language capabilities, they would not pursue opportunities to use their heritage language in situations where it was not required. Griego-Jones also pointed out that "the role that attitude plays in determining human behavior makes it critical that teachers be aware of students' attitudes and use their awareness and knowledge of those attitudes in planning for instruction." Benjamin (1997) reported that bilingual students were most interested in connecting with their culture, and were generally less than enthusiastic about topics and themes that were perceived to have no bearing on their lives. In one case, bilingual Hispanic students in New Mexico generally did not participate in Spanish discussions, despite their proficiency in the language, because the topics revolved almost exclusively around Spain, rather than Mexico, which was their cultural heritage. A similar result was garnered from the author's son, who took a Hispanic literature course in high school, only to be disappointed that discussions in the class revolved around literary genre and style, rather than the issues and experiences being explored in the writings.

A study of Canadian heritage language learners (Feuerverger 1991) revealed equal ambivalence toward further development of their language. The study found that the mere existence of heritage language programs was insufficient motivation for promoting functional reading and writing skills in the language. The three principal contributing factors were: parental education levels, strength of ethnic identity, and perceived administrative support for the program.

Parental Education Levels

Parents who had not received formal education in their native language were more likely to want their children to abandon their heritage language in favor of English. These parents tended to have greater difficulty in learning English and were, therefore, more likely to impress upon their children the need to learn English at the expense of the heritage language. Without strong parental support, there was little motivation on the part of the children to seek additional skills in the home language.

Ethnic Identity

The degree to which students felt a part of their ethnic heritage was another strong motivating factor in student success in heritage language programs. Those students who felt a strong connection with their ethnic heritage, either within the local community or in their ethnic homeland, were much more motivated to enroll and do well in heritage language programs than those who felt less connection. It was important, however, that the values of the heritage culture not conflict with their sense of being "Canadian."

Administrative Support

Students felt that there was not very much institutional support for heritage language programs. This was evidenced by a lack of materials and lack of preparation on the part of their teachers, as well as a lack of coherence and direction in the curriculum. They felt that greater organization, development of appropriate materials, and high quality teachers were needed. Despite this perceived lack of support, however, students generally found the existence of heritage language programs a positive experience:

> "Learning your ethnic language at school makes you feel like a whole person. You don't have to feel ashamed of your culture; on the contrary, you can feel that you are as good as anyone else. And it hasn't hurt my English or any other subject." [Feuerverger 1991, p.674]

Pedagogical Considerations

This section will focus on three areas of pedagogical considerations: program goals, teaching strategies and materials, and the application of the Standards for Foreign Language Learning to heritage language students.

Program Goals

There is general consensus that, wherever possible, heritage language learners should be placed in programs that are separate from the traditional foreign language student, at least at the lower levels. The goals of these programs, however, are not as clear, other than the broad goal of improving upon the skills that the students bring to the classroom. As Valdés (1980) points out, "The principal problem teaching the target language to bilingual speakers lies in developing a type of instruction that is, in essence, self-contained, that does not necessarily serve as a feeder course into more advanced courses." Consequently, program goals can be as varied as the students who take them.

Where these programs have existed in the past, they have tended to focus on literacy and the written language. Villa warns that it may be unrealistic to expect mastery of "formal" written language in the relatively short duration of most heritage language classes. Rather, students should strive toward an " 'acceptable' prose, one relatively free from 'interference' of the spoken standard" (1996, p.197-198). As discussed in the previous section, many students are motivated to pursue study of their heritage language as a means of connecting with their cultural heritage (Feuerverger 1991; Griego-Jones 1994; Benjamin 1997; Scalera 1997). The teaching of language through culture has been a focus of traditional foreign language classrooms in recent years, and it appears to hold a great deal of promise for the heritage language classroom as well. Finally, many programs focus on the expansion of the linguistic registers available to heritage language learners by focusing on more "formal" language. As was also pointed out previously, programs must be careful not to denigrate the language variety spoken by the student as part of this process.

Teaching Strategies and Materials

If we use the factors that affect student motivation as a starting point, the implications for teaching strategies and materials is clear. Instruction for heritage language learners must be connected to the student. It must start where the student is and move forward, and it must be relevant. Teachers must strive to make students feel safe to experiment with their developing language skills without fear.

The skills that students bring with them to the heritage language classroom should be incorporated into instruction wherever possible. Villa (1996) advocates using the language varieties of students as a starting point for building additional skills. Successful teachers often point out the benefit of using the linguistic diversity of the heritage classroom as a learning tool for both teachers and students.

Rodriguez Pino (1997) argues for the use of community resources in the classroom in order to connect students with their communities. Newspapers, television, and other resources from the heritage language communities can make excellent classroom materials. The use of oral history projects, the use of the literature of immigrant groups, and thematic approaches to instruction are all valuable ways of bringing the culture of their heritage alive for these students.

Collaborative and cooperative learning activities are strongly endorsed for use in heritage language classrooms (Duràn 1994; Rodriguez Pino 1997). This is especially true given the heterogeneous nature of most such classrooms.

There is very little mention in the literature of situations where there are both heritage and traditional foreign language students in the same classroom. Yet, this is the case for most teachers of heritage language learners. Mazzocco (1996) reports on a self-instructional language program that serves the needs of both heritage and foreign language learners. She notes that they were able to use the same content for both groups of students. She had students work with two sets of tasks. The heritage students generally did more advanced tasks related to the course content than those assigned to the foreign language student. For example, non-heritage students of Hindi learned standard grammatical structures and vocabulary and met in weekly conversation groups to practice what they had studied. The heritage learners did the same thing, but in their weekly groups, they were also able to discuss the variations found between the standard language they were learning and the variety of the language with which they had grown up. Similarly, videotapes of the target country's news broadcasts can be used by both groups. It was apparent that the foreign language students will need some time to decipher one or two topics, while the heritage learner will be able to gain much more substantive information and undertake more difficult assignments related to the tape.

Standards and the Heritage Language Learner

The national foreign language standards released in 1995 were designed to be applicable to all foreign language learners, including those for whom the foreign language was, in fact, a heritage language. The framework for communicative competence defined within the standards provides a means of recognizing the skills that heritage language learners bring to their studies (generally interpersonal communication skills) and a mechanism for focusing on the skills that need further work (general presentational skills). Furthermore, the inclusion of the Culture, Connections, Comparisons, and Communities standards offers teachers options for expanding the curriculum of heritage languages beyond language itself to language use in real world contexts. However, there were no specific guidelines as to how the standards might be used in the design of a heritage language program.

In 1999, the foreign language standards were reissued, this time with separate sections for each of nine language classifications: Chinese, Classics, French, German, Italian, Japanese, Portuguese, Russian, and Spanish. In the standards for several of these languages, the issue of heritage language learners is addressed. The Chinese standards include sample progress indicators targeting the heritage learner, such as this one for Standard 2.1:

> Students discuss and analyze patterns of behavior as observed in segments
> of movies, videos, news broadcasts, and articles of newspapers or maga-
> zines of Chinese culture. [Standards 1999:130]

The Russian standards (National Standards 1999, p.416-418) devotes three pages to a discussion of meeting the needs of heritage learners in the foreign language classroom. The essay raises many of the same issues discussed here. It further points out that, while the needs of heritage and foreign language learners may vary in terms of vocabulary and grammar, they very often come together again with the introduction of cultural topics. The differing needs of each group can also be used as a learning tool in addressing the standards of the fourth goal area: Comparisons.

Standards for Learning Spanish offers a learning scenario for heritage language programs. In this scenario (National Standards 1999, p.469-470), students watched a video interview with Rigoberto Manchú and, following a series of class discussions and an internet research project, they prepared responses to the interview. These included the video's key points and their students' reactions to it, as well as the new knowledge they had gleaned from it.

As with the standards and traditional foreign language programs, only implementation efforts will determine the degree to which the standards will be relevant to heritage language learners.

Implications for Teacher Preparation

What does the research tell us, then, about the preparation of the teacher of the heritage language learner, given the discussions above? Zentella (1986) prescribes a variety of coursework and other experiences that prospective teachers of heritage language learners should undertake, including:
  • Be cognizant of the different varieties of the language they are teaching.
  • Participate in the activities of nearby language minority communities.
  • Expand or refresh knowledge of that culture (or cultures) of the language(s) they are teaching.
She further notes that:
  • Courses in foreign language methodology must include training on teaching language to native speakers, with emphasis on pedagogical issues involved in language maintenance.
  • Faculty members involved in this training should experience the classroom situations their students will be facing.

Teacher attitudes have proven to be a clear determinant of success in the foreign language classroom. However, Colville-Hall, MacDonald, and Smolen (1995) acknowledge that "[l]ittle research has been conducted on how to change teachers' attitudes and behavior towards minority groups," an area that could directly impact student success in heritage language programs. They recommend providing prospective teachers with direct contact with minority groups and presentation of information through a variety of instructional formats, including films, community involvement, guest speakers, and visitations. Clair and Adger (1999) further note that:

Teachers need to understand basic constructs of bilingualism and second language development, the nature of language proficiency, the role of the first language and culture in learning, and the demands that mainstream education places on culturally diverse students. Teachers need to continually reassess what schooling means in the context of a pluralist society; the relationship between teachers and learners; and attitudes and beliefs about language, culture, and race.

Finally, teachers of heritage language learners should have access to strategies, including small group work and cooperative learning, that enable them to work more effectively with students of varying ability levels. They must be aware of the language resources in their communities and know how to access them for use in the classroom. They should have an understanding of the role of standards in guiding their programs, and they need to have a thorough understanding of who their students are and the ability to recognize the skills students bring with them to their classrooms.

Assessment

Assessment of heritage language learners can be divided into two primary areas of concerns: proper placement into language programs and progress made as a result of instruction. The arena of placement appears to garner the most concern and controversy, perhaps because charting progress in language acquisition is a more familiar topic to most language educators. Both areas, however, have a paucity of research that should be of major concern to those involved in this field.

Assessment for Purposes of Placement

The concerns regarding placement of heritage language learners appears to be centered around the need to be able to determine which students have enough language background to move beyond the traditional foreign language instructional sequence. Where specialized programs do not exist, this may mean moving students to more advanced foreign language classes. Where heritage programs do exist, the issue is more one of determining who is a "heritage" speaker and who is not.

Teschner (1983) describes an assessment tool used at the University of Texas in El Paso for separating heritage speakers from non-heritage speakers. Embedded in the instrument are "native speaker identifiers" that only a native speaker of the language would understand. When the responses to those test items were analyzed, it was determined that anyone who was able to identify eleven or more of the fourteen identifiers was a native speaker and was consequently place in an instructional sequence for native speakers. Those students who could identify no more than four of the identifiers were overwhelmingly Anglo with no or limited second language abilities. Using this tool, 75 percent of all students could be placed definitively in either the heritage or traditional language course sequence. The remaining 25 percent of the students, those in the middle, were generally allowed to place out of the first semester course of either sequence, with some students switching sequences in order to accommodate differing instructional needs.

Others (Peale 1991) call for identification of these students by what they are able to do with the language. He describes the baseline for entry into Spanish for Spanish Speakers courses in California as those who:

> are able to use Spanish to satisfy nearly all of their social and physical needs. They can express their needs for care and comfort, persuade, suggest, describe and talk about past, present, and future events. They have learned to pronounce and recognize the sounds, to construct and interpret phrases, sentences and conversations, and they have acquired an extensive vocabulary. They may not as yet have learned to read or write in Spanish nor have they necessarily learned how to think and talk about matters that lie beyond their limited world experiences.

A second factor in determining the need for a heritage language program is the advanced nature of the students' linguistic skills. On most tests, they show that they have skills that surpass what is typically developed in four years of high school Spanish classes. The tools for determining this benchmark are not discussed. The state's "Draft Foreign Language Curriculum Framework, K-12" calls for the assessment of student interpersonal, presentational, and interpretive communicative abilities in both spoken and written modes, for proper placement in heritage language programs. While not specifying particular instruments to be used, the document does note that special measures may need to be developed, as some students' abilities are well beyond the scope of instruments designed for use with traditional foreign language students.

The use of the *ACTFL Proficiency Guidelines* and the Oral Proficiency Interview has been questioned as an assessment tool for this population (Valdés, 1989), because it was designed for use with non-native speakers. Heritage learners do not fit neatly into the hierarchy of language development identified in the Guidelines: "They bring with them functional competencies at a number of levels: and, in some domains, they surpass what is expected of superior students." It does not appear that such a tool would provide adequate information as to the type or focus of instruction that would be most beneficial to the heritage language learner. Finally, there is also concern with the use of the "educated native speaker" as the norm, which has the potential to lead to the denigration of a rating based on the variety of the language spoken. This problem is all too common in the education of heritage language learners.

Assessing Progress in Heritage Language Classrooms

Reflecting current trends in classroom assessment in general, advocates of heritage language programs call for approaches that help identify progress over time, such as the use of portfolios and dialogue journals (Roca 1992; Rodriguez Pino 1997). These types of assessments can be of particular benefit in the heritage language classroom because of the heterogeneous nature of the students enrolled in these programs. Because the portfolio enables the collection of samples throughout an instructional term, it is possible to look at progress from the starting point of each student and track where progress has been made and where additional work is needed. There is no single, ideal norm against which all students are measured regardless of their starting points. Whatever assessment instrument is used, it is important that the assessment measures reflect what goes on in the classroom.

In addition to assessing progress in language abilities, some researchers (Griego-Jones 1994) have suggested that monitoring student attitudes toward developing their linguistic skills should also be assessed because of the impact of those attitudes on language acquisition. In a study designed to assess progress in writing skills in a two-way bilingual classroom, Griego-Jones found that, even in an environment that was extremely supportive of second language development, students by and large preferred to use English if given a choice, even when their first language was not English. This argues for inclusion of specific instruction on the benefits of maintaining and improving heritage language skills, as well as assessing students' attitudes on an ongoing basis in order to offset any negative feelings that may exist.

References

"Building on our Strengths" in *Classroom Leadership Online*. 1999. Vol. 3, No. 4. Washington, DC: ASCD.

National Standards in Foreign Language Education Project. 1999. *Standards for Foreign Language Learning in the 21st Century*. Yonkers, NY: National Standards in Foreign Language Education Project.

Ariza, Eileen N. 1998. Role Reversal: "The Problems of a Spanish-Speaking Anglo Teaching Spanish to English Dominant Puerto Rican Children." *Foreign Language Annals*, Vol. 31, No.3, pp. 431-436. Yonkers, NY: American Council on the Teaching of Foreign Languages.

Benjamin, Rebecca. 1997. "What do our Students Want? Some Reflections on Teaching Spanish as an Academic Subject to Bilingual Students." *ADFL Bulletin*, Vol. 29, No. 1, pp. 44-47. New York: Association of Departments of Foreign Languages.

Brecht, Richard D. and Catherine W. Ingold. 1998. "Tapping a National Resource: Heritage Languages in the United States." *ERIC Digest*. Washington, DC: ERIC Clearinghouse on Languages and Linguistics.

Brumberg, Stephen F. 1986. *Going to America, Going to School: The Jewish Immigrant, Public School Encounter in the Turn-of-the-Century*. New York: Praeger.

Campbell, Russell, and Joy Kreeft Peyton. 1998. "Heritage Language Students: A Valuable Language Resource." *The ERIC Review*, Vol. 6, No. 1, pp. 38-39. Washington, DC: ERIC Clearinghouse on Languages and Linguistics.

Checkley, Kathy. 1996. "Keeping Native Languages Alive." *Education Update*, Vol. 38, No. 2. Alexandria, VA: Association for Supervision and Curriculum Development.

Clair, Nancy and Adger, Carolyn Temple. 1999. "Professional Development for Teachers in Culturally Diverse Schools." *ERIC Digest*. Washington, DC: ERIC Clearinghouse on Languages and Linguistics.

Colville-Hall, Susan, Suzanne MacDonald, and Lynn Smolen. 1995. "Preparing Preservice Teachers for Diversity in Learners." *Journal of Teacher Education*, Vol. 46, No. 4, p. 295. Washington, DC.

Crawford, James. 1992. *Hold Your Tongue: Bilingualism and the Politics of English Only*. Addison Wesley Publishing Company.

Durán, Richard P. 1989. "Assessment and Instruction of At-Risk Hispanic Students" In *Exceptional Children*, Vol. 56, No. 2, pp. 50-54.

Durán, Richard. 1994. "Hispanic Student Achievement." In M. Justiz, R. Wilson, D.L. Björk (eds.) *Minorities in Higher Education*. Phoenix, AZ: American Council on Education and Oryx Press.

Faltis, Christian. 1990. "Spanish for Native Speakers: Freirian and Vygotskian Perspectives." *Foreign Language Annals.*, Vol. 23, No. 2, pp. 117-126. Yonkers, NY: American Council on the Teaching of Foreign Languages.

Feuerverger, Grace. "University Students' Perceptions of Heritage Language Learning and Ethnic Identity Maintenance." *Canadian Modern Language Review/LaRevue Canadienne des langues vivantes*, Vol.47, No.4, pp. 660-677.

Griego-Jones, Toni. 1994. "Assessing Students' Perceptions of Biliteracy in Two Way Bilingual Classrooms." *The Journal of Educational Issues of Language Minority Students*, Vol. 13, No. 2, pp. 79-93.

Gutierrez, John R. 1997. "Teaching Spanish as a Heritage Language: A Case for Language Awareness." *ADFL Bulletin*, Vol. 29, No. 1 pp. 34-36.

Lewelling, Vickie W., Joy Kreeft Peyton. 1999. "Spanish for Native Speakers: Developing Dual Language Proficiency." *ERIC Digest*. Washington, DC: ERIC Clearinghouse on Languages and Linguistics.

Marcos, Kathleen. 1999. "Are We Wasting Our Nation's Language Resources? Heritage Languages in America." *Language Link On-Line Newsletter*. Washington, DC: ERIC Clearinghouse on Languages and Linguistics.

Mazzocco, Elizabeth H.D. 1996. "The Heritage versus the Nonheritage Language Learner: The Five College Self-Instructional Language Program's Solutions to the Problems of Separation or Unification."

Peale, C. George. 1991. "Spanish for Spanish Speakers (and Other 'Native Languages') in California's Schools: A Rationale Statement." *Hispania*, Vol. 74, No. 2, pp. 446-451. Greeley, CO: AATSP.

Portes, Alejandro, and Lingxin Hao. 1998. "E pluribus unum: Bilingualism and Loss of Language in the Second Generation." *Sociology of Education*, Vol. 71, No. 4, pp. 269-294. October 1998. Albany, NY: American Sociological Association.

Roca, Ana. 1992. "Spanish for U.S. Hispanic Bilinguals in Higher Education." *ERIC Digest*. November 1992. Washington, DC. ERIC Clearinghouse on Foreign Languages.

Roca, Ana. 1997. "Retrospectives, Advances, and Current Needs in the Teaching of Spanish to United States Hispanic Bilingual Students." *ADFL Bulletin*, Vol. 29, pp. 37-43, Fall 1997. New York: Association of Departments of Languages and Linguistics.

Rodriguez Pino, Cecilia. 1997. "Teaching Spanish To Native Speakers: A New Perspective in the 1990s." *ERIC/CLL News Bulletin*, Vol. 21, No. 1. Washington, DC: ERIC Clearinghouse for Language and Linguistics.

Scalera, Diana. 1997. "Teacher Beliefs and the Heritage Language Learner: What Will You Teach Your Students?" New York State Association of Foreign Language Teachers Annual Meeting Series, A. Vogely (ed.), No. 14, pp. 105-112.

Soto, Lourdes Diaz, Jocelynn L. Smrekar, and Deanna L. Nekcovei. 1999. "Preserving Home Languages and Cultures." *Directions in Language & Education* , National Clearinghouse for Bilingual Education. No. 13, Spring 1999.

Teschner, Richard V. 1983. "Spanish Placement for Native Speakers, Nonnative Speakers, and Others." *ADFL Bulletin*, Vol. 14, No. 3, pp. 37-42. New York: Association of Departments of Foreign Languages.

Valdés, Guadalupe. 1980. "Teaching Ethnic Languages in the United States: Implications for Curriculum and Faculty Development." *ADFL Bulletin*, Vol. 11, No. 3, pp. 31-35.

Valdés, Guadalupe. 1989. "Teaching Spanish to Hispanic Bilinguals: A Look at Oral Proficiency Testing and the Proficiency Movement." *Hispania*. Vol 79, No. 2. American Association of Teachers of Spanish and Portuguese.

Valdés, Guadalupe. 1995. "The Teaching of Minority Languages as Academic Subjects: Pedagogical and Theoretical Challenges." *The Modern Language Journal*, Vol. 79, No. 3, p. 299-328.

Valdés, Guadalupe. 1997. "Dual-Language Immersion Programs: A Cautionary Note Concerning the Education of Language-Minority Students." *Harvard Educational Review*, Vol. 67, No. 3. Cambridge, MA: President and Fellows of Harvard College.

Valdés, Guadalupe. 1998. "The Construct of the Near-Native Speaker in the Foreign Language Profession: Perspectives and Ideologies about Language." *Profession 1998: Perspectives on Ideologies about Languages*, pp. 151-160. New York, NY: Modern Language Association.

Valdés, Guadalupe. 1999. "Nonnative English Speakers: Language Bigotry in English Mainstream Classrooms. *ADFL Bulletin,* Vol. 31, No. 1. pp. 43-48. New York: Association of Departments of Foreign Languages.

Villa, Daniel J. 1996. "Choosing a 'Standard' Variety of Spanish for the Instruction of Native Spanish Speakers in the U.S." *Foreign Language Annals,* Vol. 29, No. 2. pp. 191-200. Yonkers, NY: ACTFL.

Zentella, Ana Celia. 1986. "Language Minorities and the National Commitment to Foreign Language Competence: Resolving the Contradiction." *ADFL Bulletin*, Vol. 17, No. 3, pp. 32-42. New York: Association of Departments of Foreign Languages.

A Texas Framework for Languages Other Than English, Project ExCELL. 1997. *Excellence and Challenge: Expectations of Language Learners.* Southwest Educational Development Laboratory. Austin, Texas: Texas Education Agency, 1997.

Bibliography

Abu-Rabia, Salim. 1999. "Attitudes and Psycholinguistic Aspects of First Language Maintenance Among Russian-Jewish Immigrants in Israel." *Educational Psychology,* Vol. 19, No. 2, June 1999, pp. 133-148. Dorchechester-on-Thames, UK: Carfax Publishing.

Garcia, Georgia Earnest. 1999. "Bilingual Children's Reading: An Overview of Recent Research." *ERIC/CLL News Bulletin*, Vol. 23, No. 1 pp. 1-5. Washington, DC: ERIC Clearinghouse on Languages and Linguistics.

McQuillan, Jeff. 1996. "How Should Heritage Languages Be Taught?: The Effects of a Free Voluntary Reading Program." *Foreign Language Annals*, Vol. 29, No. 1, pp. 56-72.

Peregoy, Suzanne F. 1991. "Environmental Scaffolds and Learner Responses in a Two-Way Spanish Immersion Kindergarten." *The Canadian Modern Language Review/LaRevue Canadienne des langues vivantes*, Vol. 47, No. 3, April 1999, pp. 463-476.

Schrauf, Robert W. 1999. "Mother Tongue Maintenance Among North American Ethnic Groups." *Cross Cultural Research,* Vol. 33, No. 2, pp. 175-192. May 1999. Thousand Oaks, CA: Sage Publications.

Valdés, Guadalupe. 1991. "Bilingual Minorities and Language Issues in Writing: Toward Profession-Wide Responses to a New Challenge." *Technical Report No. 54. Center of the Study of Writing*. October 1991, pp. 1-38. Washington, DC: Office of Educational Research and Improvement.

Valdés, Guadalupe. 1991. "Minority and Majority Members in Foreign Language Departments: Toward the Examination of Established Attitudes and Values." *ADFL Bulletin*, Vol. 22, No. 2. pp. 10-14. New York: Association of Departments of Foreign Languages.

Chapter 2

Getting to Know the Heritage Language Learner

Editors' Notes

People have a tendency to make assumptions about others based on what they believe or know about themselves. Although this tendency is highly problematic because of the fundamental individual differences that exist from one person to another, when people share a common culture, language, community, and a common set of formative experiences, many of these assumptions can prove to be fairly accurate. In the absence of this commonality, however, such assumptions can lead to serious misinterpretations and misunderstandings with grave societal consequences.

In like manner, it is not uncommon for teachers to make assumptions about their students based upon their own backgrounds and experiences, the character of the communities where they teach, their students' appearances, and the impressions that those students make in the classroom or the school in general. Just as in the world beyond the classroom, if there is a shared commonality, many of those assumptions can prove to be accurate. In the case of heritage language learners, however, their complexity defies assumptions. As a result, if uninformed educators design and deliver instruction and interact with the students and their families based on assumptions about what those students, their world, and their educational needs are like, the whole instructional process will not only be inadequate, it may very likely do harm to those students and, in turn, damage the institutions themselves as they attempt to educate.

Teachers of foreign languages, particularly those accustomed to working primarily with English-speaking students learning that language for the first time, traditionally have been able to make certain assumptions. They have assumed that their students come to them knowing little or nothing about the language they are being taught, and curriculum and teaching practices have reflected that assumption. When foreign language teachers make such assumptions about heritage language learners, their effectiveness as teachers is diminished, because the learners' needs are decidedly different, both in content and methodology. For this reason, teachers must engage actively in a discovery process so as to grasp and understand the complexity of their heritage language learners. Their discoveries will equip them to teach with greater awareness and develop curriculum, teaching strategies, and materials that respond meaningfully to that complexity.

As the Project Development Team explored the elements that contribute to teacher effectiveness, they found time and again that teachers who knew their students well taught more successfully. Rather than making assumptions about them, oftentimes based on their immediate appearance, their grammar, their knowledge of vocabulary, or their particular language variety, the successful teachers saw them more holistically. This enabled those teachers to recognize the students' talents, and to see their proficiency in their heritage language as a strength rather than a deficiency.

In this chapter, you will have a glimpse of learners through four profiles written by teachers of actual students in their classes. We provide you with a framework that you can use to get to know your own students by asking the right questions. The chapter concludes with three retrospectives in which adult heritage language learners look back. Their accounts help us to realize that our heritage languages and cultures are indeed an indelible part of who we are; they never disappear. This is why the teaching of the heritage language learner in the foreign language classroom has such human significance.

Student Profiles

Jason

Diana Scalera

Jason was a special education student who at my request was placed in the Heritage Language Arts class. He was fifteen at the time and had spent half his life in Puerto Rico and half in New York City, moving from one area to the other at one to two year intervals. Most of his family members are bilingual. He was classified as a MIS II student, one with serious emotional and behavioral problems. It was very difficult to teach a class with Jason in it. He would constantly interrupt students, talk loudly to people across the room, and generally not pay attention to the lesson. When he spoke Spanish in class, he stumbled on words and seemed unsure of himself.

I thought he was a student who did not speak much Spanish but understood what he heard. I noticed, however, that when I gave a test with dictation, he would not be able to answer any of the questions. When I let him read the part dictated, he was able to answer the questions with 100 percent accuracy.

I gave this information to the school-based evaluation team. When they rewrote Jason's Individualized Education Plan (IEP), they wrote "Jason cannot speak, read, or write in Spanish." When I asked the assistant principal what criteria were used to draw that conclusion, she was not sure. Fortunately, in this case, there was little correlation between Jason's IEP and the services he actually received. Jason remained in the Heritage Language Arts class.

At the end of the year, we began to prepare for the New York State Regents Comprehensive Examination in Spanish. This is an exam that consists of 24 percent spontaneous conversation, 30 percent reading, 30 percent listening and 16 percent writing. It measures what a high school foreign language student should know after three years of instruction. I knew that Jason would do well on the reading. I also that knew if he had someone sit with him to help him focus he would do well on the writing portion. He could even pass the dictation portion if it were read to him individually rather than with the entire group of test takers. What I had learned over time was that Jason was unable to understand instructions that were given to the group. If I spoke to him directly and individually, he was able to comprehend and follow instructions. This may have accounted for some of his behavioral problems. I was concerned, however, with the dialogue portion, because I had never heard Jason sustain a conversation in Spanish.

As we were practicing the dialogues in class, Jason asked if he could present a dialogue in front of the class with another student instead of having me as his partner. This is generally what I would do, but, with several students with behavioral problems in the class, I tended to maintain tight teacher-centered control. I was reluctant but relented because he was very insistent. He and another student played the parts of a shopkeeper and a customer who had broken an item in the store. The dialogue they created was truly amazing. Both students were completely fluent in a Spanish that came from the Puerto Rican countryside. They were not only fluent, they were very funny and creative. They had the class in stitches. I felt as if I was watching a very funny Spanish-language sitcom. Neither of these students had ever spoken with such fluency before. They had chosen this moment to "be themselves."

What I learned from Jason is that during most of the school year he was trying to approximate my "educated" Spanish. Even though we had spoken often about the acceptability of all varieties of Spanish, what he understood was that he should not speak "his" Spanish in class. His Spanish belonged among friends and family. This incident made me realize what an impact my variety of Spanish had on my students.

Just being the teacher set up my Spanish as the standard even though I am a non-native speaker of Spanish. Although I was careful never to criticize any student for his or her variety of Spanish, Jason considered me the authority and would not allow what he knew to appear in class until the end of the year. His sharing was a wonderful gift and a powerful lesson to me. It made me acutely aware of the impact of the relationship between teacher and student, especially for a special education student who is also a heritage language speaker.

Jason passed the exam at the end of the year. It was the only statewide test Jason would ever pass before graduation.

Manny

John Figueroa

Manny was born in the United States to a Dominican Father and a Nicaraguan Mother. He mainly communicates with his parents in Spanish, and he uses Spanglish with his friends and classmates in school. When he speaks, he often uses slang and idioms that are commonly used in the Dominican Republic. He is also able to switch code/languages with his teachers.

At first, he preferred to speak only in English, but as he became more comfortable, he had no problem speaking in either English or Spanish or both (Spanglish).

Manny does not feel that knowing a second language is a big advantage, since he does not write or read Spanish as well as he speaks it. However, as he has learned more about his heritage language, he has become more proud, comfortable, and appreciative of his parents' language.

Manny is able to speak about any topic since both his parents and grandparents always exposed him to Spanish at home. His level of reading in Spanish is average, because he reads mostly in English. However, since he has been reading in Spanish more consistently, he has definitely improved, and now he is reading literature in Spanish. Manny's writing experience has not been up to par. Prior to coming to this school, and all of the way through middle school, his teachers have been very critical of his poor grammar and level of writing. Even though the syntax and grammar still are in need of improvement, his interest in writing has definitely increased, as has the amount of writing he can do effectively.

Pierre L. and Abdoulaye C.

Jocelyne Daniel

Pierre

Pierre is fifteen years old. He was born in Haiti. When he came to New York, he was only seven years old. Because he was born in December, he had the opportunity of going to school in Port-au-Prince for two years before coming to New York City. When he came to the United States, he went to elementary school and junior high school in Brooklyn. During those years, he did not study French at school.

At home he speaks mostly Créole with his parents and with other adults, but when he speaks to his brother or his sisters, he speaks only English. Pierre is highly motivated. He studied a year of Créole before he started to study French.

Pierre understands simple conversation in French, simple dialogue. He is at the beginner/intermediate level in reading and writing, but he is a beginner in speaking. He knows that speaking is his weak point. He is always looking for an opportunity to say something in French, even if it is not perfect.

Pierre wants to be a chef in order to create Haitian and French cuisine.

Abdoulaye

Abdou is now sixteen years old. He was born in Sénégal. He came to New York five years ago. In Sénégal, French is one of the main languages used, so Abdou speaks French, but his reading and writing skills are weak. When he was in Sénégal, he did not go to a French-speaking school. He was taught in his native language, but he was exposed to the French language. When he attended junior high school in Brooklyn, he found that French was not offered, so he started to study Spanish.

When he started high school, he requested French. He is very interested in learning and sharing with other students. He is eager to learn and share, because he understands that speaking French helps him to connect with many French speakers whom he probably would not have met otherwise.

José

Dora Villani

José was a student in my Level III Heritage Language Learner class last year. He was born in the Dominican Republic and presently lives in a Dominican neighborhood, although his school friends come from all different ethnic groups. José returned to live in the Dominican Republic for a short time since he came to this country. When he was barely three years old, he learned Spanish from his mother who spoke to him only in Spanish, and from watching *novelas* on television with her. Due to family circumstances, he returned to the Dominican Republic at the age of five. He remained there for one year, during which time he attended kindergarten. As one would imagine, his kindergarten education was limited to simple reading and simple vocabulary acquisition.

Before José entered high school in the Bronx as a freshman, he took a placement test in intermediate school, which determined his placement in the Level II Heritage Language learner sequence. The placement test is given to incoming ninth grade students. It is a written test preceded by questions that are sociolinguistic in nature. Ideally it would be a better assessment for placement if the students also received an oral interview. This would give the teachers the opportunity to also assess the communicative ability of the students. However, since the ninth grade incoming class is usually comprised of 900 students, mostly Hispanic, it has been rather difficult to also conduct individual interviews. Even with the placement test, the classes on any given level in the Heritage Language Learner sequence have diverse cognitive and communicative abilities in the heritage language.

When José first came to my class, he was very shy and reluctant to participate. At first, whenever he did participate, he spoke English. I did not correct him, but rather encouraged him to speak Spanish. Several students follow this pattern no matter what the level. As José became more comfortable with the class and with Spanish, there was a change in him. He participated more frequently, and he spoke Spanish. He was able to read fluently, but his writing needed to improve, and it did.

Unfortunately, this class, in which Jose was blossoming, was canceled due to programming problems. José ended up in another Level III Heritage Learner class where I was not the teacher. However, José's enthusiasm for learning Spanish continued. He attended the Spanish class in which he had been scheduled as well as my class every day, even though my class was at the end of his day. And he participated actively. He wanted to learn as much Spanish as possible. I admired him for that and for his enthusiasm. I learned that when he was in the Level III class, it was more difficult for him because of the teacher's teaching and the level of Spanish she used. During the second term, José was in a class where the teacher only spoke English, even though it was a Heritage Language Learner class, and it was too easy for him. In order to get more practice in Spanish, he joined the club, *Orgullo Hispano*, in which the participants are all heritage language learners.

This year José is in Level IV Spanish and is improving continuously. Once again, he is attending my Level III Heritage Language class. He has acquired cognitive ability in Spanish but has also learned a lot about his culture. José is a wonderful young man and a teacher's dream because of his enthusiasm and his thirst for knowledge.

A Framework for Learning about Your Students

All students bring with them to the classroom a set of personal stories, experiences, and emotions that affect how they behave, interact, and learn. By asking the right questions, teachers can acquire the essential insights into the minds and the worlds of their learners and, in so doing, develop the sensitivity and the responsiveness that will help them to achieve success in school. Knowing the right questions to ask can be elusive, particularly when there is no sound basis for shared commonality.

The lists of questions presented here have been divided into six categories. All of the questions were devised by the Project Development Team, checked for validity by teachers experienced in working with heritage language learners and in a variety of school settings. In the six categories, there are questions relating to:

1. *Linguistic proficiency,* that give the teacher a view of the strengths that the learners bring to class with them and the areas where they need further instruction.
2. *Motivation,* that take into account the nature of the learners' identification with the heritage language that make them interested in studying it in school.
3. *Academic preparedness,* that enable the teacher to understand the types of prior educational experiences the students have had as well as their areas of strengths and areas in need of further development.
4. *Cultural connectedness,* that provide insights to the relationship that the learners have with their culture, the extent of their actual involvement with the culture at home and in the community, and their attitudes about that relationship.
5. *Emotional factors,* that help teachers to understand how the learners feel about themselves as people and as students within the context of the classroom and the school.
6. *Societal factors,* that yield information about the place of the students and their families in the larger community.

A Framework for
Learning about Your Students

Linguistic Proficiency

General Questions about Language Use

1. What language does the learner speak? Does the learner use a particular identifiable variety of that language?
2. What is the purpose of language for heritage language learners? Do they see it as a social tool, a political tool, a means of acquiring knowledge, a means of communication? With whom do they use their heritage language for these various purposes? In what settings?
3. In the case of immigrants, what was the nature of their prior school experience before coming to the United States? What attitudes do they have toward schooling that may have emanated from those prior experiences?
4. To what extent are the learners actually successful when engaging in the interpersonal, interpretive, and presentational modes of communication for personal purposes? For academic purposes?
   (Some learners, for example, may have a high degree of proficiency in the interpretive mode but be unwilling to use the language in either the interpersonal or presentational modes. This unwillingness may give a mistaken notion that the student does not know the language.)
5. To what extent are the learners willing to engage in each of these three modes of communication?
6. How successful do they think they are when engaging in these three modes of communication?
7. What are their attitudes regarding their heritage language? How do they feel about using it?
8. How do they feel about being from that heritage language background? How are those feelings expressed?
9. To what extent do the students use the heritage language for communication in school? Describe the situations in which they tend to use the heritage language in school.
10. To what extent are the students engaged in the use of the interpersonal mode of communication in the heritage language outside of the school?

Understanding/Receptivity

1. In what ways do students expose themselves to their heritage language through media (for example, television, radio, motion pictures, theater, music, newspapers, and magazines)? When? Where? What type?
2. Is there a difference between their ability to see/hear/comprehend the various forms of media and their ability to react or respond? In what ways are the students able to demonstrate their comprehension of what is seen/heard?
3. In what types of media do the students tend to express and demonstrate the most interest?
4. For recent immigrants, what exposure did they have to the various media prior to coming to the United States?
5. What types of media are students best able to understand? What is the level of language used in the media that they are best able to understand?
6. What forms of media tend to be the most difficult for the students to understand?

Oral Proficiency

1. What are the students able to speak about? What topics do they speak about and what communicative functions are they able to perform?
2. What is the range of comprehensibility and appropriateness (fluency) of the language used when they are engaged in the interpersonal and presentational modes of communication?
3. What is the degree of linguistic accuracy in their use of the interpersonal and presentational modes of communication? What types of grammatical structures do the students tend to be able to use correctly, and what types of grammatical errors do they tend to make? Are there any discernable patterns in their correct or incorrect use of the language?

Reading

1. What prior exposure has the learner had to reading? What degree of reading readiness has the child achieved prior to entering the school or prior to coming to this particular class?
2. What role does reading play in the student's culture or country of origin?
3. What level of interest in reading do the students appear to have? How much interest do they express?

4. With what reading topics are the students most familiar from their everyday lives? What topics are the students most interested in reading about?

5. What types of texts (for example, newspapers, signs, announcements, advertisements, short stories, and books) are students able to read in the heritage language? What is the level of language of those texts? What subject material do students tend to read most? What is the degree of facility with which they can read?

6. To what extent do students actually engage in reading the heritage language outside of school? What types of reading materials are found in the home? Where do they obtain the material that they read in their heritage language?

7. How are the students best able to demonstrate the degree to which they have understood a text?

Writing

1. What role does writing play in the students' cultures and countries of origin? What has been students' experience with writing prior to coming to this school? To this class?

2. What are the students able to write about? How comfortable are they with writing? How successful are they in accomplishing their writing tasks?

3. What is the range of comprehensibility and appropriateness (fluency) of their language when writing?

4. What is the degree of their linguistic accuracy in writing? What types of grammatical structures do the students tend to be able to use correctly? What types of errors in writing do they tend to make? Are there any discernable patterns in their correct or incorrect use of the heritage language when they are writing?

5. To what extent do the students engage in writing? For what purposes do they tend to write when they are outside of school?

6. What level of interest in writing do the students express? What level of interest in writing do they demonstrate in class?

Motivation

General Interest

1. To what extent and in what ways do the learners demonstrate an interest

in maintaining association with their heritage language at home? In the community? With other students of the same background in school?

2. How willing are the students to learn in general and to learn their heritage language in particular? How is that willingness demonstrated?

3. To what degree do the students demonstrate interest in heritage language classes, and how this interest is actually shown?

Learners' Goals

1. What types of overall academic and life goals do the students seem to have? If the students and their families are recent immigrants, is there any apparent connection between their choice of goals and the immigration experience? Is there any apparent connection between their choice of goals and their proficiency in their heritage language?

2. What do the students want to be able to do in their heritage language? Are there any discernable patterns in their choice of linguistic goals as they move through their years in school or as they are exposed to their heritage language classes?

3. What connection do they see between their heritage language and the world of work? The world of higher education? What influence does their awareness of this connection have on their performance in heritage language classes? In their performance in school in general?

4. What is the nature of the relationship that the students have with their heritage language teachers? Their teachers of other subjects? To what extent does this student-teacher relationship influence the students' attitudes and their performance in the heritage language class? In school in general?

Academic Preparedness

1. For immigrant students, what was the nature of their exposure to formal schooling in and through the heritage language before coming to the United States? What skills do the students bring with them?

2. What study skills and learning strategies do the students tend to use? Where/how did they acquire those skills and strategies?

3. What study skills and learning strategies do the students need to acquire in order to be successful in school in general? In heritage language classes?

4. To what extent do the learners know what to expect in terms of classroom procedures? Course requirements? Teacher expectations?

5. What kinds of stress do the students experience when dealing with their academic subjects? With different/unfamiliar teaching strategies? How does this stress manifest itself?

6. In which courses do the students tend to excel? What are the reasons for their success in these courses?

7. Which courses tend to be the most difficult/problematic? What are the sources of their difficulties?

8. How do the students view themselves academically in relation to others? To what extent are the students able to evaluate their academic performance in relationship to that of their peers? To what extent are they able to evaluate their heritage language proficiency in relationship to that of others?

Cultural Connectedness

1. What is the nature and extent of the students' involvement with the practices of their heritage cultures outside of school? To what extent do they participate in the cultural life of the community? What type of social life do they lead after school?

2. What is the nature of the students' family lives? Are the students living with their biological parents? To what degree do they participate in the cultural lives of their families?

3. To what extent and in what ways is family life associated with the heritage culture?

4. To what degree are the students involved with the tangible products of their heritage culture?

5. To what extent are their life perspectives and their goals associated with their heritage culture? How comfortable are the students with their perspectives and goals within the school setting? Within the larger social context? In what ways do their perspectives and goals tend to change over time?

6. How aware are the students of the political, social, and economic events that surround them?

7. Do the students have a perception of themselves as a minority or as a minority within a minority? If so, how does this perception manifest itself in the classroom? In the school?

8. Are there forces/influences at work in their environment that affect their willingness to learn their heritage language? If so what are those forces/influences?

9. How long have the students and their families been in the United States? If they are recent immigrants, why and how did they come here? What are their families' plans vis-à-vis their future and their country of origin?

10. What are the attitudes/perceptions of parents toward their own language in the United States? In what ways do these attitudes/perceptions affect their children?

Emotional Factors

1. What is the nature of the students' life experiences outside of school? In what ways do those experiences affect their academic performance and/or general behavior in school?

2. What is the nature of the relationship among students of the same heritage language background? What attitudes do they have toward each other's language varieties? Toward each other's socioeconomic status? In what ways do those relationships and attitudes affect their academic performance and/or general behavior in school?

3. What types of emotional support do heritage language students tend to need in class? In school in general? Are there any discernable patterns in the way in which these needs are expressed?

4. What degree of self-awareness do students exhibit in relationship to the learning task and to the learning environment?

5. How do students feel about what they already know in their heritage language?

Societal Factors

1. Where do the students and their families tend to reside? What is the nature of their living conditions?

2. What is the nature of the family structure in the heritage culture? How does this compare to the family structure as it exists here in the United States?

3. What is the employment history of the students' families? How does this employment profile affect their life style? What are the students' attitudes/perceptions regarding their families' socioeconomic status? How do those attitudes and perceptions manifest themselves in class? In school in general?

4. What is the nature of the relationship between the heritage language stu-

dents and students of other language backgrounds? What attitudes do they have regarding other students' languages and cultures? In what ways do the relationships and attitudes affect their academic performance and/or general behavior in school?

5. What are the attitudes of the non-heritage language students and teachers toward the heritage language students and their culture? How do those attitudes manifest themselves in the school setting?

6. In what kinds of extra-curricular activities do the heritage language students become involved? To what extent do language and culture issues affect that involvement?

Teachers who are able to answer these questions about their students will have an adequate understanding of the backgrounds and experiences that they bring to class, thus enabling them to approach the entire teaching/learning process in a more informed and, therefore, a more effective manner.

It is important to keep in mind that some of the questions can be answered for entire groups of learners, but that it is often necessary to seek specific answers for individual learners, recognizing that each learner may have a particular set of characteristics that will impact uniquely on the teaching/learning process. It is also important to remember that the answers will not be found in a week, a month, or even a year. There are many questions and answers. Over time, as teachers keep asking and probing, they will become more adept at seeking out information. Gradually, they will build a valuable information base that will inform them in their work and prevent them from basing what they do on mistaken personal assumptions about the learners.

Heritage Language Learners Look Back

Emily: A Life Lived in Two Worlds

Andrew Parker

This language barrier has fossilized Emily's relationship with her parents at a kind of infantile level of development, which is unlikely to improve until either they improve their English or she works on her Korean.

My friend Emily was born in New York about a year after her parents moved here from Korea. Rather than living in a Korean enclave like Fort Lee, New Jersey, or in the neighborhoods of Elmhurst or Flushing in Queens, her family settled down in the almost all-white borough of Staten Island, where she lived until the age of seventeen, when she went to an out-of-town college.

She grew up isolated from other Koreans geographically, and also isolated from her white American neighbors culturally and linguistically. Her parents barely spoke any English at all when they first arrived, and they were mistrustful and afraid of non-Koreans. So, Emily virtually had no exposure to English or to anyone outside of her family until she went to a public-school kindergarten at the age of five. She was pretty much the only ESL (English as a Second Language) student in her school, and it took her a while to assimilate with her classmates and learn English. Ultimately, by the time she was in second or third grade, she learned to get by in English, a product of the "sink-or-swim" method of English instruction. She maintained a mild Korean accent into the early years of high school, but eventually she was able to eliminate it by mimicking the strong (and much-stigmatized) Staten Island accent of her neighborhood friends. When she got to college, she quickly learned that the regional accent in which she had learned to speak English was low in social prestige, so she almost immediately adopted a more neutral American accent, like a TV-anchor person, which she maintains to this day.

An interesting by-product of her particular sort of bilingualism and her self-consciousness about being perceived as having an accent is that she possesses an uncanny ability to imitate other peoples' accents and verbal mannerisms. She mimicked an authentic British accent, for instance, within several minutes of stepping off the plane at Heathrow. Now, at the age of twenty-four, Emily speaks English like any other middle-class, educated native. The only glitch in her English competence, which might betray her as a non-native speaker, is her utter inability to comprehend certain American idioms and folk expressions. For instance, if someone were to characterize the even-sidedness of a trivial decision by saying, "It's six of one and a half dozen of the other," she would nod her head in utter incomprehension. (Interestingly enough, one does not realize just how large a component of our language is composed of such expressions until one spends time with someone who does not understand any of them.)

Anyway, regrettably, Emily's Korean-language ability has not kept pace with her ability to communicate in English. She never learned to read or write in Korean, even though Korean is written in a simple phonetic alphabet. Her ability to understand spoken Korean is much better than her ability to produce Korean utterances on her own, and she is unable, for the most part, to speak more than a sentence or two without code-mixing to supply the vocabulary she lacks. What is interesting, though, is that she possesses the higher-order language abilities in Korean, which most second-language learner's lack. For example, she has the ability to process Korean in an automatic and unconscious way, and she has a remarkable degree of intuitive mastery of the social functions of the language. She can be meticulously polite, for instance, in Korean, even when her vocabulary and grammar fail her. (It should be noted that politeness in Korean requires a subtle and complex awareness of social relationships and a knowledge of how to adjust a bewildering array of politeness morphemes and relationship markers depending on the person to whom one is speaking.) She can understand Korean humor and go into fits of laughter over Korean-language sitcoms on UHF television, but she understands very little of the Korean nightly news. Often when we encounter Koreans at restaurants or stores, or overhear strangers speaking Korean on the street, she will be unable to decipher the explicit content of their utterances, but she can immediately jump to a conclusion about whether they are being nice or not. This happens all the time. She will beam all over after exchanging a few words with a shopkeeper if he uses what she considers to be appropriate or kind politeness markers, such as calling her "little sister" rather than "madam." At other times she will scowl in disgust at what appears to me to be an identical situation, except in those cases, the shopkeeper may have sounded patronizing, forward, or dismissive. She makes up for her lack of vocabulary and grammar skills by being super-sensitive to culturally specific paralinguistic features like tone of voice and body language.

The contexts or social domains in which Emily is comfortable communicating in Korean, understandably, are restricted mostly to interactions with her family. She says that she understands her parents perfectly when they are admonishing her or ordering her around. The traditional Korean culture in which she was raised is patriarchal and observes a rigid hierarchy of social relationships. When she is being spoken to as an adult speaks to a child, with blandishments, commands, or sharp reprimands, she understands Korean perfectly. However, she is unable to communicate adequately in Korean with her parents when she is trying to explain an opinion, justify a personal choice, or disagree with them about something, because as a young girl, she never had occasion to employ such linguistic functions. She code-mixes to supplement her inadequate Korean vocabulary with English words, but she code-switches into Korean when she is getting yelled at and has to defend herself.

Unfortunately, because of her parents' inadequate English and her inadequate Korean, they tend to communicate with each other within the linguistic constraints of parent–child language, the language that she understood and spoke as a little girl before she learned English. Emily and her parents understand each other completely when they are making meaningless sweet-talk or when they are yelling at her and she is trying to talk her way out of getting in trouble. This language barrier has, to borrow a linguistic term, fossilized Emily's relationship with her parents at a kind of infantile level of development, which is unlikely to improve until either they improve their English or she works on her Korean.

On some level, though, Emily feels a lack of motivation to improve her own ability to speak Korean, and part of the reason for this lack of motivation is that, unlike more egalitarian languages such as Spanish, the Korean language encodes social status differences, and a young woman in Korean culture (and, hence, language) has inferior social status. The Confucian hierarchy is reflected in the grammar, lexicon, and pragmatics of the language. For instance, it is inappropriate on a pragmatic level for a young woman to speak in a forceful, self-assured way to someone who is older, or male or, in some other way, a social superior. A young woman like Emily is expected to use a more tentative, supplicating tone of voice, and make the necessary lexical and grammatical changes, when expressing an opinion to someone to whom she owes respect, such as her parents or boss. When Emily tries to express a point of view to her parents in her imperfect Korean, they often get angry at her and refuse to listen because they feel that she is using an "American tone of voice," that she sounds inappropriately strong or challenging. When she expresses herself to them in English with the appropriate Korean-style deference and affected tone of uncertainty, they will listen to her without getting offended, but she feels that she is unable to say adequately what is on her mind. She lacks the command of Korean necessary to use both the paralinguistic features of the language and the language itself to express herself to her parents, and she is unable to know for sure whether or not it would even make a difference.

A friend who grew up in Korea told Emily recently that there is no equivalent word in the Korean language to express the concept of personal boundary. Therefore, even if Emily could speak perfect Korean, she would still have trouble asserting some of the values that she grew up with in the United States, and which, as an adult, she would like her parents to respect.

Emily and her parents face an obvious language barrier, one that impedes communication and exacerbates the misunderstandings that most children and parents experience as the children grow into adulthood and try to carve out adult identities for themselves. Of course, there is usually some sort of "generation gap" between parents and their children, but in Emily's case the gap is particularly wide. Most of the parents of Emily's friends came of age in America in the sixties, experiencing the social revolution first-hand and absorbing at least some of the sixties' counter-cultural values. Emily's parents, however, came to the United States in the early seventies after the anti-traditionalism of the hippies had influenced American values but before it had had any influence on Korean values. Emily's parents always are lecturing her about what it means to be a good Korean, but the traditional values that they try to impart are somewhat anachronistic at this point. Emily's Korean-born friends are always telling her that things have changed over in Korea, that women have gained a greater degree of equality, that they are free to take on nontraditional roles for themselves, and that the once-rigid social hierarchy is becoming more flexible. But Emily's parents, who are themselves now caught between two cultures, think that things ought to be the way they were. They see contemporary American values as being antithetical to their traditional Korean values, and they see in their daughter the embodiment of much of what they loathe.

Emily, for her part, is also trying to straddle two worlds. She grew up with the progressive values of American youth culture, and she developed, through hard personal experience, an intense sensitivity to the plight of the social outsider. As the only Asian child in an all-white school, she transgressed social boundaries and, perhaps as a result, has adopted, as a supreme social and moral value, the importance of being open-minded about the permeability of social categories, a value is not shared by her parents. Emily's feminism and her political commitment to social equality for all racial and ethnic groups seem to have their provenance in her awkward experience as a Korean girl growing up in white suburbia, but it is precisely these values which strike her parents as being so un-Korean.

It is easy to imagine, then, that much of Emily's attitude toward her bilingualism, toward her home language, is bound up in her feelings about her relationship with her parents. She has a deep ambivalence toward the Korean language and culture. She says that she wants to live in Korea for a while to get better at the language. She also says that she would like her children to grow up speaking English and Korean, but, at the same time, she really lives her life with a hard-to-conceal mistrust of all things Korean. For her, on some level, Korean is the language of domestic disputes, reprimands, and childhood beatings. She has every intention of improving her Korean-language ability, but it is unlikely to happen until she develops a more positive perspective on Korean-ness in general.

Learning My Heritage Language:
An Odyssey of Self-Discovery

Vincent Giangreco

Perhaps it is Virgil and Cicero coming home to roost, coming to reclaim me and to remind me that my cultural affiliation started a long time ago with Grandpa, discussing the different ways of cooking and eating a tomato.

Although my journey with and in the Italian language did not begin until I was thirty-three years old, I guess I could say that it had its roots in a kind of minimalist bilingualism that I engaged in as a very young child with my grandfather who spoke no English. There were words and phrases exchanged, the meanings of which were immediately felt and realized, since they lay in the concreteness of everyday things and actions, like food and eating, and in the very physical displays of affection. I should say that my bilingualism at this stage was Sicilian and English because Sicilian is what my grandfather and parents spoke, and it is a very distinct dialect of Italian. Actually, Sicilian and standard Italian can be thought of as different languages, since they are essentially mutually unintelligible.

My grandfather, then, was my Sicilian language target, with the living room and kitchen being the exclusive domains in which we spoke. English was by far my dominant language, since it was the only one I spoke with my parents, sisters, other relatives and friends. So, in these domains I engaged in an active, albeit very limited, functional bilingualism—Sicilian with my grandfather and English with my parents and everyone else. Given the clear-cut division in terms of language targets and domains, this rightfully could be thought of as an example of diglossia on an individual level (Baker, p.36).

A distinction needs to be made between my functional bilingualism and my language background. In my family, Sicilian was used in a variety of contexts and for a variety of purposes. My grandfather used Sicilian to speak to me about food and cooking. My parents, on the other hand, used it to speak to each other and to relatives when I was not around, and it was what they occasionally spoke to each other when my sisters and I were around, to avoid having us understand what they were saying to each other. However, they never spoke to my sisters or to me in what was their native language. Sicilian was part of my nonparticipative language background. As my grandfather became more and more absent from the family, my listening and speaking skills were limited and never went beyond what they were when I was six or seven years old. Eventually, they were lost completely. My parents, however, had come to the United States when they were twelve years old, and learned to speak English quite as fluently as native born English speakers. Consequently, my not having learned Sicilian as my first language is a classic example of Fishman's three generation hypothesis (Baker, p.46) whereby the heritage language is completely lost by the third generation. My parents, who were second generation and intent on assimilating, spoke exclusively in English with their children (who were third generation) and in domains that were once reserved only for Sicilian.

This was my parents' attitude toward their first language as well as toward English, which led to the loss of Sicilian as a language of communication at home across generations. Our home was split between two languages. English was perceived as the language of prestige, and thus success, integration, and assimilation. Sicilian was the language not only associated with discrimination and poverty, but was also the language associated with the innocence and happiness of a childhood from which they were suddenly and brutally alienated, as well as with the consequent trauma of abandonment from their native land. To speak to their children in Sicilian meant to be reminded of their own childhood alienation.

I think that the exclusion from their language, which was often present, provided me with the necessary condition to want, eventually, to establish a connection with a culture that has reflected my identity in certain respects, but a culture from which I have been deprived of full participation. Perhaps like my parents, I, too, have kept a distance from their first language by becoming deeply involved with Italian and not with Sicilian. Of course it was the logical thing to do, to learn the prestige variety spoken by the great majority. But I cannot help wondering, almost twenty years after I first started studying Italian, whether getting close to their language might have meant getting closer to the pain and trauma they so very much wanted to forget but which deeply affected them throughout their lives.

Even though some words, phrases, and sounds in Sicilian always remained with me from my early childhood experiences, my receptive and productive skills were at an elementary level when I began studying Italian. In a way, I was a classic heritage language learner returning to my roots or at least close to my roots—Italian rather than Sicilian. My "fifth area of language competence"(Baker, p.7), my ability to think in the language, did not begin to develop until I made several trips to Italy for a few months at a time and lived with only Italian speakers. This was also after I had already been studying the language for two years in New York.

My attitude toward the Italian language was very positive since the language represented the cultural link to an identity that I both had been part of and cut off from. Consequently, my motivation to study systematically was very high. The only formal training I had in Italian was a year of private lessons, once or twice a week, and one year of conversational practice in a private school in New York, after I made several trips to Italy. I consistently studied on my own, avidly reading newspapers, books, mostly literature and history, listening to radio and television, watching movies, going to museums, and engaging in discussions whenever I could. In terms of ability, I certainly was more able, at least in the earlier years, to read the language than to speak or understand it. My writing ability also exceeded my speaking and listening skills, since I spent much time engaging in creative writing as a way of studying the grammar during my private lessons. Although I did make progress in understanding and speaking during my semi-formal training, I was still burdened by my inability to "think" in Italian.

It was not until after I had spent my first year in Italy, that I really began to think in the language and to feel a concomitant increase in my listening skills. I experienced this "thinking" in the language as a quantum leap rather than a gradual development, as if a Gestalt of the language emerged and represented itself in thought. However, after this took place, I became more aware of the content and context of thought. I also realized that it was easier for me to think and speak in Italian in certain domains and with certain people than others. For example, it was easier for me to think in Italian and speak the language if the discussions focused on current events, immediate problems of city living, issues of the neighborhood, or any other topics that were generally more familiar and concrete, and less abstract and philosophical. If the circumstances were relaxed and familiar, and if I perceived the person to whom I spoke as patient and willing to take into consideration that I was not a native speaker, then I could use the language with greater ease and comfort. In short, anything that would interfere with the fluency of my own native English would interfere even more so with my ability to use my Italian. All these differences notwithstanding, I realized at this point that I was functionally bilingual. I was able to say what I wanted to say and understand what was said with a variety of people in various domains such as a stranger on a bus, or the local bar owner at the bar, or a friend at a dinner party. My performance level, however, was not the same across all of those domains, nor was it at the same level as a native speaker.

As the years passed, my performance level in all skills increased, but it certainly did not increase equally across skills. A difference between meaning and form became more evident. My ability to speak with grammatical accuracy was not systematic; it was more related to whom I was speaking and the domain in which the conversation was taking place than in the content of the conversation. If I felt any antagonism toward me because I was a foreigner, or any impatience because I was not from the neighborhood, and, therefore, unable to use the local dialect and slang, then I might trip up on my words and my grammar, but I could still make my self completely understood. My ability to express meaning, regardless of topic and level of abstraction, surpassed my grammatical form. In general, although my sentence structure often equaled that of a native speaker, I would still occasionally make elementary mistakes, such as using the wrong preposition or using a feminine article with a masculine noun. These were mistakes that a native speaker, who was not as conversant as I on topics of art, literature, and politics, would never make.

My flaws and idiosyncrasies led to an identification dilemma. People would often think that I was from some place outside of Italy, somewhere in northern Europe. Occasionally, I was pegged as an American who happens to have very good pronunciation in Italian. Since I lived in Rome, the Roman accent began to influence my pronunciation of certain words, and, eventually, the accent was present in my general speech patterns. So I became the northern Italian or northern European who obviously lived in Rome, and, occasionally, the American who obviously lived in Rome. I became more and more aware that my accent varied according to how much I concentrated on Italian phonology while I was speaking. It also varied depending upon how Italian, or non-Italian, I felt in relation the person or people to whom I was speaking, and whether I was being perceived as more Italian or American culturally. Even though I was certainly interested in the aesthetics of proper pronunciation, that was not the only point of consideration. An equally important issue was one of identity. This was an identity from which I felt cut off, or an identity with which I very much wanted to be associated. In short, my accent would vary according to the extent to which I identified with the people and situations around me.

As I grew more confident in my overall language competence and in myself as an identity emerging in my own right, my need for native-like pronunciation diminished. This language and its culture were and are part of my identity, but not to the exclusion of all other influences of my life. They interact and combine in ways that are difficult to grasp, and they continue to interact and combine to produce a new emergent identity, namely me.

The only formal evidence I have of language achievement is a language proficiency exam I took for twelve credits in order to enter the TESOL (Teachers of English to Speakers of Other Languages) program. Although I received all twelve credits and am capable of another twelve, my language skills are certainly not equally distributed across the four skill areas. If I watch a more complicated film or theater piece, I miss about 10 to 15 percent that would not be missed by a native speaker. Even though I have read more than forty books on literature, art, politics, and history and even though I read at least one or two newspapers a day during the six years that I lived in Rome and, perhaps, one newspaper a week during the seventeen years since I left there, I still cannot process the language as quickly as I can in English. Perhaps I just have not had enough experience in the language.

The quantity of my experience in Italian, which is much less than that of a native speaker, is only one variable. I also have not had the quality of experience that a more formal academic environment can provide. In all the years that I have been involved with the Italian language, I have actually done very little writing compared to my experience speaking, listening, reading, and, of course, thinking. Perhaps a more academically focused writing experience in writing essays and papers would have helped me in the other areas of my language ability.

My six years living in Italy were not all consecutive. On three occasions, I spent one year in Italy and one year in New York. When I was in New York, I did not speak Italian much, although I regularly read and listened to the radio and watched movies. Perhaps these interruptions affected my overall language performance. However, when I lived in Italy, I spent at least 80 percent of the time with very cultured, educated, native speakers. I became very fluent because I lived and breathed the language. I used it most of the day to speak about, read about, and listen to everything ranging from the mundane to the abstract. Although I had the ability to write about all of those things, I did not use my writing skills and, consequently, did not improve and refine it. Perhaps that affected my other skills as well. Now, I can write an essay or an informal letter, but I cannot adequately write a very formal letter in Italian without help. Of course I can do it in English, because my schooling was all in English. I cannot play with the Italian language and make puns with double meanings as I can in English, because I lack the depth of knowledge of the semantic differences of words and phrases. I lack the richness of idioms and idiomatic phrases, and my use of slang is very limited.

In conclusion, from my personal experience, I am convinced that motivation plays a very major role in language learning. The desire to relate to and identify with another culture is also of prime importance on the motivational continuum. Even though I have not arrived at native-like proficiency in all skills in all situations, I have arrived at the point where I feel more emotionally connected and centered speaking Italian rather than English under certain circumstances. Perhaps this relates to one of the things that language represents, namely, a cultural perspective. Italians are rhetorical by nature and have been throughout history. Every topic has as many points of view as there are people discussing it. I realize, through my journey with the language, that I have always been rhetorical and love to discuss all of the possible aspects of a subject, an attitude that occasionally meets with impatience and ire among Americans, who have much more dog-matic opinions about "how it is." Perhaps it is Virgil and Cicero coming home to roost, coming to reclaim me and to remind me that my cultural affiliation start-ed a long time ago with Grandpa, discussing the different ways of cooking and eating a tomato.

I think that the most powerful implications of my journey with the Italian language are the crucial roles of motivation in learning the language and main-taining it. Working at maintaining and developing one's heritage language or lan-guages is an enriching experience. Even though some adolescents go through a period of rejecting their heritage language in favor of the majority language for prestige, fashion, peer pressure and/or rebellion against parental authority (Romero), I cannot imagine any adult not feeling good about themselves for being able to speak the language of their parents.

As a child, I always felt bad about not being able to understand my parents when they spoke in Sicilian to each other and to relatives. I felt cut off and excluded. I remember how much I wanted to know what was going on and how frustrated I felt not being able to do so. Consequently, I felt inadequate, because I was not empowered to fully negotiate in a language that was very important to my parents and very much a part of my linguistic, my cultural, my psychologi-cal background. Should we not help students maintain this connection? How could it not empower children psychologically if they are able to interact fully with the world inside and outside of their own home? Why was I so motivated to reconnect with my heritage language if it were not to regain some sense of the personal empowerment from which I had been cut off? Should not one of the goals of education be to empower children so that they can negotiate adequate-ly with the world around them and thus develop a greater sense of self-esteem? How can children develop a deeper sense of self-esteem if they are cut off from interacting with their parents in the only language that their parents can use to truly express their love, the language that guards the precious memories of their own childhood?

Cummins (1989) speaks about empowering children psychologically and emotionally so that they will go on to develop positive self-concepts and break the vicious circle of the negative self-fulfilling prophecy incurred by an often inherently racist educational system. If the educational system, not only in indi-vidual cities but nationwide, does not adequately address the issues of cultural identity as expressed and formed through the students' heritage language, then this will disempower the children, as it did to me, by creating, at least on some level, a sense of inadequacy, a loss of pride and, to some extent, a negative self-concept. If students are not given the opportunity to identify more profoundly with their heritage language as a means of empowerment, then is this not an act of institutional racism?

References

Baker, Colin. 1997. *Foundations of Bilingual Education and Bilingualism, 2nd Edition.* Multilingual Matters Ltd.

Cummins, J. 1989. *Empowering Minority Students.* Sacramento, CA: California Association of Bilingual Education (CABE).

Romero, M. 1999. Class notes for the course Principles and Practices of Bilingual Education. Fall 1999. New York: Hunter College of the City University of New York.

Keeping One's Language: Looking Back with Regret

Jacqueline Rizk

I can communicate my love for my grandmother but, since I cannot converse freely with her, I feel cheated of fully knowing her.

My parents were born, raised, and married in Egypt. My sister was six months old when they decided to emigrate to America. I was born here four and one-half years later.

When my parents first came to this country, they struggled with English. They always spoke Arabic at home. For this reason, my sister, Dahlia, learned to speak Arabic. When I came along, five years later, Dahlia was already attending school.

In elementary school, Dahlia sometimes confused the two languages, which she then spoke with the same level of fluency. Her teacher saw this as a problem. She advised my mother of her worries that Dahlia would not be able to learn English fluently if they continued to speak to her in another language. My parents took this very seriously. They did not want to limit their children's opportunities or learning abilities. For this reason, they spoke to my sister and me in English while we were growing up.

Now, I look back with amazement on the impact that one person, my sister's elementary school teacher, had on our lives. Once I was in my later years of elementary school, when my parents were no longer worried that I would have difficulty with English, they made several attempts to teach me Arabic. At that time in my life, however, I felt that being Egyptian made me "different," and not many young children enjoy being different from their peers. I used to get angry with my parents when they spoke to me in Arabic. I would remind them that they were in America and that I was American.

I am a first generation American, and I did not acquire my parents' native language. The impact that my inability to communicate in Arabic has had on my life has been tremendous. While I am with my parents, I cannot always understand the conversations they are having. My extended family is very large, so that at our many family functions, I constantly have to ask, "What's going on?" While I am very close to my family, my inability to speak and understand Arabic does create a communication barrier for me. My only living grandparent, my mother's mother, lives here, but she does not speak English. I can communicate my love for her, but, since I cannot converse freely with her, I feel cheated of fully knowing her.

Now that I understand what I have missed by not learning my parent's native language, I regret the loss. I realize that it will be much more difficult to retrieve Arabic as an adult than if I had learned it as a child and maintained it from that point. I am trying. I have asked my parents to speak to me only in Arabic while I am at home. It constantly amazes me how little I know of a language that was spoken around me my entire life.

As I learn more about language education, I find it very interesting how different countries value and utilize language instruction in schools. Of course, there are reasons for this. My father emerged from schooling in Egypt as a bilingual. My mother is a trilingual. I emerged from schooling as a monolingual. I acquired a second language, but it required an additional academic major and study abroad. These efforts were costly in terms of time and money.

My parents' education was very different from mine. In Egypt, there was, and still is, a huge focus on second and third language acquisition. My mother attended French schools until she reached the college level. She then attended the American University of Cairo. My father attended the same university. My parents feel that the reason for the push toward bilingualism and multiculturalism can be attributed to political and financial factors. Egypt's number one source of income is tourism. Without it, the economy would suffer greatly. By learning other languages you can communicate with tourists. This makes you more marketable, and it strengthens the economy of the country.

Throughout time, it seems that the United States has changed its stance on the issue of language education. Most of my education took place in the 1980s and 1990s. A movement toward a more global education influenced this time period. A second language was mandatory in order to fulfill high school graduation requirements. The three years of Spanish that I took still did not compare to the dual language schooling that my parents experienced.

I began to learn Spanish at the high school level and continued throughout college. My goal was to learn the language and be able to communicate fluently. I wanted to become bilingual. While in college, I realized that study abroad was necessary in order to achieve that goal. I spent every summer during college in Mexico. I realize that learning Spanish has made me more marketable in today's society, but it was more of a personal achievement for me. If Arabic had been available in my curriculum, I probably would have studied it. Unfortunately, it was not.

As I continue my studies, I realize how important it is to allow children to hold on to their heritage language. Good heritage language programs will encourage them to do so. This will not only provide students with an opportunity to be more marketable in today's society; it will also allow them to hold on to their culture.

Chapter 3
Goals and Fundamental Beliefs

Editors' Notes

As the Project Development Team proceeded in their efforts to identify what teachers should know and be able to do when working with heritage language learners, it became increasingly apparent that, as Parker J. Palmer states in his book *The Courage to Teach*, "teaching emerges from one's inwardness."

As teachers, our attitudes toward our students, the way in which we interact with them, our degree of effectiveness in reaching their needs through instruction, the way the students feel in our presence, and the goals that we identify for them all are based fundamentally on our system of beliefs. Virtually every aspect of what we do with and for our students stems from our beliefs about them as learners and as people.

The Team members found that they could not address the challenge of developing a teacher preparation program until they explored and stated what they believed about themselves as teachers of heritage language learners, about the learners themselves, about the nature of the learning environment, and about the qualities of an effective curriculum.

This chapter of the volume allows you, the reader, to explore this issue of beliefs and the goals that emanate from them. Diana Scalera takes you into the classroom on a voyage of self-discovery that gave rise to her own set of beliefs, beliefs that changed her life as a teacher, enabling her to teach and her students to learn. Her voice and the voices of the students that speak in her article provide a clear understanding of the fundamental role that beliefs play, particularly when it comes to the heritage language learner. They will resonate with any teacher who has ever faced a class not knowing what to do.

The Statement of Goals and Fundamental Beliefs that follows is the product of the Team's own self-examination. We hope that the Statement will guide and inform you, the reader, in your own consideration of what you believe.

Teacher Beliefs and the Heritage Language Learner: What Will You Teach Your Students?

Diana Scalera ✳

You have just been told that you will teach Spanish to heritage speakers, a new course in your school. After the initial panic wears away, serious fear takes hold. There is no state curriculum. There is no local curriculum. Your academic training never mentioned that you would have to teach this group of students. A review of the few textbooks available convinces you that you will have to find other resources to establish realistic goals and outcomes for your students. When you ask for help, your supervisor suggests that this is an opportunity to be creative. The choices you make while teaching this course will depend on who you are, the training you have had, and what you believe about heritage language learners.

It is recognized that student motivation is one of the main determinants of second/foreign language acquisition (Dörnyei 1994; Gardner and Trembly 1994; Oxford and Shearin 1994). However, we know very little about the impact of teacher motivation. Given the lack of all other types of support, the teacher of heritage language learners is the single most important element that will determine the success of his or her students. Each teacher's beliefs about how to teach and about the abilities of heritage language learners will have a major impact on the decisions he and she makes in terms of use of class time, types of assignments, and how and why students are motivated to learn (Vanpatten 1997).

This article will examine the initiation of this teacher into the field of heritage language teaching as a prototype of what many teachers experience in light of the social context in which courses for heritage language learners are created and taught, the lack of institutional support for these programs and the dearth of materials available. Given the changing demographics of the United States, all foreign language teachers should be prepared to teach heritage language learners. I will discuss some of the essential components of that preparation.

Social Context

One method used to analyze the social context in which heritage languages are taught is to measure the vitality of the heritage language— "that which makes a group likely to behave as a distinctive and active collective entity in intergroup situations" (Giles, Bourhis, and Taylor 1977, p. 308). Vitality has been studied by many researchers when two languages coexist in one geographical location. The vitality of a language can be measured in two manners: subjective and objective. Researchers who measure both find that subjective and objective factors are highly correlated. The vitality rating of an ethnolinguistic group can suggest the likelihood of survival of that group in an interethnic situation (p. 198).

Subjective factors relate to the perceptions of the different linguistic groups toward speakers of their own and the other language. These conditions may be at least as important as objective factors in determining ethnic vitality (p. 198). What does society-at-large believe about speakers of particular language? How have speakers of that language internalized those messages?

When high school freshmen, for example, are first placed into a Spanish heritage language classroom and notice that all their classmates are Hispanic, they often ask, "Is this a remedial class?" Students have been conditioned to believe that being Hispanic is a liability in the U.S. school system, so this becomes their first conclusion (Scalera, personal communication, 1994-1999).

The objective vitality can be measured by three main factors: economic and social status variables, demographic variables, and institutional support variables (Scalera 1994-1999, p. 197). The objective vitality of languages other than English in the United States can be very low in certain parts of the United States.

The New York Times recently examined how this plays out in Mount Kisco, a small town in Westchester County, New York. Thirteen percent of this town's population of 9,100 is now of Latin American origin. The Hispanic population is mostly made up of workers who clean houses, manicure lawns, or work in construction, while the majority of the town's residents are of the profession-al class. During the mid-nineties racist letters appeared in the local newspaper denouncing the presence of Hispanics in the town. There has also been grad-ual white flight from this town. One local resident said, "I bought a half-mil-lion dollar house up here to get away from people like that." Mount Kisco has asked surrounding communities to help pay for social services that this popu-lation needs, because they, too, benefit from the labor of these immigrant workers. Even some of those who have befriended the Hispanic community have suggested that the community alter its cultural practices to alleviate the discomfort it causes the non-Hispanic population. A local clergyman helped create a storefront community center where Hispanics can go inside and watch television, instead of congregating in the streets to socialize, which is a normal practice in most Latin American countries. A retired teacher is quoted in this article, lamenting that "our town is not what it used to be" (Gross 2000). These attitudes do not stop at the school house door. Even when schools create pro-grams to address the needs of heritage language learners, as has been done suc-cessfully in this town's schools, the attitudes of neighbors, teachers, and class-mates will have a lasting impact on the psyche's of the children of these immi-grant workers.

Institutional Support

The federal support for the teaching of heritage languages is limited to students who have been categorized as English Language Learners. These students may receive instruction in their heritage language until such time as they have been determined to have achieved a sufficient proficiency in English (Bilingual Educa-tion Act 2000).

The *Standards for Foreign Language Learning: Preparing for the 21st Century*, more commonly known as the "National Standards" mentions heritage language learners in a few paragraphs concerning diverse learners. These standards do not provide specific goals for heritage language learners that are different from sec-ond language learners (1996).

A review of state curricula from states with large populations of heritage speakers reveals that there is concern for heritage language learners who need to learn English, but there is no evidence that students who are also English dominant have a place in the curriculum. Texas, for example, has a well-developed native Spanish curriculum for children who are learning English up until these students reach high school. During high school, all learners become foreign language learners (Texas Essential Knowledge and Skills 2000).

California's Draft Foreign Language Curriculum Framework K-12 (2000) includes recognition of the existence of heritage learners, but once again defines them as English language learners. There are, however, several references to the needs of heritage learners and the need for professional development. There are no separate goals or instructional mandates, but this document suggests that students be placed in levels of foreign language appropriate to their skills.

New York City has created a document that includes learning standards for Spanish Language Arts. Eighty-six percent of the heritage speakers in New York City are Spanish-speaking. Its *New Standards™ Performance Standards* (1997) include Spanish Language Arts for all levels of instruction and explain that these standards parallel the English Language Arts curriculum and can be applied to other languages that are taught in the city. Once again, these standards are presented as support for English language learners.

Canada has a very different approach to heritage language learners. Its International Language Program has a national curriculum to provide home language enrichment to all heritage language learners. This curriculum is designed for any student with native ability in a language other than English. In Ontario alone, the International Language Program has an enrollment of over 120,000 students, most of whom attend two and a half hours per week, or eighty hours per year. There are more than 4,500 heritage language classes in sixty-three different languages. It is believed that every language in the world is taught somewhere in Canada (Oketani, 1997).

Teacher training for heritage language courses is mostly unavailable at the university level. Hunter College, however, is piloting a heritage language methods course that may become a requirement for all foreign language teachers. Because of the history of the lack of training, in many cases, a teacher fluent in the needed language is asked to teach a heritage language course. Little consideration can be given to that particular teacher's preparation because there is not a large enough pool of teachers who have the high level of proficiency necessary to teach such a course. With more commonly taught languages, a foreign language teacher is usually the best candidate. With the less commonly taught languages, a math teacher from Hong Kong or a science teacher from Russia may be the best choice.

Textbooks

Without attempting a book-by-book review of the products available, some generalizations can be made about publishers' priorities. Because several key states with large populations, such as Texas, New York, and California, also have large numbers of Spanish heritage language learners, several publishers have begun to recognize this group and create materials for them.

These books fall into two main categories: Spanish foreign language textbooks that have support materials for heritage language learners, and books that are prepared for English language learners. The limitation of the former is that they are grammar driven, and follow the priorities that relate mostly to the foreign language curriculum. Beginning lessons include word agreement and present tense conjugation. Intermediate books include past tense verbs, etc. They will often confuse heritage language learners and make them feel unsuccessful at using their own language. They are asking heritage language learners to approach their native language as if it were a foreign language. It would be as if an English department adopted a first-level English text as a second language textbook for their incoming native English speaking freshman.

While some textbooks in the latter category are excellent, one of the limitations of these books might be that their main purpose is to support English language acquisition. Such books often include translations of the short stories, plays, and poetry that are generally taught in English language classrooms. They are not dangerous to use. However, they lack imagination, and limit the use of the heritage culture as a medium for language learning. In addition, many of these books focus on spelling and accent rules, and other isolated writing rules before there is much actual authentic use of the language. Students, therefore, spend much of their time studying about the language instead of using it for authentic purposes (Faltis, p. 118).

There are textbooks that teach Chinese as a heritage language because there is a long history of community support for weekend language schools. These books often follow the pedagogical practices used in China, in which a certain number of characters learned reflect the achievement of certain grade levels. Those student born and educated in the United States who attend these schools often complain of the boredom and difficulty of learning in this manner.

If you have heritage learners who speak a language other than Spanish or Chinese, you may be out of luck unless you have a personal lifeline to the countries or origin of your heritage language learners. The internet, however, has helped improve access to such materials.

Additional Limiting Factors

Every district and sometimes every school define heritage language learners differently. John F. Kennedy High School in the Bronx, for example, has over five thousand students. They have eight levels of Native Language Arts in Spanish for English language learners, a literacy track for English language learners who are Spanish speakers with little formal academic training, a special track for English-dominant Spanish speakers and a foreign language track. The move to reduce the size of large schools in New York City is threatening the diversity that can be accommodated in this program. When schools are broken down into smaller schools, teachers are often concerned that a program that might have taken twenty years to build will be dismantled.

In a smaller school in Manhattan, High School for Environmental Studies (approximately 1,100 students), there are one-year courses for Spanish, Chinese, and Polish heritage language learners. Spanish-speaking students can then proceed to the Advanced Placement Spanish Language and Literature courses, where they will be joined by fifth- and sixth-year students who are studying Spanish as a foreign language.

The criteria used to designate students as heritage language learners is a politically determined decision. Some of the factors that can influence these decisions are based on the demographics, budget considerations, teacher beliefs, and the needs of any particular school community.

Depending on these considerations, a class of heritage language learners can have a range of students with high-level Cognitive Academic Language Proficiency (CALP), to students who are receptive bilinguals, that is, who are only able to understand the spoken language. It can be said that our educational system has created a hybrid language learner, one who is neither a native speaker of a language nor a second language learner. These students have been schooled in a language different from the one in which they had their first thoughts. They were not taught to read or write in their first language and, in high school, when our society finally concedes to provide foreign language instruction, they are being asked to learn to read and write in their primary language.

Reflective Practice Model Case Study

Given the lack of traditional supports that heritage language teachers face, it would be beneficial for teachers of this specialty within our profession to use a "reflective practice" model for analyzing success. This is a model in which the instructor develops skills through practice and reflection of that practice

(Kinginger 1997).

Kinginger points to two different reflective practice models that can help teachers improve their professionalism. They are:

> The *craft model*, emphasizing imitation and emulation of the expert's professional wisdom, and the *applied science model* ... accentuating implications of the profession's received knowledge, such as can be found in journals, textbooks, and courses on education. [p. 8-9]

This article would encourage a combination of both models of reflective practice. However, it recognizes that there is a third model: the baptism-by-fire model, which is highly popular in urban schools. This model proliferates in the absence of available experts and the profession's "received knowledge." Teachers must draw on their own accumulated expertise, test their assumptions, and alter their practice accordingly. All three models rely on ongoing cycles of theory-building, practical application, and reflection (See Figure 1).

When my assistant principal first told me that I would be teaching the Spanish Heritage Language Learner class, I was panic-stricken. I did not believe I had the proficiency to teach the class. He assured me that I did. He, however, did not speak Spanish. I am not a native speaker of Spanish, and although I have spent extended periods in Spanish-speaking countries and had my New York State 7-12 teacher certification in Spanish, I did not believe that my proficiency could sustain a class of heritage language learners. Up until this point, I had taught the first two levels of the New York State curriculum. There were always several native speakers in these classes, so I was not unfamiliar with their needs and abilities. It was clear to me that the class needed to be taught entirely in Spanish. I was not

---

Figure 1. Reflective Practice Model of Professional Education and Development.

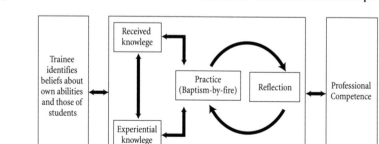

Adapted from *Heritage Language Teacher Training.* (Wallace 1991, p. 49).
Reprinted with the permission of Cambridge University Press.

sure that I could do that.

I was also afraid that I would not be able to understand the rapid-fire Caribbean Spanish that most of the students spoke. My students' dialects had nothing to do with all the Romantic and Modern Spanish literature I had read in my undergraduate training. I still understood only about two-thirds of what I heard, if I were to be honest. How could I, with all these deficiencies, pretend to teach these students their own language.

My instincts told me that the only way to get through this experience was to be well prepared. I called every publisher I knew and asked them to send me any book that might be appropriate for this group of students. All the books I found, at that time, were filled with drill-and-practice spelling activities or short readings, and drill-and-practice spelling activities at the end of each reading. I thought that spelling was something I could teach because I really did know how to spell in Spanish, and my students definitely did not. My insecurities led me to look for deficiencies in my students, so I would not feel so deficient.

I also called upon friends. The two most helpful were a high school ESL teacher, and a college remedial writing teacher. They introduced me to the writing process. They suggested several good books and articles on process writing and reader response. In addition, they directed me to the Adult Literacy Center. This is a center that is devoted to teaching adults to read and write in the language that they speak. Literacy classes are conducted in English, Spanish, and Chinese. I met with their teacher trainer, was allowed to borrow books from their extensive library and was given samples of student work and projects. The truth is, I did not have any intention of using any of this material because I would be required to explain these practices to my students.

For the first two months of the course, I sustained a posture of "I am here to teach you how to use your language properly." I taught the Spanish sound system, I tested my students, and they failed the tests. They snickered and made fun of my Spanish. I began to have nightmares about this class. I taught *"diptongos"* and *"triptongos"*; I tested them, and they failed. Disciplinary problems were reaching dangerous levels. I had stopped having nightmares about the class because I was no longer sleeping. I taught accent marks; I tested them, and they failed. I was miserable; they were miserable; something had to change!

I finally threw myself on the mercy of the court. I told the students that I was very uncomfortable teaching the class because I knew that they could speak Spanish with much more ease than I could. In addition, I was uncomfortable being a non-Hispanic telling Hispanics what was correct and incorrect. I felt that the racism involved in the power relationship was not what I wanted to perpetuate. I admitted that I often did not understand what they said. I told them that I sincerely wanted to help them enrich what they already knew, but that I would no longer pretend that I knew more than they did. We began to find some common ground.

I remembered some of the suggestions that my teacher friends had given me and began implementing them. I gave my students the first page of a short story. I asked them to finish writing the story. They read their stories to each other. They gave each other feedback using some guiding questions. They clapped for each other. They encouraged each other. I ignored the errors. Some of the stories were so moving, errors and all, that I felt compelled to call friends and read them my students' work. The students felt successful, I felt successful, we had joined the same team.

Some students turned the story into a Gothic horror. I gave them a short story by Horacio Quiroga to read as their next assignment. Others wrote love stories so I gave them Corin Tellado novels to read. Another had a sports angle. His assignment was to read the sports page and report on it. I realized that this was the first time that most of them had been asked to write something in Spanish. They did not need to hear about all the spelling errors. They needed to hear that what they wrote in the language of their soul could be powerful and compelling. It was, and we all could tell.

We continued to work together on reading and writing assignments. I was learning much more than any of them. I was becoming more accustomed to their Spanish, and they were learning to understand me. I realized that I often used unfamiliar vocabulary. My vocabulary came from novels, not real life. They learned some of my vocabulary, and I learned theirs. I still had not figured out how to approach the question of error correction. However, they were experiencing Spanish as a written language for the first time with very little difficulty.

The final project of the semester was to create a small booklet. I showed them some examples from the Adult Literacy Center of student work. I asked my students to work in groups, write stories, and illustrate them. They wrote the stories on the computer so that we could cut and paste the text with their drawings. As they were working on the computers, I began sitting with each group of students and correcting some of their errors. The students began asking me for explanations of why certain things were errors. They were extremely possessive of this project, and wanted it to be perfect. I began giving them individual explanations of what they were ready to hear. The final projects were not error free, but there had been a major improvement over the first days of the class when everyone was failing because the information I was teaching was of no use to them.

Without realizing what was happening, I was participating in a reflective practice model with elements of craft, applied science, and baptism-by-fire. I searched out teachers who I knew were expert at teaching writing. I also consulted textbooks and a community center dedicated to teaching literacy, and I read theoretical works. I began by theory-building. Unfortunately, my personal insecurities got in the way and I made poor choices at first. I implemented my plan and failed utterly. I continued to consult experts and theoretical works and to develop better plans and to evaluate their success.

I learned many important lessons that semester. First, my insecurities should not drive the curriculum nor could I look at my students from a deficit model. It served no one. I did not have to be the dispenser of all knowledge (Faltis 1990, p. 118). We were all much more successful when I set the stage for the students to examine what they had done. Collectively, we had a tremendous amount of knowledge about the language, the culture, and how to communicate. Once the students started responding to each other's work, the class was no longer about me (that is, what I knew or did not know, or what my skills were). It was about what the students had produced.

It became evident that I had to start my curriculum from the point of what my students could do well. My job was to enhance what they did know and to get them excited enough about the language to want to discover what they did not know. When I was teaching isolated grammar points, no one found any use for them and the students were unwilling or unable to digest the material. When an individual youngster recognized a need for a particular grammar point, it became imperative that he or she have the necessary information.

It also became apparent that the social context that placed all of us in this classroom had an important impact on our experience. This class had been created by a programming accident. No one really considered a class for Spanish heritage language learners necessary, even though this school's population was 45 percent Hispanic. I was chosen to teach the class simply because I had a Spanish teaching license. No one seemed concerned that I had no special training or expertise in this area. Neither New York State nor New York City had any curriculum to offer at that time. In addition, the textbooks available were severely flawed. When I discussed the difficulties I was having with the class with my supervisor, he assured me that it would work itself out. I could have continued using my drill-and-practice materials and sent all the "troublemakers" to the dean, and no one would have been the wiser. The students got the message loud and clear that what they were able to do, that is, communicate in Spanish, was not a valuable skill. I had even begun confirming this belief through my own poor curricular choices.

Conclusion

Educators who work with pre-service teachers cannot predict the situations in which any particular teacher will be required to function. Many schools, however, are reporting growing numbers of heritage speakers. Foreign Language teacher preparation needs to include preparation to teach heritage language learners. In addition, all teachers need to be trained to uncover and actively choose the theories and beliefs systems that they will use to create their lessons. They must also learn that they need to evaluate not only their students' work but also their own assumptions about what and how they are teaching.

To improve institutional support, we need to pressure the state and local school communities to begin to recognize all parts of this diverse group of language learners so that all teachers will have the tools they need to be successful. Several states now have standards for instruction of heritage languages for students who are in federally funded programs to learn English. These students are only a small number of heritage learners in this country. There is a need to broaden the definition of "heritage language learner" to include all students with native or near-native abilities in languages other than English, regardless of their abilities in English.

Many strides have been made since those first days ten years ago when I struggled in front of my class. Heritage learners now appear in curricula and there are new textbooks coming out every year written by teachers who have worked with this population. The most important leap a teacher or community can make, however, is to identify the rich linguistic abilities of heritage learners. These students, while sometimes limited in their use of one or both languages in comparison with a monolingual person of each language, usually have the deep syntactic and cultural understanding in both languages that we strive for in our foreign language students. As their talents differ from foreign language students, so do their needs. This volume discusses these needs and identifies specific methodology that emphasizes and enriches each heritage learner's linguistic abilities. To be successful as a heritage language teacher, one must first help his or her students perceive their language skills as assets, recognize what they already know, and provide a forum for each student to want to fill in his or her own gaps in usage. When curricula, teacher training, and actual practice reflect these considerations, many more of our heritage learners will be able to more fully realize their dreams.

References

Bilingual Education Act. 2000. Section 3283, 20, U.S.C.

Dörnyei, Z. 1994. "Motivation and Motivating in the Foreign Language Classroom." *Modern Language Journal*, Vol. 7, No. 3, pp. 273-284.

Faltis, C. 1990. "Spanish for Native Speakers: Freirian and Vygotskian perspectives." *Foreign Language Annals*, Vol. 23, No. 2, pp. 117-126.

Field Review of Draft Foreign Language Curriculum Framework K-12. 1999. *Foreign Language Curriculum Frameworks and Criteria Committee. California Department of Education.* At www.cde.ca.gov/cilbranch/eltdiv/flfw/forlangfw/htm.

Gardner, R.C. and P. F. Tremblay. 1994. "On Motivation: Measurement and Conceptual Consideration." *Modern Language Journal*, Vol. 78, No. 4, pp. 524-527.

Giles, H., R. Y. Bourhis, and D. M. Taylor. 1977. "Towards a Theory of Language in Ethnic Relations." In H. Giles (ed.) *Language, Ethnicity, and Intergroup Relations.* New York: Academic Press.

Gross, J. 2000. "For Latino Laborers, Dual Lives; Welcomed at Work but Shunned at Home in Suburbs." *New York Times.* January 5, 2000.

Kinginger, C. 1997. "A Discourse Approach to the Study of Language Educators' Coherence Systems." *Modern Language Journal*, Vol. 81, No. 1, pp. 6-13.

Learning Standards for Languages Other Than English. 1996. The University of the State of New York.

New Standards™ Performance Standards. 1997. New York City: Board of Education of the City of New York.

Oketani, H. 1997. "Japanese-Canadian Youths as Additive Bilinguals: A Case Study." *Mosaic*, Vol. 4, No. 2, pp. 14-18.

Oxford, R., and J. Shearin. 1994. "Language Learning Motivation: Expanding the Theoretical Framework." *Modern Language Journal*, Vol. 78, No. 1, pp. 12-28.

Standards for Foreign Language Learning: Preparing for the 21st Century. 1996. U.S. Department of Education and the National Endowment for the Humanities. P. 18.

Syllabus for Modern Languages. 1988. The University of the State of New York.

Texas Essential Knowledge and Skills for Spanish Language Arts and English as a Second Language. 1997. At www.tea.state.tx.us/rules/tac/ch110_128toc.html.

Vanpatten, B. 1997. "How Language Teaching is Constructed." *Modern Language Journal*, Vol. 81, No. 1, pp. 1-5.

Wallace, M. J. 1991. *Training Foreign Language Teachers: A Reflective Approach.* New York: Cambridge University Press.

Statement of Shared Goals and Fundamental Beliefs

Teachers of heritage languages should:

- understand how complex heritage language learners are.
- have high standards and expectations for their students and believe that the students can achieve those standards.
- have a high level of proficiency in the heritage language they teach.
- acquire the sociolinguistic foundations that enable them to be respectful of the language origins and ever-evolving language varieties, dialects, registers and styles that students bring with them to class and build upon them.
- understand the social, political, and emotional issues associated with having various degrees of proficiency in one's heritage language.
- be aware of their students' attitudes toward and degree of receptivity to learning their heritage languages.
- be sensitive to the cultural backgrounds of their students and incorporate those cultures into their instruction.
- help students to recognize the uses and purposes of their heritage language both in their immediate environment and in a global society.
- enrich the lives of students by giving them options of variety in register so they can communicate with a variety of audiences in the heritage language.
- encourage students to actively engage in exploring and discovering the richness of their linguistic and cultural heritage.
- use the language skills and cultural experiences that students bring with them as an integral part of instruction.
- use a variety of instructional approaches to accommodate the variety of levels of language proficiency in the same classroom.
- incorporate personal voice into the instructional program.
- nurture their own sense of self-esteem and communicate it to their students.
- be an advocate for the heritage language learner and promote the importance of the heritage language program within the school.

Students of heritage languages should:

- develop the sociolinguistic competence necessary to enable them to use their heritage languages to communicate with a variety of audiences and for a variety of purposes: personal, social, academic, and beyond.
- learn what roles their heritage countries have played in the world, what each's role is in the world's technology and economy.
- learn what roles their heritage countries and languages may play in the next century and how they themselves can become important in the society of the future.
- learn how their cultures, customs, and religions were developed.
- be aware of the usefulness of their heritage languages and the reasons for learning them.
- understand and become increasingly confident that continued use of a language both inside and outside of school will result in the re-emergence of "forgotten" lexical and structural elements of the language.
- be able to self-monitor and reflect upon their use of the heritage language.
- be encouraged to teach their teachers as well as their peers the individual or unique characteristics of their heritage languages.
- become independent learners.

A successful heritage language learning environment is one in which:

- the differences among the cultures represented in each language group are recognized and respected.
- the multiple perspectives that arise from students' lived experiences and prior knowledge are respected and validated.
- interaction among the school, the family unit, and the community is ongoing.
- mutual respect between and among teachers and learners is fostered.
- students are guaranteed an opportunity to comment freely and participate in discussions as equals.
- students' attempts at communication are valued; they are allowed to take risks and make mistakes knowing that making errors is part of learning.
- all learning styles are acknowledged and addressed in a variety of ways and settings.

• learning is student-centered and interactive, and makes use of the most effective strategies and technology.

An effective heritage language curriculum:

• is based upon recognized standards for both language arts and foreign language.
• has clearly stated goals that are understood by teachers, administrators, and students and that guide student assessment.
• includes literature, history, geography, social science, and cultural activities related to students' countries, as well as current material related to their daily lives.
• makes use of current technologies to improve students language skills and cultural understanding.
• includes real-life situations that involve the students in the heritage language communities.
• integrates language experiences across the curriculum to ensure the development and use of language skills and concepts necessary to all subject areas.
• combines the language arts skills of reading, writing, viewing, speaking and listening in an integrated process of making meaning. They are not taught in isolation from each other.
• reflects the understanding that language learning is progressive and that students will progress to higher levels in given aspects of a language at different rates.
• uses multiple and varied measures to assess student performance, including listening, speaking, reading, writing, and viewing.
• provides opportunities at regular intervals for students to demonstrate what they know and are able to do.

PART TWO

Voices from the Classroom

Introduction ❋

I was delighted when, just over two years ago, my friend and colleague, John Webb, asked if I would be interested in sharing with the ACTFL/ Hunter College FIPSE grant team some of my insights regarding language development and learning as they pertain to all of us who are language teachers. As an English teacher with almost thirty years of experience—from middle school through post-graduate programs— I was especially interested in the topic that John asked me to address: How, in the English language arts, do we identify our curriculum and how do we go about delivering it to students from widely divergent English language backgrounds? As states move toward full implementation of more rigorous standards in all subject areas, it is essential that we have clarity about what it is that we are teaching, and why, and how. Too often, well-intentioned curriculum reforms have failed because teachers were unclear about their goals or felt unsupported in their most effective implementation. It was impressive to me that this project, which had as its ambitious goal the development of a teaching and learning paradigm for heritage language teachers and students, called upon the talents and expertise of experienced teachers and administrators of secondary foreign language programs, as well as experts in foreign language education at the university level, to identify its objectives and to frame its curriculum. I was doubly impressed that this group, in seeking to develop an innovative and effective program for this challenging group of students, would be interested in hearing how some of these issues were being addressed in the parallel field of English language arts. I was intrigued with the potential for both teaching and learning in my involvement with the heritage language learner project, and I was not disappointed.

It has been apparent to me for some time, in my work both as an English teacher and researcher at the secondary level, and in my capacity as a supervisor of English instruction at the secondary level, that language learning is a recursive process that is best achieved through integrated instruction in all of the language arts skills—reading, writing, listening, speaking, and viewing. My basic premise in speaking with the ACTFL /Hunter College team that day was that the standards for effective English language arts instruction form the basis for language instruction standards of any kind, especially for those students whom the team identified as heritage language learners.

Like many English language arts students, heritage language learners bring with them into the language classroom a level of exposure to, and familiarity with, the language of instruction. This exposure may be from their homes or communities. It may have occurred early on or have been sustained over time. It may or may not include oral or written literacy or proficiency. It may or may not reflect reading competency or fluency. The truth is that just as students coming into the English language arts classroom run the gamut from possessing the barest proficiency in the skills of language arts instruction to the most sophisticated, heritage language learners entering heritage language classrooms present the same range of confidence and ability in their heritage languages and the same sense of familiarity with the language, which may keep them from focusing on what they still need to learn rather than on what they already know. How does a foreign language teacher adequately address this range of needs and stimulate necessary learning? I was reminded of an experience that I had in the late 1970s in a remedial reading class that I had been assigned to in a large city high school.

All of the students in this particular class shared two characteristics: They all had scored below the eighth grade reading level on standardized tests, and they were all older than sixteen, the cutoff for compulsory education in New York. Most, in fact, were over eighteen years of age, though their transcripts reflected few high school credits earned to date. My chairperson directed me to "do what you can with them," and handed me one of the then-ubiquitous, prepackaged remedial reading kits, with fragmented reading comprehension passages accompanied by questions. As I came into class the first day of the semester, reading kit opened on my desk, and began to explain to the students what we would be working on this term, some heads immediately went down on the desks while groans emanated from the mouths of others.

"Oh, no, not again!"

"Why do we have to do this boring stuff?"

I started to explain how these were the materials that were appropriate for people who read at a basic level, that once they had mastered these concepts, they would go on to more interesting work. As I looked around, I could see that no one believed me. Their previous school experiences had just about convinced them that school was not for them, and my speech was proving the truth of their thinking. I looked at their disappointed faces, rapidly hardening into indifferent masks, and blurted out a question: "If we don't read this stuff," pointing at the materials in the kits, "what would you like to read?"

"I want to read one of those books that they read in the real English classes," one girl offered.

"Which book?" I asked, curious now in spite of my misgivings. It had never occurred to me before this that students tracked in remedial English had any knowledge of, let alone desire to read, books studied in the academic English classes.

"You know, that Shakespeare one about that guy and his girlfriend."

"You mean, *Romeo and Juliet*?" I asked somewhat incredulously.

"Yeah, that's the one," she asserted, nodding her head vigorously, as other students began to chime in: "Yeah, why don't we ever get to read any real books?"

By the end of the period, I had agreed that our class would read *Romeo and Juliet*. There were a few problems, though. I had no books; I had no experience adapting Shakespeare for students with reading levels this low; I had no sources of teaching materials to accomplish this task. I felt that I couldn't ask for help from my supervisor, because I would be going outside of the prescribed curriculum in pursuing this unit with remedial students. For the first time in my teaching career, I felt totally alone. But I also felt strongly that if I could find a way to bring these students to this material, something very exciting could happen, and so I set to work planning.

What resulted was an experience that changed my life as a teacher. We spent eight weeks on *Romeo and Juliet*. Students read, re-wrote, talked about, and drew responses to every part of Shakespeare's play. They explored the notion of gangs and the effects that they had on communities and on families. They talked about expectations for boys and for girls, and why people can't talk about personal problems with their families. They talked and wrote about good advice and bad advice, without worrying, for once, whether their English was good enough. They looked at parts of *West Side Story* and compared it to Shakespeare's tale. They performed adaptations of scenes. They wrote diary entries. They designed costumes and sets. And they read every word of Shakespeare's play. When we finished, I asked them whether they wanted to see a video of the play, Franco Zefferelli's lush version. They agreed eagerly to attend an afterschool viewing one day, so that we could watch the entire film in one sitting.

I provided the popcorn and darkened the room as the opening credits rolled. Not one student was absent from this unrequired class session. Just as they had questioned, fought with, and disputed each of the characters' decisions during our reading of the play, they now engaged actively with the video before them. I had anticipated the intensity of their response to the film and had brought along a box of tissues for the weeping that I knew would ensue when Juliet woke up to find her young husband dead. Few eyes were dry by the time the video ended. Everyone in that room knew that we had shared something very special.

That experience was pivotal to my development as a teacher. Never before had I realized how important it is to listen to what students say that they need and then to give it to them. I realized that a good English teacher needs to be a juggler—of time, of resources, and sometimes, of constituencies. By the time my students had completed the play, word had gotten out that I was doing Shakespeare, successfully, with a remedial reading class. Eventually, my chairman came by and was amazed to see what the students were doing. He never did figure out, however, where I had gotten that set of books!

In order to serve the learning needs of all of the students I teach, I need to have many balls in the air simultaneously. I need first to realize that all students want to do work that they consider to be authentic, whether or not their scores reflect certain competencies. I need to convince my students that this is work that they can do and that I will help them to do it. I need to introduce classroom experiences that offer them a number of options for engaging—speaking, viewing, writing, listening, and reading. I need to convince them that I will not worry too much about correctness at the outset of our time together—the point is for them to engage. I know that once they are engaged, they too will see what they still need to learn, and will go about that task by becoming jugglers themselves. This doesn't happen easily or immediately. As a teacher, I know that I must stay focused on the goals—true oral, reading, and written proficiency—

but I must also be attentive to how each student whom I teach juggles the process of getting there.

The goals of language learning, whether English or other, are identical—to promote communication, fluency, literacy, and eventually, proficiency—in reading, writing, and speaking the target language. The New York State English Language Arts Performance Standards outline competencies in reading, writing—including grammar and usage—speaking, listening, and viewing. What has changed in the past twenty-five years of English language arts instruction, and what my experience teaching Shakespeare to remedial English students demonstrated so vividly to me, is that methods of instruction had to change to meet the learning needs of increasingly diverse groups of limited-English-proficient students.

When I began to teach, almost thirty years ago, I was trained to use a linear proficiency model—moving from oral proficiency, to textual literacy, to written proficiency, with an emphasis on correctness of expression. As the research on whole language (and my own classroom experiences) began to demonstrate so clearly, language learning is not linear; it is recursive. Not only does fluency generate literacy and proficiency, but that proficiency—in each of the language arts competencies of reading, writing, speaking, listening, and viewing—engenders new levels of fluency, which produce further literacy and proficiency. The recursive process continues infinitely, so long as learners continue to be engaged. What are the characteristics of a curriculum with the potential to keep students engaged? The experiences will vary according to subject matter, but respect for the learner and what the learner brings into the classroom is at the heart of every successful curriculum.

In its preliminary "Statement of Shared Goals and Fundamental Beliefs," the ACTFL/ Hunter College team laid the groundwork for the development of a student-centered curriculum that respected and celebrated the heritages of its students. It seemed to me that day two years ago, when I first presented to this group, and still seems to me today, that these goals and beliefs form the basis of all effective language arts instruction and, as such, form a good basis for dialogue about the relationships between English language arts learning and heritage language learning.

I feel privileged, therefore, to have been invited to help the ACTFL/ Hunter College participants shape their stories of effective heritage language learning and teaching experiences, and to act, along with John Webb, as co-editor of this book. As I read, with growing excitement, the stories of participants and the results of their research, I became more convinced than ever of the value of working together to discover the elements of effective instruction. That knowledge continues to enrich my life both as a teacher and as a mentor of others whose stories of teaching and learning are just unfolding.

Barbara L. Miller, Ph.D., Co-Editor
Hunter College High School,
City University of New York

Chapter 4

Standards and Heritage Language Learners

Editors' Notes

Responding to the heritage language learners' complexity is one of the challenges that teachers face when designing programs and planning instruction. Once teachers begin to seek answers to the questions presented in "A Framework for Learning About Your Students" in Chapter 2, it becomes apparent that neither a standard foreign language curriculum nor the teaching strategies used in standard foreign language programs are adequate for heritage language learners. The richness of their language varieties and their lived experiences, both social and academic, that they bring with them to class are different from those of foreign language learners. As one teacher pointed out in an interview conducted as part of the ACTFL/Hunter College Project, "Heritage language students are the ones who know more." They are proficient in their language in ways that foreign language learners, and sometimes even their foreign language teachers, are not and may never be. At the same time, they may have gaps in their knowledge of their heritage languages that foreign language learners do not have, and these gaps prevent them from performing certain kinds of communicative tasks, reading and writing in particular. As a result, when teachers attempt to apply a standard foreign language curriculum and foreign language teaching strategies to the teaching of a heritage language, it can lead to discomfort, if not frustration and failure, for both students and teachers alike. Foreign language learners and heritage language learners are two different groups of students, each with many special needs.

Early in their discussions, the members of the ACTFL/Hunter College FIPSE Project Development Team decided that it might be informative to meet with teachers of English to explore the possible similarities between the teaching of language arts and the teaching of heritage languages. Striking similarities became apparent immediately, whether the two groups were comparing standards and goals of instruction, learners' characteristics, teaching strategies and classroom activities, or the types of assessment that could be used most effectively. It turns out that American students studying English have many traits in common with heritage language learners, so it is logical for the teaching of heritage languages and the teaching of language arts to be close relatives in the pedagogical family. Of course, this relationship has many implications. Teachers of foreign languages have been prepared to teach foreign languages; they have not necessarily been prepared to teach language arts. Therefore, if foreign language teachers are to design effective curriculum, identify successful teaching strategies, and develop appropriate assessment techniques for heritage language learners, they will have to study the standards that apply to language arts classes and begin to learn what teachers of language arts do.

In this section, Maria Giacone will lead you through a consideration of the issues associated with standards and the heritage language learner. She will ask you to consider answers to two overarching questions: "What do you want your heritage language learners to be able to do?" and "How will you assess their success?" She proposes a set of essential elements of a standards-based curriculum and, in so doing, highlights the similarities between the teaching of language arts and the teaching of heritage languages.

Cynthia McCallister presents a clearly detailed picture of a language arts class, including the teacher's expectations, the kinds of practice opportunities that students have, the nature of the interaction between a student and the language arts teacher, the actual instructional procedures used, and the culture of the learning environment that will foster student language development. As a foreign language teacher, you will find her description valuable, because it can be used as a model for your own planning and instruction with your heritage language learners.

Standards and the Teaching of Heritage Languages

Maria C. Giacone ✳

*I*n my career as a teacher of French, I remember the challenge to the profession as the numbers of students enrolled in foreign language classes dwindled. As registers decreased but prescribed class size did not, the composition of classes became increasingly multilevel and multitrack. The crisis hit home for me when I found myself facing a class of some twenty students collectively enrolled in French 3,4,5,6, including nonnative speakers as well as students who had received most of their formal education in a French language school system. The class included intermediate to advanced students, some of whom would be taking the New York State Regents Comprehensive Examination in French. Some students were studying French for the first time, while others were already quite fluent. In my greetings to the class that day, I explained the situation. There was some silence. Then one student, who sat up front, raised her hand: "How do you propose to teach this class?" she asked.

I do not remember the exact words of my response to her. But I do remember that I had come to some fundamental conclusions. I asked myself four basic questions:

1. *What were my instructional goals?* No single curriculum could tell me that. I had to look at a variety of curriculum documents available to me, and beyond those documents into the hearts and minds of my students and into the depths of my discipline. What does it mean to study French? What does it mean to know it? What should students be able to do? Why is that important?

2. *How would I convince myself that my students had achieved the goals?* Test scores couldn't accurately reflect the achievements of such a diverse group of students. I knew that I was going to teach differently, therefore, I had to test differently: paper and pencil tests alone would be inadequate.

3. *How would I shape my instructional agenda?* What would classroom activities look like? What language behaviors did I want students to demonstrate? Decisions about how to set up classroom activities would be contingent upon where my students were along the continuum of instructional goals in French language acquisition—goals that I would make explicit to them at the outset of our work together. Such instruction would look different, sound different, be approached differently, and would be learned differently. The "typical" lesson format with which I had been familiar would be significantly changed, or done away with altogether.

4. What specific instructional strategies and student strengths would I draw upon? What did my students know of the language we were studying and of other things? What did I know from my other teaching experiences about successful instruction? What did I need to know and study further?

Instructional planning based on an assessment of educational resources and outcomes is sometimes described as "backward design." One starts with the end in mind—the instructional goals—and then goes on to determine evidence of accomplishment—student products and behaviors. The final consideration is to see where students are in the continuum of their learning and to identify appropriate instructional strategies that will help them to achieve the desired goals.

Instructional Planning

- Identify instructional goals.
- Determine evidence of accomplishment.
- Determine where students are in their learning.
- Identify appropriate instructional tools and strategies.

With acknowlegment to Wiggins & McTighe, 1998.

Those four preliminary questions lay the groundwork for my thinking and planning and generated my overarching concerns as a teacher. These two concerns lay at the heart of what we now call standards. They are:

1. What do you want your students to know and be able to do by the time they leave your class/your school?
2. How will you assess their success? What evidence do students need to produce to demonstrate that they have mastered what you have taught them? How will you determine what constitutes an acceptable quality of work? How good is good enough?

Most educators of heritage language learners have a notion of what is meant by "standards." Generally, we understand the concept to include the idea of having high expectations for all of our students, accepting the premise that given time and quality instruction, all students can achieve at comparable high levels.

Let us test that notion by reacting to the following statement: *All heritage language learners achieve the same standards.*

Reaction to this vision of student success will depend upon how we define the heritage language learner, what we mean by "achieve" and what we understand standards to be.

Standards can be described in two ways:

1. *Content* or *Learning* standards are those that address what students need to know and be able to do.
2. *Performance* standards address the nature of the evidence that demonstrates what students know and are able to do. That is to say, performance standards determine what constitutes work that meets the standards one has set.

Naturally, content standards and performance standards overlap. Performance indicators usually accompany content standards, and content is implicit in performance standards. Standards in themselves are not new. What is new is the notion that academic standards need to be made explicit and familiar to everyone affected by them, teachers, students, and members of the community, so that everyone can be clear on the rationale for curriculum, assessment and instruction. Clear articulation of educational standards accomplishes several important objectives:

- Standards provide a common understanding of what we want all students to know and to be able to do.
- Teachers, students, and families are clear about the quality of student performance that meets the standards. Teachers' high expectations are reflect-

ed in students' and families' understanding that achieving the goals of education requires rigorous work.
- Schools and communities are committed to the notion that all students can understand and achieve the standards given time, appropriate resources, and quality instruction.

Adopting standards is not about adapting something new to the old way of doing things. Rather, it is about weaving together the many strands of education reform in order to provide a unifying, cohesive conversation that spans all disciplines. A standards-driven curriculum often challenges assumptions about what we can expect from students while staying away from prescriptions of how to teach. It requires from students new types of evidence and multiple types of evidence in order to demonstrate knowledge and competence. Assessment of instruction of this nature is ongoing. It does not rely solely on single, high-stakes testing opportunities that offer either a "good grade" or a "bad grade." A standards-driven curriculum establishes an educational setting that reflects a culture of "revision and redemption" (Darling-Hammond 1998) where students grow in knowledge through revisions of their work, and where through mechanisms that encourage effort, students can redeem themselves of "failed" attempts as they struggle through the complex process of learning. Finally, and especially for teachers of heritage language learners, articulating a standards-driven curriculum forces us to answer the question: "What is our content?" in a new and deeper way.

Toward a Deep and Lasting Understanding

When I was in high school, French was one of my favorite subjects. I liked it for two main reasons: I thought it was "fun" to speak another language and I was good at it! Preparing for the Regents exam (New York State Comprehensive Examination in French) was not exceedingly difficult. Taking post-Regents classes was technically unnecessary, but would offer me a pleasurable thing to do while adding academic spice to my transcript.

In the last two years of my high school study of French, I found myself in what I would later discover to be quite an unusual class. Most of us had started French in junior high school. Some of us had been "exposed" to it in elementary school. Some of us came from French-speaking countries or spoke it at home. While some of us were in the honors program, some of us were in "regular" classes, and some in "nonacademic" programs. None of us could imagine the journey we would be undertaking together, led by a remarkable teacher.

The day that our teacher, Mrs. Rose, introduced Baudelaire, she did so by reading the poem *"Correspondances"* to us toward the end of the period and asking us to react to it on paper and with our peers. The next day, she called upon us to share our ideas with the class. We had done a careful reading of the poem, and, free from restrictive guidelines, we brought to the text our own experiences and perspectives. She acknowledged our responses. Through an ensuing series of lessons, we examined other poems by Baudelaire and the literary era in which he lived. By the end of that unit, many of us had revised our original notions and interpretations. Throughout, we were engaged and eager to proceed—to test our assumptions because they had been validated and had become the basis of lessons whereby the teacher and her students could construct a richer understanding of Baudelaire's work.

Then there was the time we read Voltaire's *Candide*—cover to cover. It was a raunchy philosophical tale of adventures that we thought, at first, could lay only in the realm of fantasy. We cynically scorned the nature of optimism captured in *"le meilleur des mondes possibles"* when calamity after calamity struck Candide and his cohort. Our final task was to look for a recent event that had been written about in the press and use it as the basis for a "final" chapter of *Candide*. The event, though current, had to be of the type that would appear as a logical fit in the stream of events as Voltaire had depicted them. Naturally, the chapter had to be written in the *passé simple* and in a literary style close to that of Voltaire.

After days of searching, I chose an article about a church in Lisbon that had taken issue with a local abortion clinic. The setting and the issue seemed to cry out for Voltaire's hand and so writing the chapter not only gave me practical insight as to the literary style and philosophical thought of this eighteenth-century writer, but gave me the perfect opportunity to apply them to a current issue.

Finally, we were given time and opportunity for revision. Through this experience, each of us found that the issues we had chosen had received a thorough analysis that led to a deeper understanding than we otherwise would have gained.

At the end of my final semester in high school, my French teacher learned that the English class had just finished reading *Crime and Punishment*. Our French class had just finished reading *L'Etranger* and had explored facets of existentialism. Among the three options offered to us for our final paper that semester was a comparison of Raskolnikov and Meursault as existentialist characters in two very different novels. Those of us who chose to write this paper gained insight into the concept of existentialism not relegated to one specific text or author, or to the literature of a particular culture. We compared a French novel set in Algeria to a Russian novel read in English translation in our English class, and we wrote about them in French.

What we had come to understand, accept, and value as high school students during our post-Regents years was that French demanded as much work and as much creative and rigorous thinking as was demanded of us in other academic subjects. In fact, some of our other "academic" classes paled in comparison. What we experienced in that class served us well in all of our disciplines. We also knew that everything we had done in our pre-Regents years was purposefully planned not only to help us pass that examination, but to prepare us for the immensely engaging and rich learning experiences of the post-Regents years. Thus, French was not a "frill"—an unnecessary luxury—but an academic "must." And each of us—of varying academic levels—succeeded because, as a community of learners, we were engaged as thinkers. We were familiar with each other's patterns of thought and reasoning. We challenged each other and depended on each other for feedback and to provide further stimuli. Thus, it had become important to us that each of us succeed.

What "success" meant became apparent the day I presented myself for my Master's oral examination. All of my professors greeted me, save the one responsible for questioning me on twentieth-century literature. We waited. Then the committee decided to proceed without her by agreeing that each of the professors present would ask me a question on modern literature as well as questions in their own areas of specialty. For a moment, I panicked. I had made it a point to immerse myself in modern literature. I could speak about the esteemed though obscure authors not yet widely recognized. These professors surely would not ask me about them.

They didn't. They were not particularly familiar with current authors and literary trends, so they resorted to what they knew. They asked me about Camus! I had in-depth knowledge of his signature work from what we had done in high school. I did not have to go digging into recesses of memory. It was all still fresh and vivid for me, for I had achieved the ultimate goal of all successful education: I had gained what we hope for all students—a deep and lasting understanding.

The Heart of a Standards-Based Curriculum for Heritage Language Learners

At the heart of standards-based education lies the idea that what we choose as important enough to teach is transmitted in such a way that it becomes for the student, in the words of Wiggins and McTighe, enduring understanding (1998).

Knowledge may come by way of facts and procedures or by way of concepts and processes. But alone and discreet, and seen as instructional ends in and of themselves, these aspects run the risk of soon being forgotten. How these aspects are interwoven into interesting and stimulating tasks and activities is what makes the essence of a learning experience an integral part of who we become.

Deciding which standards are appropriate for heritage language learners may be an exhausting task, for in truth, all content and performance standards apply across disciplines. If we see ourselves primarily as teachers of language acquisition and language arts, then an interesting activity would be to examine some standards that particularly deal with these aspects of curriculum. In the spring of 1999, the teachers enrolled in the Heritage Language Learner Academy at Hunter College specifically examined samples from five different standards documents. Some of these were documents of content standards; others were of performance standards. We looked at the ACTFL Performance Guidelines, New York State Languages Other Than English (LOTE) Standards, New York State English Language Arts (ELA) Standards, New York City ELA/ESL/Spanish Native Language Arts (NLA) Performance Standards, and the National Foreign Language Standards.

To familiarize ourselves with the various standards to a greater extent, we proceeded to sort them into categories not by affiliation or discipline but by commonalities among the five groups. We were not surprised to find that there were indeed common aspects linking the various types of standards. What was startling, however, was the wide variety of organizing themes under which these groups of varying standards could be assembled. We considered standards that went from situational/functional uses of language to standards that stressed conceptual knowledge and core understandings and found bridges that might not have been apparent before participating in this exercise. Heritage language instruction is not simply language acquisition, nor is it simply language arts. Language acquisition standards and language arts standards are both requisite in what we do, for the way in which we communicate cannot be divorced from the substance of what we communicate.

Certainly, there is a continuum. The work on the profiles of heritage language learners found in Chapter Two clearly demonstrates that there are markedly different student needs at each point along the continuum of language development. Language acquisition may need to be the major focus for some students at one point on the continuum and language arts at another point. The intermingling of both in various configurations, however, needs to occur at each point if our students are to be fluent, literate thinkers, readers and writers in the target language.

Surely the statement "All heritage language Learners achieve the same standards," remains vague. But perhaps it begins to take on a resonance when we consider that there are ultimate common goals for all our students: fluency as *thinkers* who read, write, and speak for a variety of purposes and a variety of audiences. The vision for each of them is the same. Where they are along the continuum of language development varies greatly. How we get our students from where they are to where we envision them to be will demand a new, rigorous look at what is at the heart of what we teach and how we teach it.

This issue becomes especially critical in the area of literacy. Increasingly, we are faced with teaching adolescents who are below grade level in academic performance. It is the language arts class (whether English or a language other than English) where literacy skills and practices are most often addressed and developed that will serve students in all their academic studies. Heritage language learners who are in an adolescent literacy program may be part of a bilingual program where they study native language arts as well as English as a second language. This is sometimes referred to as a dual literacy program. Some heritage language learners who are not bilingual program students and who are studying a language other than English as their "foreign" language may be in "remedial English" classes or in specially designed literacy block programs.

When a colleague and I were faced with providing instruction for high school bilingual students who were performing at the bottom quartile at our school, we knew we needed to abandon all "conventional" types of instruction. Up to that point, the Native Language Arts class had focused primarily on reading and writing through literature—mostly short stories in anthologies with vocabulary exercises and reading comprehension questions. That approach had not produced significant results. We developed instead a program that had clear curricular goals for developing literacy and that responded to students' interests and curiosity. It provided engaging and appropriately leveled pieces of literature and articles, videos, and hands-on experiences on topics related to science, nature, social studies, and the arts as well. Connections to respective disciplines were made to the extent possible so that reading and writing across the disciplines could be developed.

When there is a solid foundation in literacy in the native language, native language proficiency can be tapped and transferred into the learning and development of a second language. For recently arrived students who have had gaps in their education, the Native Language Arts class becomes critical in developing literacy. ESL instruction builds upon the program in native language adolescent literacy. Similarly, teachers of languages other than English to students in "remedial" English programs or literacy block programs must be aware of the instruction in those programs and make appropriate connections to the second/"foreign" language curriculum. While, ultimately, the educational goals are the same for all students, there are critical intermediary goals that require a keen understanding of adolescent literacy issues.

Clearly envisioning what standards-meeting performance looks like and then informing ourselves of where our students are so that we can make available appropriate and rich opportunities to meet and exceed standards, involves carefully examining student work in all of its forms and looking at the instructional tasks that engender student work. Aligning our assessments (tests, assignments, extended tasks) to our standards-supported goals will necessarily change the nature of instruction. Communication skills; thinking processes that include reasoning and analysis, decision-making, problem-solving, inquiry and design; work habits and attitudes such as collaboration and cooperation, self-monitoring and self-regulation, reflection and self-evaluation, responsibility, creativity and imagination; awareness of diverse cultures, cultural contributions and cross-cultural skills are all integral elements vividly present in every heritage language learning experience (New York State Integrated Learning 1997). Students can make connections to viable career options and life-long learning skills through various learning opportunities and experiences that are authentic in nature. In effective heritage language classes, students reach out to audiences other than teachers and peers for authentic purposes that are meaningful to a community.

Thus, standards-based instruction becomes a tightly woven tapestry that blends many strands into a coherent and desired result. One cannot assume that

---

Successful Practices that Promote Literacy and Literate Behaviors Include:

- extended time.
- skills instruction that is *contextualized.*
- sustained reading.
- writing process (drafting, revising, editing).
- immersion in reading and writing through reading/writing workshops.
- theme-based activities that arise from and relate meaningfully to students' lives and experiences.
- immediate reflection on and "real world" application and practice of skills, knowledge and processes acquired.

standards-driven lessons or units alone can optimally achieve the desired results intended by the standards. Instruction must mirror the *design and intent of curriculum and corresponding notions of assessment* that are standards-based. In such a system, student work in a variety of forms is constantly examined against the instructional tasks that engender the work. This insures that clearly understood expectations are aligned with assigned tasks, student products, assessments, and curricular goals. It also serves to build on students' strengths and to uncover the "logic of error" (Rose 1989) where error reflects an attempt on the learner's part to think things through, to reach, discover, apply, construct, and create. Examining student work in order to recognize and build on those attempts is a valuable, indispensable tool in shaping instructional practices. Learning experiences are designed to develop thinking and literacy and ultimately recognize that disciplines are not isolated entities—even though each has its own set of particular skills and factual information—but are distinct parts of an integrated body of knowledge.

Elements of a Standards-Based Curriculum for Heritage Language Learners

At the heart of a standards-based curriculum for Heritage Language Learners lay several key notions. A standards-based curriculum for Heritage Language Learners:

• shifts traditional approaches to teaching/learning, assessment/evaluation/"testing," and curriculum design.

• examines student work in a variety of forms against the instructional tasks that engender the work.

• acknowledges that error proceeds from logical assumptions and reflects the attempt to think things through, to reach, discover, apply, construct, and create.

• insures that there are multiple assessments. It is not about preparation for one high-stakes test.

• is structured to include both language acquisition and language arts.

• allows for students to be engaged in instructional tasks for authentic purposes that are meaningful to a community.

• is designed so that each learning experience becomes integral to developing language as a tool for thinking and critically negotiating the world.

• understands that all standards are interconnected.

• believes that people acquire intelligence by interacting in situations that require thinking skills including problem-solving skills, where they are guided and assisted in their attempts and for their successes.

An Academic Belief System

Implicit in a standards-driven curriculum is a belief system that is grounded in a notion that Lauren Resnick of the University of Pittsburgh puts forth as the underpinning of nine Principles of Learning (1995, 1999). The notion is simply this: It is effort, not aptitude, that determines success. This notion alone will find opposition in the form of structures already present in many schools that dictate how, when, and to whom we teach "foreign" languages and heritage languages, and even which languages should be taught. There is a widely held belief that certain students are not endowed with an aptitude for languages and therefore cannot "master" them. This is an idea that is in direct opposition to a standards-based system of education, which, if it is to succeed, requires that educational systems reorganize themselves to support the expectation that every student will achieve the same high standards.

At the outset, we contemplated two overarching questions: What do you want students to know and to be able to do? How will you assess their success? To those we add a third question: What do we envision our students to be? The heritage language learner already possesses a unique gift—often not perceived as such. Heritage language learners bring to their study of a language the knowledge of particular varieties of language and perspectives of culture that are sometimes devalued if they do not conform to "standard" conventions. Recognizing and utilizing students' strengths and knowledge rather than focusing on their "deficiencies" allows students to explore many more connections between strands of knowledge and experience. It emphasizes the importance of open-mindedness, inquisitiveness, flexibility, and tolerance as it fosters critical and analytical thinking skills.

Within the framework of a larger school instructional policy that often relegates the study of other languages to the category of the almost useless, the study of a heritage language may seem at best an interesting pastime, at worst, a waste of time. When it is accountable to language acquisition and language arts standards, integrated and connected meaningfully to the academic curriculum as a whole, the undeniable value of the study of a heritage language becomes apparent to all.

What does it mean to speak a language? Within the boundaries of its semantic and lexical expression, it presents a frame through which to view the world. It provides a social key; it is a tool we require in order to negotiate thought and the complexities of communication; it is the living expression of a culture. Language is permeable, mutable, in a constant state of evolution, and always open to social scrutiny, evaluation, and judgment. It is what unites us and divides us and keeps us uniquely human.

A second language provides another view, another tool, and a testament to human capacity and experience. Language, in large measure, is how we learn, transcend limitations, continually become more than we are. As teachers and learners of heritage languages, we must constantly examine what we are teaching and learning. What lies at the core of our endeavors to teach such things as vocabulary, grammar, and literature? Why are we teaching it, learning it?

Ultimately, our vision is to make the study of a heritage language a viable and forceful tool to frame and negotiate the world. With that vision as a goal, we proclaim that all heritage language learners are on the road to achieving the same standards—standards of language acquisition and of language arts, standards that speak to acquiring facility in listening, speaking, reading, writing, and viewing, as well as standards that speak to thinking, analyzing, and reasoning. If standards are seen to serve only an ideal, then we are lost. When standards help to elucidate a commonly understood and desired vision, then we begin the conscious work that enables teachers and learners to walk the road that will get us to our destination.

References

Darling-Hammond, L. 1998. "Using Standards and Assessments to Support Student Learning." (Keynote address, April 23, 1998.) *Promoting High Standards: From Concept to Reality.* Board of Education Conference, New York City.

Resnick, L.B. 1999. "Making America Smarter." *Education Week,* Vol. 18, No. 40, 38-40. June 16,1999.

Rose, M. 1989. *Lives on the Boundary.* New York: Free Press.

University of Pittsburgh. 1999. *Overview of Principles of Learning.* Pittsburgh, PA: Institute for Learning.

Wiggins, G., and J. McTighe. 1999. *Understanding By Design.* Alexandria, VA: Association for Supervision and Curriculum Development.

The New Essence of "Teacher Stuff": An Orientation to Language Arts Instruction

Cynthia McCallister ✳

I recently thumbed through the writing notebook a child had brought from school. The quality and quantity of his notebook entries made me curious about how interactions he'd had with his teacher influenced his writing. Out of curiosity I asked, "What does your teacher do during writing time?" He responded, "Teacher stuff, you know, working at the computer and filing and stuff."

I was vexed that this student's notion of teacher stuff involved the teacher working in isolation from her students. The image of teacher cast in my mind by this child's interpretation of teacher stuff is that of a clerk or technician—someone primarily concerned with the dual demands of administering units of knowledge and then monitoring learners' mastery of content.

This image aligns with the traditional role of the American teacher, a role that has been dictated by common assumptions about how children learn and how schools should teach. According to these assumptions, it is commonly believed that humans think, learn and understand in universally similar ways. From this assumption it is reasoned that principles about learning can be developed and applied to all human populations. Based on these principles, optimal educational treatments can be specified through experimental means, incorporated into formal curricula, and applied to larger student populations. According to this logic, a school system could adopt a "one-size-fits-all" curriculum and proceed confidently in the belief that, if the teacher executes the curriculum accurately and skillfully, all children will learn through a process of information transfer.

The "one-size-fits-all" approach has dominated patterns of language arts curriculum development and implementation throughout most of the last century. But in our present era of early twenty-first century school reform, there is broad consensus among educators that the assumptions governing these approaches are seriously flawed, as are the schooling practices they encouraged. Common and still prevailing assumptions that have inspired education practice for most of the twentieth century are now being rigorously challenged by the evolution of ideas in various disciplines in the social sciences that are allied to education. A new profile of the learning person has emerged based on new assumptions.

Constructivism: Humans do not learn in universally predictable ways. Instead, individuals construct personal understanding through experience, and one's history of experience has significant consequences for learning.

Social interaction: Learning is a socially constructive process. Learners actively build understanding in the company of other members of their learning communities. Through experience, learners construct understandings that emerge from social interactions.

Learning through practice and use: Individuals don't acquire new knowledge and skill through rote learning and isolated drill, but learn novel ways of thinking and acting as active participants in the valued social practices of the larger culture. New social and intellective competencies are acquired through use as learners take active part in the culture's valued social practices.

Reflection and self-regulation: Learners have the capacity to reflect on their thoughts and actions, and to self-regulate behavior in order to adapt to the expectations of the larger culture.

Relevance of culture and context: Since an individual's meaning interpretations derive from socially oriented, contextualized experience, culture is a significant consideration in the teacher-learner dynamic. It is increasingly understood that social interactions provide a medium for learning, and that all social contexts are influenced by culture and history. A culture privileges certain ways of being and knowing above others, and has mechanisms to perpetuate cultural knowledge. Each culture possesses its own canon of knowledge; and domains of knowledge prized in one culture might have only marginal importance to another culture.

As the demands made upon schooling by a society that is increasingly concerned with the potential for school to successfully educate all of its citizens, education's constituencies are now particularly intent on reforming the traditions of American schooling to reflect new knowledge about thinking and learning. Across the United States, state departments of education, local school districts, and professional and research organizations in education have sponsored reform initiatives designed to transform traditional schooling practices. Some of these initiatives reflect a new conception of the role of the teacher as one who possesses deep expertise of subject, educational practices and traditions, individual students and human development. The expert teacher can simultaneously draw from this expertise in order to accomplish the following:

- Establish a classroom learning culture that supports the developmental, social, intellectual, and emotional needs of all learners.
- Design learning environments and experiences that provide learners with sufficient opportunity to learn desired skills and knowledge.
- Assess and monitor learner progress.
- Provide feedback and deliberate teaching necessary to guide mastery of academic content and its generative use.

The language arts teacher's role has become one of analyst, mediator, assistant, and facilitator, working alongside learners as they try to master the unfamiliar demands of increasingly sophisticated text-based practices. Recent conceptions of literacy teaching challenge teachers to move out from behind the desk and into the social space of the classroom where they can interact with students as they facilitate literacy development through participation in the learning culture of the classroom. The teacher cultivates a "mutual learning community"—an environment of collaboration, cooperation, and inquiry that is rich with social interactions that offer children the opportunity to learn the concepts and practices that matter in the larger culture (Bruner 1996).

In this chapter, I will explore what literacy teaching looks like when it is situated in the social space of the classroom. I will describe the dynamics of the reading component of a language arts classroom that is reconceptualized according to contemporary assumptions about teaching and learning. From a perspective that is responsive to social and cultural considerations, I will explain how a classroom functions within established time-space structures, the roles that teacher and students assume within those structures, and their modes of interaction and accomplishments. Then I will conclude the chapter with a theoretical overlay that will help illuminate the rationale that supports these practices.

The Changing Face of "Teacher Stuff"

It is reading time in Ms. Meltzer's eighth-grade classroom. In class today the room is quiet as her students sit at their tables in groups of four, silently reading self-selected literature. Ms. Meltzer sits next to a student and together they talk quietly about a book he has been reading. She and her students know this discussion format as a *reading conference* (Graves 1983)—a time when she meets one-on-one with her students to discuss their experiences as readers and writers. As Ms. Meltzer talks with the child, she guides him through a process of reflection over the content of what he has read and helps him identify the particular challenges he has recently experienced in his reading. In this conference she is helping him to discover the gaps in his understanding of the story, and to decide on the next steps he will take as an independent reader. When their conversation is finished, the student resumes his reading as Ms. Meltzer moves to conference with another child.

Later in the period, during the end-of-class group discussion, known as *reading share*, when the class debriefs together about their experiences during the day's reading workshop, the student offers to his classmates, "Now I have to go back and re-read my whole book. When I conferenced with the teacher I found out I didn't understand a thing!"

In this scenario, *teacher stuff* involved Ms. Meltzer working alongside one of her students and assuming the role of guide, model, mentor, helper, and assistant. Through discussion, she helped the child come to identify portions of the story that he did not understand. In conferences such as these, Ms. Meltzer introduces new information that has relevance to children as they engage in the daily routines and practices of classroom life.

Ms. Meltzer organizes her literacy program in a way that is a departure from conventional teaching practices, where every student is instructed according to a set curriculum designed without regard to the individual learning needs. The standardized, one-size-fits-all curriculum is particularly unresponsive to the "diverse learner"—the student who speaks English as a second language or who speaks a dialect other than non-standard American English, the child whose learning style deviates from the cognitive-linguistic modes of learning that are privileged in school, the child who is not accustomed to the middle-class, Eurocentric values and practices that shape and distinguish American schooling practices. The majority of learners in Ms. Meltzer's classroom can be classified as diverse by one or more of these definitions.

Ms. Meltzer teaches in a public intermediate school in northern Manhattan in a community where in 1990 more than 40 percent of the population were foreign born (*New York Times*). The large majority of her students are first- or second-generation immigrants. Nearly 85 percent are first- or second-generation Afro-Caribbean native Spanish speakers for whom English is a second language. A number of other students are also recent immigrants from Eastern Europe or Southeast Asia, who are learning English as a second language. According to the 1998 Class Ethnic Census Report for the school, the student body is 85 percent Hispanic; 5 percent White; 7 percent African American; and 3 percent Asian/Pacific Islander. Seventy-four percent of the students are eligible for the Federal free lunch program. Students for whom English is a first language— African-American and European-American children—represent a minority in her classroom. Regardless of their linguistic background, all of these students are enrolled in Ms. Meltzer's English language arts class, and this is the discourse of instruction and communication in the classroom.

Diverse learners such as those who are members of Ms. Meltzer's classroom often require additional resources sufficient to meet the diverse learner's needs and characteristics. All students need teachers who are able to use their expertise in order to make reasonable assessments of learning and to obtain the resources necessary to potentiate growth in light of specific learner characteristics and needs. Students need teachers who possess sufficient skill and expertise to identify needs and sufficient latitude to deliver resources. These resources might come in the form of extra practice, more instruction, or simply more inspiration. The language arts program Ms. Meltzer has adopted creates opportunities for her to notice her students needs and then to respond in ways that nurture their growth. I will explain how these opportunities unfold through an examination of the time-space structures and the principles that explain language and literacy learning within these structures.

The Literacy Workshop: Time-Space Structures

As class begins on a typical Reading Workshop day in Ms. Meltzer's class, the students enter the room and sit at their seats. One child begins handing out the students' individual reading folders, each containing the particular book the child is reading at the time, assessment notebooks in which Ms. Meltzer writes her observations of students' progress (after Tabersky 1996), and reading journals in which the students record their reactions to books they are reading. These are the tools that Ms. Meltzer and her students will need as they engage in the practices that this learning culture has come to know as "reading."

After folders are distributed and students have settled in, the class begins. Ms. Meltzer has built her literacy program around the workshop approach to literacy instruction (Graves 1985; Atwell 1987; Tabersky 1996). The literacy workshop is modeled after the principles that structure the artist's studio. The workshop honors the importance of daily reading and writing practice, the value of mentoring and the sharing of expertise, the power of creation, and the relationship between the values of the learning culture to the intentions, motivation, and productivity of learners. The workshop includes the following components:

- Whole-class lesson (10 minutes)—Ms. Meltzer presents the whole class with a lesson on a topic of relevance. This lesson focuses on students' specific needs, the content of which is determined by Ms. Meltzer in her assessment of her students' needs informed against the curriculum and learning standards documents. These lessons focus on wide-ranging topics from procedural concerns that aim to help students develop independent work habits to teaching points that target thinking processes involved in reading and writing.
- Independent reading and reading conferences (30-40 minutes)—Once Ms. Meltzer gives her lesson, students begin independent reading. This daily time block provides students with a daily, sustained opportunity to engage in the literacy practices that are targeted as learning outcomes of the program. Students read self-selected titles or common books that small groups of students have collectively selected and which they will later discuss as a group in what is known in the classroom as a literature circle. The independent reading format ensures that all children enjoy a daily opportunity to practice newly acquired reading skills and strategies.

During independent reading, Ms. Meltzer conducts individualized assessment and instruction in one-on-one formats called conferences. When conferences begin, in Ms. Meltzer's words, "I move to the students." She takes a seat beside a student and engages him or her in a conversation about the practice of being a reader. These conversations are initially exploratory in nature. But it doesn't take long for Ms. Meltzer to identify an overriding need and begin to focus the interaction around this need. During conferences Ms. Meltzer is trying to assess the students' overall attitude toward their reading. She asks herself: Is this child engaged in the book? Is she having difficulty with processing text or comprehension? How can I help?

When Ms. Meltzer identifies several students with a common need, she also uses this time to organize small instructional groups to target these needs. When the skill or topic has been successfully learned, the group is dismissed and students return to independent reading.

> • Whole-group share (10 minutes)—An opportunity for students to discuss their goals, experiences and accomplishments as readers. This daily ritual promotes a collective awareness of the habits and practices that distinguish avid readers. This sharing session is essential in helping to cultivate a shared literary culture.

The workshop program is designed to provide students with engaging classroom experiences and enable growth in reading and writing, together with a framework of assessment and instruction that is responsive to the needs of individual students. It accomplishes this aim through several principles that operate simultaneously within the classroom structure. These principles are expectations, practice, interaction and assessment, instruction, and culture.

Expectations

Learning outcomes have their origin in the expectations of both teacher and student. For the teacher, expectations set a course of action and interaction with students, and have a powerful influence on what students will accomplish.

Unfortunately, because the American teacher's role has historically been more technical than professional, the cultivation of expertise as a force in shaping teacher expectations has been hindered by the lock-step system of curriculum design and implementation (Darling-Hammond). Professional expertise is held captive when teachers are required strictly to adhere to rigid curricula. For example, in the past, Ms. Meltzer's teaching was tightly controlled by a district-level mandate strictly to adhere to a commercially published textbook curriculum. She referred to this curriculum as she executed a prescribed sequence and pacing of instruction. In such a program there is little room for teachers to tailor the demands of the curriculum to meet the needs of students.

But recently, Ms. Meltzer and her colleagues have taken advantage of reform-oriented curriculum policy and have used it to defend their teaching practices. After persuading the district that their proposed reading plan addresses the learning standards that were recently adopted by the Board of Education, Ms. Meltzer and her colleagues were permitted to reshape their approach to the teaching of reading.

The new freedom Ms. Meltzer is enjoying is due in part to the fact that the formal bureaucratic expectations have undergone a transformation in recent years. With the advent of the accountability movement, standards and expectations have been made explicit and available in the form of learning and teaching standards documents that originated in the deliberations of educators, researchers, administrators, parents and the private sector. These documents are often informed by contemporary theory, and can be used meaningfully to reshape classroom practice. Ms. Meltzer uses the Board of Education's new learning standards for English language arts to clarify the expectations through which she navigates her teaching. She is cognizant of the escalating pressure on her students to master particular domains of academic knowledge. The standards specify performance expectations in the domains of reading, writing, listening, and speaking in specific terms. They state which tasks students should accomplish throughout the year and provide evaluative criteria against which student performances can be compared. Ms. Meltzer refers to these expectations as she plans lessons to present to the whole class. (See Figure 1 on page 119, for an excerpt of the reading portion of these standards.)

Ms. Meltzer no longer follows a published language arts curriculum. Instead, she determines the content of group lessons based on the needs of her students measured against the expectations derived from her expertise as a teacher of over twenty years. She uses her professional judgment to determine what lessons are most relevant for students at the time and has the freedom to plan lessons that she deems appropriate.

Practice

> Nowhere in the higher animal kingdom are highly skilled and recombinable acts ever learned "automatically" or by rote.... For their full development, they all depend upon being practiced and shaped by use. [Bruner 1990, p. 72]

Underlying Ms. Meltzer's reading program is the principle of practice. It is assumed that in order to cultivate expertise in any given activity, the learner needs consistent and extensive opportunity to practice that skill. Ms. Meltzer's students enjoy extended daily opportunities to practice reading, writing, listening and speaking around authentic and personally relevant texts. Her students know from the beginning of the school year that they will be expected to use the independent reading time in order to expand their ability as readers, and are reminded continually to use the workshop time to their advantage.

The particular tasks students will be asked to practice during their independent reading time are specified in general terms in the standards documents. For example, throughout the year students are required to read twenty-five books or book equivalents, produce accompanying responses to literature, and read and comprehend four books or book equivalents that lead to an in-depth exploration of a subject, an author or a literary genre. (Refer to the italicized portions in Figure 1 for reference.) These flexible requirements leave ample latitude for Ms. Meltzer to tailor projects and assignments to meet the needs of her students and the curriculum. Students are required to read daily for thirty minutes both at school and at home. Three times during the week they are required to compose

---

Figure 1. Board of Education of the City of New York, New Performance Standards for English Language Arts in Reading

Read at least 25 books (or book equivalents) per year, including traditional and contemporary literature, magazines, newspapers, textbooks and text obtained on-line, representing a diverse selection of pieces from at least three different literary genres and five different authors. Produce written responses that demonstrate students' ability to use reading as a means to learn, to explore issues in depth, and to utilize reading as a means to exercise rights and responsibilities as a member of a democratic society.

Read and comprehend four books about one issue or subject, or four books by a single writer, or four books in one genre. Responses to readings should produce evidence that the student:

- Makes and supports warranted and responsible assertions about the texts.
- Supports assertions with elaborated and convincing evidence.
- Draws the texts together to compare and contrast themes, characters, and ideas.
- Makes perceptive and well-developed connections.
- Evaluates writing strategies and elements of the author's craft.

The student reads *informational materials and produces written work* that demonstrates the student can:

- Restate or summarize information.
- Relate new information to prior knowledge and experience.
- Extend ideas.
- Make connections to related topics or information.

Adapted and reprinted with permission from: Board of Education of the City of New York. *New Performance Standards for English Language Arts in Reading, Appendix I* [italics added].

---

a written response to their reading in a journal. In their independent reading, students are free to choose titles from the classroom library, the school library, or to bring books from home. Periodically throughout the year, Ms. Meltzer organizes unit studies around significant issues, events and people in American history, integrating the subjects of social studies and language arts.

Ms. Meltzer provides her students with guidance concerning the procedural aspects of these expectations so that they are able to select books, pace themselves in their reading, and complete responses to literature with relative independence soon after the year begins. Journals are distributed early in the year, and Ms. Meltzer instructs her students how they should keep their journals. She provides instruction throughout the year in which she prompts and cultivates specific modes of response or comprehension processes. The system of performance-based independent practice composed of reading and response work provides a context in which she can conduct assessment and respond with appropriate instruction.

Interaction: A Context for Assessment

One-on-one interactions are at the heart of the Ms. Meltzer's reading program, because they provide the opportunity for her to respond to her students in ways that are directly relevant for each learner. Responsivity begins with assessment, and personal interaction is the most basic and essential means to gather critical insights concerning how students are progressing in their learning.

Authentic reading situations create the social space in which Ms. Meltzer can work. Within the context of independent reading and literature discussion groups, she can interact with students and monitor their progress. The reading program features differential modes of interaction. Ms. Meltzer interacts with the class as a whole group during the introductory lesson and end-of-class sharing time, providing opportunities to assess group dynamics, cohesion, and understanding. As students respond to literature in their journals, she uses these journals as a tool for literary interaction and instruction, inviting children to practice their fluency in written discourse. The face-to-face interactions she has with students during the reading conferences provide a chance to closely assess how students are progressing.

In her interactions with students, Ms. Meltzer makes judgments about their growth against her own expectations that are grounded in her expertise and also informed by the learning standards. Refer once again to Figure 1, page 119. The evaluative criteria Ms. Meltzer uses to assess student progress appear next to the bullets. She has used the language of the standards expectations to create evalua-tive tools she uses in her interactions with students. For example, as she interacts with her students, she might consider the extent to which a child is making asser-tions about the text, whether he is supporting assertions with evidence, or if he is making comparisons between the themes, characters and ideas in texts. These types of criteria inform the judgments Ms. Meltzer makes about her students as readers and provides her with a greater sense of direction as she considers how to plan instruction that is best suited to meet students' needs.

Documentation is the product of Ms. Meltzer's informal assessments of stu-dents. As she sits with students and converses with them about their reading, writing, and thinking, she jots down her observations in a conference book that students keep in their reading folders (see Tabersky 1996). She judges the confer-ence interactions and her students' responses against both her internal sense of expectations as well as the more formal sources of expectations that structure schoolroom practices. By documenting her observations Ms. Meltzer brackets her impressions and composes them into a physical form. This action signals to each student in the classroom community that the work they do is important and worthy of consideration. The written notes become a tool for the reflective dis-course of learning as she shares her insights with students. Ms. Meltzer believes the process of recording causes her students to respond with more seriousness to the demands of the reading program. She explains,

> Documentation in my conferences with students is a solution to their not listening. I can say to them, "Now look, this is what I have written down." Then they look at you with this serious look and say, "Now I've done everything you said to do."

All of these modes of interaction model self-reflection and self-regulation for students, and guide them to consider the manner in which they are thinking through reading, prompting them to make adjustments in their actions. Before she restructured her reading program to include the close interactions that are a function of reading conferences Ms. Melzer explains:

> I feel that what I was missing was part of the assessment piece. It occurs to me that I hadn't reached some children because I hadn't been assessing them. And because I wasn't assessing them, I wasn't able to plan in order to address their individual needs. [My current approach to reading instruction] allows for interaction between student and teacher in a dif-ferent way than I had been used to instructing. I realize that this interac-tion was also part of what had been missing in other literacy plans and models. I also see that this model allows the teacher to observe and guide

the child as an individual reader.

The one-on-one interactions are probably the most demanding aspect of her teaching, she explains. They force her to confront the nettlesome challenges that present themselves in her students' learning. Ms. Meltzer explains that sometimes, after the large group lesson, she just wants to sit and work at her desk, "and then I think, oy, conferences. They're the hardest part of teaching! You teach something, and then you discover it did not sink in, and then you teach it again …it's repetitive. In conferences, you use your *kistches*—a Yiddish word meaning your guts. Conferences are gut wrenching!"

Instruction

The large-group lesson, individual practice time, conferences, and large-group sharing formats of the reading workshop provide ample opportunity for Ms. Meltzer to provide her students with direct teaching that guides them toward learning targets. Instruction that is both focused on learning objectives but also targeted on students' real needs more efficiently closes the gap between what learners are presently capable of doing independently as readers and what they will eventually be expected to be able to accomplish independently.

Conference formats offer an opportunity for Ms. Meltzer to share her expertise and offer direct teaching that is tailored to the individual and diverse needs of her students. In her conversations with students about the books they are reading, Ms. Meltzer can provide assistance to students that is specific to their needs, resulting in instruction that is more direct, explicit, and fast-paced than would be the case in a programmed method of instruction. In Ms. Meltzer's words, the purpose of the conference is to nestle close to kids in order to force and expand their understanding. She comments:

> It gives me a chance to clarify things I'm not sure they understood. What I presented at the front of the room. Some kids can't follow along. Did you understand when I said this or that? It's a good time for them to tell you their understanding of what's been going on. This morning I had a chance to make sure they knew what they were supposed to write in their journals—because it was a new thing. It's about developing close and intimate relationships to kids in the classroom, and clarifying.

Throughout the year, as she monitors students' reading processes and their responses to the books they have read, Ms. Meltzer gleans insights that have enabled her to plan teaching in ways that are responsive to her students' needs. In conferences, she documents her insights, then uses the data generated to inform instructional planning for large-group instruction. The content of whole-group lesson topics include community rules and workshop procedures, comprehension strategies and modes of response to literature, and dynamics of the reading process.

Modeling, demonstrating, discussing, showing, telling, and reflecting are all strategies that Ms. Meltzer uses to provide direct teaching. But again, the source of decision-making in regard to which teaching strategies or approaches to employ stems from her expertise rather than a mandated, prescriptive curriculum. The power of the instructional model employed by Ms. Meltzer is its potential to provide learners with instructional resources that are specifically geared to address their particular and individual needs.

Culture of the Learning Environment

Teaching historically has been concerned with the academic development of individual students, with little regard paid to the connection between group cohesion and individual development. Until recently, pedagogical approaches have devoted only marginal concern to the relationship between culture, the learner's perception of herself in culture, and the learner's rate of progress. But recent conceptions of social and intellective development are increasingly aware that the fit between the learner and the surrounding environment is a critical factor in learning.

Ms. Meltzer sees her role as teacher first and foremost as a builder of a learning culture—one who is primarily responsible for helping her students contribute toward the creation of a community ethos that will provide learning experiences that are beneficial to all members of the class. By establishing classroom rituals, habits, rules, customs, and procedures that build student independence around meaningful text-based activity, Ms. Meltzer can better accomplish the principal task of cultivating academic development. Involvement in day-to-day reading practices that are pleasurable in their own right contributes to the development of positive attitudes and intentions in students. A strong positive learning culture instills motivation and enthusiasm. Reading workshop allows students to build a community of shared values, preferences, interests, and practices around the activities of reading and writing. The learner improves his or her expertise by watching and learning from others who possess greater expertise.

Individuals who read every day and who discuss and share their interests with fellow readers have the opportunity to let their identity form around the act of reading and to accumulate more self-knowledge and world knowledge through reading. The reading program works in harmony with the social and emotional needs of Ms. Meltzer's students. Flexible guided reading groups prevent stigmas and labeling. Literature circles provide for independence, sharing and assumption of responsibilities. The whole thrust of the program pushes the child to become independent—a strategy needed in order to become a functioning adult.

Once a robust learning culture has developed, Ms. Meltzer can capitalize on the natural momentum for learning that it provides. Once students are able to engage independently in activities that will facilitate academic development, she can harness the native human capacity for interpersonal learning and the desire for collaboration. If her students are capable of independent engagement in reading, she is freed from the demands of coordinating daily group activities and managing disruptive student behavior and is, thereby, better able to attend to the task of nurturing literate behaviors in her students.

Conclusion

From infancy forward, social interaction is the foundation for language and language-based activity (Stern 1990); and language-based activity forms the foundation of literacy. This principle is particularly relevant to heritage language teachers for whom many of the concerns of praxis center on the connections between language and learning. It should be understood by heritage language educators who are seeking to reform language education practices that social interaction is a crucial factor in literacy development. Effective models of literacy education will accommodate the social dynamics of the learning process. As I conclude, I will offer a summary of how the model presented in this chapter speaks to these demands.

Conventional social interactions that are bounded by the constraints of social convention can be defined as formats. Formats provide the opportunity for human interchange and the possibility for understanding to emerge through inter-mental connections (Bruner cited in Cole 1996). Connections between adult and child or expert and novice are the means by which the learner discovers how to negotiate the demands of unfamiliar contexts. The reading workshop can be seen as an integrated, multifaceted learning culture comprised of a web of learning formats—conferences, journals, literature discussion groups, group sharing, and large-group lessons—each serving to enforce the aims and purposes of the learning culture. With accumulated experience of participation in these formats, and with the expanded understanding that accompanies such participation, academic competency develops.

Ms. Meltzer and several of her colleagues have taken deliberate steps to restructure their approach to literacy teaching in order to provide each student with the best possible opportunity to become proficient in their reading, writing, listening, and speaking. Ms. Meltzer's reading program respects the principles of *expectations, practice, interaction and assessment, instruction,* and *culture* just described. Her program invites students to join in creating their own learning culture through daily reading practice, to learn about themselves as readers though interaction with others. The model presented here can serve as a model for an approach to language education which respects the notion that literacy is socially defined and, once acquired, becomes equipment for survival in society.

The emphasis in education has shifted from a concern with the process of content transfer and mastery to a concern for how learners master academic content as a means to develop intellective competence (Gordon 1999). Given the fact that mastery of text- and technology-based modes of communication is a significant factor toward the achievement of intellective competence and greatly impacts one's life chances, schools are under increasing pressure to reform the common practices of schooling so that all children have sufficient opportunity to learn. It is hoped that Ms. Meltzer's work can serve as a model for the kind of classroom-based reform that needs to occur in order to respond to the needs and characteristics of diverse learners and provide all learners with the opportunity to learn.

References

Atwell, N. 1987. *In the Middle: Writing, Reading and Learning with Adolescents.* Portsmouth, NH: Heinemann.

Board of Education of the City of New York. 1998. *New Performance Standards in English Language Arts.*

Bruner, J. 1996. *The Culture of Education.* Cambridge, MA: Harvard University Press.

Cole, M. 1996. *Cultural Psychology: A Once and Future Discipline.* Cambridge, MA: Harvard University Press.

Darling-Hammond, L. 1997. *The Right to Learn: A Blueprint for Creating Schools that Work.* San Francisco: Jossey-Bass.

Elmore, R. F. 1996. "Getting to Scale with Good Educational Practice." In "Working Together toward Reform." *Harvard Educational Review.* P.1-27.

Gordon, E. W. 1999. *Education and Justice: A View from the Back of the Bus.* New York: Teachers College Press.

Graves, D.H. 1983. *Writing: Teachers and Children at Work.* Portsmouth, NH: Heinemann.

New York Times. December 26, 1999. Susan Sachs. "From a Babel of Tongues, a Neighborhood." Front page, continued on p. 32. Queens College Sociology Department as source cited.

Stern, D. N. 1990. *Diary of a Baby.* New York: Basic Books.

Chapter 5
Inside the Heritage Language Classroom

Editors' Notes

In Part One of this volume and in the preceding chapters of Part Two, we have considered the issues that, according to experienced teachers, are at the very core of a successful instructional program for heritage language learners: the identity and experiences that the learners bring to school, the goals and beliefs that influence teachers in their work, the standards that guide curriculum and assessment, and the language arts orientation that appears to be most effective in meeting the learners' needs. Now it is time to take a look inside of actual classrooms where heritage languages are being taught to learn how all of those core issues come together to form a coherent picture of what teachers do and how their students learn. Once again, we will be informed by the voices of teachers and students.

Migdalia Romero and Claire Elaine Sylvan report the findings of their research on successful classroom practices in three diverse school settings. That research was conducted as a part of the ACTFL/Hunter College FIPSE Grant Project. Through their examination of the interaction that they observed between teachers and learners in everyday classroom situations, we see a paradigm for successful heritage language instruction emerge, a paradigm that speaks of a shared set of goals and beliefs that guides successful teaching. Although that paradigm may resonate with teachers of foreign languages, it may not be reflected in their regular day-to-day work. Therefore, what Romero and Sylvan found can have far-reaching impact on the instructional program that foreign language teachers can create and the kinds of experiences that heritage language learners can have in their classes.

The chapter concludes with a series of seven wonderful stories, written by classroom teachers, in which they share their experiences working with their own heritage language learners. These deeply personal and often moving accounts of their interactions with their students will give you a very special and privileged first-hand view of the challenges, the goals and strategies, the hopes and doubts, the strengths and insecurities, the successes and failures, and always the dynamic human encounters experienced by teachers and students alike.

Heritage Language Classrooms in Action— Three Case Studies: An Introduction to the Research

Migdalia Romero ※

During the 1998-1999 academic year, as part of the ACTFL/Hunter College FIPSE Project, a team of three researchers began an exploratory study that took them into three high schools in New York City where there were special classes for heritage language learners. The members of the team included Migdalia Romero, Professor at Hunter College, Claire Sylvan, humanities teacher and administrator at International High School, and Cecilia Calderon, a returning student at Hunter College majoring in Romance languages. The team set out to explore what effective teachers are doing instinctively and intuitively with heritage language learners in the absence of formal training or of a specialized curriculum. The goal was to contribute to a paradigm for instruction that differentiates foreign language instruction from effective heritage language instruction. The question the research team set out to answer was what works with heritage language learners and to speculate on why this was so.

While the size of the sample in the study that is described in this section mitigates against making broad-based generalizations, data from multiple sources shed light on effective instructional practice among heritage language learners.

What is being proposed is a reconceptualization of heritage language instruction that distinguishes it, in fundamental ways, from foreign language instruction.

The Sites

Three inner-city schools participated in this study. Two were comprehensive academic high schools with a population of over 3,000 students, and the third was a small experimental school for students who had not been successful in comprehensive high school settings. Two schools offered Spanish to Spanish speakers and the third offered French to Haitian Créole and French speaking students.

Riverside High School is a small alternative high school serving students in grades 9 through 12. It is at least the second high school that many of its students have attended. Eighty percent of the families are below the poverty level, receive free lunch, and live in projects. Most students are African-American (46 percent) or Hispanic (46 percent). The remaining 8 percent are Asian or white. Most students are between sixteen and twenty-one years of age. Heritage language learners in this school come from many countries, including the Dominican Republic, Puerto Rico, Colombia, Ecuador, Peru, Chile, Mexico, El Salvador, and Honduras. The majority (80 percent) was born in the United States and have lived here most, if not all, of their lives. A very small number (5 percent) are ESL students, some of whom are literate in Spanish. However, 98 percent have strong receptive skills in Spanish, understanding most spoken Spanish. Productive capacity is more limited with 50 to 60 percent able to speak limited Spanish and another 20-30 percent unable or unwilling to speak it at all, either because they lack the skill or are afraid to exhibit their limited proficiency.

The heritage language program at Riverside High School is the work and vision of one person—John Figueroa. On his second day at the school in 1992, John made a proposal for restructuring the foreign language program. From 1992 to 1997, the school grew from four Spanish classes to eight, with two full-time teachers. Of the eight classes, only one is a heritage language class, taught by John Figueroa, the teacher targeted for this study. The heritage language class he teaches is organized around content—the history and literature of Latin America. It is taught through the medium of Spanish and students may opt to take it for social studies credit or foreign language credit.

Midtown High School is a comprehensive high school with 3,500 students. The French class designated as a heritage language class is made up of French speaking students from Haiti and Africa, as well as advanced French students from the foreign language track.

Uptown High School has an enrollment of 5,300 students. Seventy percent of the students are Hispanic and the remainder, African American, Asian, and other. The school offers a traditional academic program, requiring one to three credits of foreign language for graduation. Students can choose from Italian, French, and Spanish. Those who choose Spanish are placed in one of three tracks: the foreign language track, the heritage language track, or the bilingual track. The foreign language track is designed for students with no prior knowledge of the language. They can take up to four years of Spanish. In their last year they can be recommended for Advanced Placement Spanish that would give them college credit. A bilingual track targets Spanish dominant students, offering them English as a second language, together with a full complement of bilingual classes in which Spanish and English are used.

The heritage language track at Uptown High School was designed for students who had some knowledge of the language obtained from outside of school. Students in this track are described as English dominant bilinguals. Their ability in Spanish runs the gamut from limited ability, or resistance to speaking the language but with some receptive skills, to strong receptive and productive ability. Heritage language students may also take Advanced Placement Spanish in their fourth year of study, along with the foreign language track students. The heritage language program at Uptown is over twenty years old, with up to fifteen teachers serving its student body. The students in the heritage track test into it, or they are recommended by teachers in their junior high schools. The largest group is from the Dominican Republic, followed by Mexicans, South Americans, Central Americans, and Puerto Ricans.

The Teachers

The three New York City high school classroom teachers who volunteered to be observed for this study were all members of the ACTFL/Hunter College FIPSE Project Development Team. They had been nominated originally by their supervisors to participate in an invitational conference on heritage language learners in September 1997, as part of the initiation for that Project. The nomination of these teachers to the conference reflected their interest and commitment to heritage language learners, as well as their creativity in the classroom, and it was because of the quality of their contributions at that conference that they were asked to join the Project Development Team.

The teacher at Riverside High School was born in Columbia, South America. He came to the United States twelve years ago after finishing high school in

131

his native country and, at the time of the study, he had been teaching at Riverside for seven years.

Jocelyne Daniel, the heritage language teacher at Midtown High School, was born in Haiti where she was schooled in Créole and French through her second year in high school. She came to this country at the age of seventeen and finished her last two years of high school in New York as an ESL student. She remembers her experience in high school in this country favorably. There were teachers who taught her to plan and to look ahead, and who showed her how to go about getting into college. While attending Brooklyn College, she went to France for a year to study sociology. At the time of the study, she had been teaching in New York for twelve years.

Dora Villani, the teacher at Uptown High School, came to the United States from Italy with her parents at the age of six, after having attended a few months of first grade in her hometown of Calabria. She completed first grade in the United States. While she had the opportunity to study Italian in junior and senior high school, she chose French in junior high and Spanish in high school. In college, she was placed in an advance Italian class because of her "oral proficiency" and her perceived comprehension of the language. In her words, "It was the worst thing that happened to me." She realized that while she understood Italian, she could not really speak it. She found herself not speaking in class and frustrated with the work. Her experiences with Spanish in junior and senior high school had been much more fulfilling academically and socially, and so she pursued Spanish as a major in college. She also spent a year abroad in Spain. Dora's experience with the Italian language and with her Italian identity was not unlike the experience of many heritage language students in the school in which she was teaching. It became evident in interviewing Dora that she had a great deal of affinity for, and empathy with, the heritage language student. At the time of the study, she had been teaching at the same high school for over twenty-five years and was instrumental in establishing the school's heritage language program.

Source of Data

Data were collected from three sources: teachers, students, and Heritage Language Program coordinators at the three sites. Teachers were observed, and teachers and students were interviewed. The goal was to seek out convergence of data between what teachers did (as gleaned from observations) and what teachers and students said about what works. The research team was able to document the ways in which teachers acted on their belief systems and goals for their students.

Teachers were observed using an observation protocol generated by the research team. (See "Classroom Observation Checklist," Appendix 1, page 155). It highlighted areas in the research that were considered important in language acquisition research. The objective was to describe the environment and the physical evidence of "culture" in the classroom. It focused heavily on how teachers used language, encouraged its use in the classroom, and responded to students' use of language. It also was intended to describe the strategies used by teachers as reflected in their methods.

Teachers were interviewed after the observation. They were asked to discuss a "best class scenario" in order to understand what teachers thought about their practices and about their students. In addition, they were asked about their goals for their students, the ways in which they handled linguistic diversity in the class, and how they monitored student progress. Overall, the intent was to understand the ways in which teacher's attitudes and knowledge of their students informed their practice. (See "Teacher Interview Protocol," Appendix 2, page 156.)

Selected students were interviewed at each school. Group interviews of up to six students were designed with two purposes in mind. The first was to tap students' feelings about their heritage language class and its relative impact outside of school. The second goal was to understand a student's perspective on what works. Students were prompted to speak about their teachers' attitudes, expectations, and the nature of their interaction with their students, data that could not be captured easily by an observation. Participants in the student interviews were selected by the teacher to reflect different levels of heritage language proficiency. (See "Student Interview Protocol," Appendix 3, page 157.)

An interview with the Program coordinator was conducted to provide organizational and historical information about the Program. (See "Coordinator's Interview Protocol," Appendix 4, page 158.)

Two members of the research team carried out all interviews and observations. This provided some assurance that the two observers had seen the same events and behaviors (inter-rater reliability). Members of the observation team wrote up their observations. In addition, interviews were audiotaped, and tapes were transcribed.

Analysis of Findings

Findings were analyzed in three phases. Immediately after each site visit, the two members of the research team met to debrief. During this debriefing, they focused on their initial impressions, discussed what they had gleaned from the day, and sought clarification of discrepancies in what was observed. At the second phase, when all of the data from a school were compiled and tapes transcribed, the three members of the research team met with transcripts in hand. The data set from each school was discussed in order to shed light on the question of what works. To this end, strategies, patterns of behavior, and belief systems were described and analyzed. By focusing on one school at a time, it was possible to see the ways in which teachers' and students' voices coalesced on effective instruction for heritage language learners.

The third phase of analysis involved the comparison of each data set across sites. To this end, student data were compared across sites, as were teacher interview data, and observation data. Through a process of continuous comparative analysis, patterns and idiosyncrasies across sites were noted.

In analyzing the data, the research team looked at the interface between what students brought to the task of learning their heritage language and what teachers did to foster their language development. Through an analysis of that interaction, the research team was able to propose a paradigm for heritage language instruction that differs in some fundamental ways from that of foreign language instruction. The following two articles, "Instructional Practice in Heritage Language Classrooms" and "Teachers' Belief Systems in Exemplary Heritage Language Classes" reflect this analysis.

Instructional Practice in Heritage Language Classrooms

Migdalia Romero 米

"When in junior high school, I was enrolled in a Spanish course that was absolutely too easy! I was bored to death. They were learning "casa" and "perro" when I was reading Latin American literature."
Rita Martinez, bilingual teacher, New York City

This quotation epitomizes one problem heritage language learners encounter in foreign language classrooms. It represents New York City during the eighties when Rita Martinez was attending public school. But it is also very much like my experience in the sixties and of countless foreign language students today. For some heritage language learners, foreign language classes represent an easy "A." However, in some of these classes, the forms of Spanish these students bring to school from their home and community are denigrated, leaving them with less self-esteem than when they entered and with less willingness to use the language.

Overall, many of these classes ignore the receptive and productive ability that these students bring in their heritage language. This travesty is an indictment of the prescriptive, one-size-fits-all, foreign language curriculum designed for students with no prior experience in a language, and driven by the goal of acquiring academic literacy. While a worthy objective, academic literacy is often pursued in a way that disengages students who bring prior knowledge of the language. In promoting this prescriptive curriculum, teachers focus on what is perceived to be missing or spoken "poorly," ignoring the rich dialect varieties spoken by diverse ethnolinguistic groups throughout the United States.

Until recently there have been very few training programs or classes that focus on preparing foreign language teachers to work with heritage language learners. Teachers asked to teach these students often do so reluctantly, for a variety of reasons. Some teachers are intimidated by the native-like proficiency of some of the students. Others resent the attitude of students who feel they know more of the language than the teacher does, or that they can speak it with greater fluency. Yet other conscientious teachers are overwhelmed by the range of receptive and productive skills that these students bring, the lack of an appropriate course of study, the paucity of appropriate materials, and the need to make major adaptations to a curriculum designed with a totally different population in mind (Valdés 1995).

The heritage language learner however, provides creative foreign language teachers with an opportunity and a challenge. When faced with a new population, especially one for whom there may be no curriculum, teachers want to know what to do next. Their focus is most often on activities, lessons, and/or units of study that work. These may fill a void and solve an immediate problem, but they do not get at the essence of effective instruction. While there is comfort in knowing what to do, there is power in having a sense of what can make any activity or lesson work, that is, the strategies that drive minute-to-minute decision making in a classroom and that define good language instruction.

This article documents three foreign language teachers who accepted that challenge. More specifically, it describes the strategies these teachers developed in response to making their classes work on behalf of their heritage language learners.

Thumbnail Sketches of the Schools and Teachers

All three high schools that were part of this descriptive study were located in New York City. They are described in greater detail in the introduction to this section.

Riverside High School is a small experimental school. The teacher-in-charge designed a program that enabled heritage language learners to take a Caribbean history and culture class taught in Spanish for either social studies or Spanish credit. The focus of the class was simultaneously on Spanish language development and history. The size of the school and the nature of its students contributed to this teacher being able to experiment with a content-based language course. The teacher, a native of Columbia, South America, came to this country at the age of eighteen, after having completed high school.

Midtown High School, in contrast, is a comprehensive high school serving 3,500 students. It offers a full complement of foreign language classes and a much smaller complement of heritage language classes. The class that was observed as part of this study was an advanced French class comprised of native speakers of French from French speaking African countries, French speaking Haitian students, and advanced French foreign language students. The teacher was a native of Haiti, having been schooled in both Créole and French, until coming to this country at the age of seventeen, where she finished her last two years in high school as an ESL student.

Uptown High School is also a comprehensive high school with over 5,000 students. It offers three tracks for language study: a foreign language track, a native track, and a heritage track. In the heritage track, there are fifteen teachers, some of whom also teach in the foreign language track. The teacher who participated in this study was a native of Calabria, Italy. She came to the United States at the age of five, after having attended a few months of first grade in her home country. While she maintained her native language at home, she chose to study Spanish in junior and senior high school, and to major in it in college. Her experience with Italian was very much like the experience of many of her Spanish students with their home language.

Sources of Data

As noted earlier, three sources of data were used to document the instructional practices of the three subjects of this study. The first source was direct classroom observation. The second was an interview with the observed teachers, and the third, a group interview with selected students. The observation gave the researchers the opportunity to view the learning environment the teacher had created and to see how the teacher carried out the activities that comprised the lesson. In the interviews with both teachers and students, the question of what constitutes effective practice was raised. The discussion with teachers revolved around what had worked for them over time, what they took into consideration as they planned lessons, and the strategies they used to ensure student engage-

137

ment. With students, the focus was on what worked in the classroom from their perspective. They were encouraged to talk about their teachers, the classroom environment, lessons, and assignments, as well as their goals and the gains they felt they had made.

It was not easy for the teachers to talk about their strategies, for while strategies are overt and observable, teachers were not always conscious of their use. When asked to describe the strategies they used most effectively, the teachers in our study often described "activities" that worked for them. When strategies they had used during an observation were brought to their attention, teachers often commented on not being aware that they had done what was observed. In effect, many of the strategies that teachers used in these classrooms evolved unwittingly and over time as a spontaneous reaction to instruction, the circumstances of the moment, and the reality of their students and classrooms.

Overview of Instruction

Kauchak and Eggen (1993) define teaching strategy as "an interconnected set of teaching behaviors designed to accomplish specific goals." Effective instruction, however, does not begin in the classroom; it culminates there. It starts long before teachers set foot in their rooms. It commences when teachers receive their roster of students, start thinking about the room in which they will be teaching, the content they must cover and/or choose to cover, and how they decide to cover it. In addition to planning the environment, effective instruction encompasses the planning of lessons, that is, how teachers select to introduce, motivate, develop their aims, and monitor their students' growth.

Once in school, but before actual teaching takes place, effective instruction includes how teachers greet their students as they enter the room and as they leave class. It may also include how they get to know their students personally in and out of school, and what they choose to learn about their students. In the classroom, effective instruction focuses on the day-to-day and minute-to-minute responses to students that promote engagement and learning, minimize digression, and ensure success.

For the purposes of this analysis, strategies have been redefined to include not only teaching behaviors embodied in the implementation of lessons and activities, but also those that figure in teachers' planning and their interaction with students as well. As such, the analysis of strategies has been divided into three categories, each representing one dimension of the teaching-learning process: planning, instruction, and interpersonal communication.

Planning strategies encompass the way in which teachers structure the learning environment, the goals they establish for their students, the choices they make about the content to include and how to cover that content, and the ways they incorporate their student's prior knowledge into their plans.

Instructional strategies include the ways in which teachers deliver instruction. These strategies incorporate how teachers seize the moment, especially in the teaching of grammar, how they engage students, use language in class and respond to the students' use of language (both heritage language and English) including their "errors," keep students on task, and handle digressions during instruction. At the instructional level, strategies focus on a teacher's minute-to-minute responses to students and to the teaching moment.

Interpersonal communication strategies look at how teachers get to know their students and how they socially interact with them.

Planning Strategies

In creating an environment conducive to learning, the teachers we observed had to work within the constraints of the programs in which they were teaching. In addition, they had to take into account the physical structure of the classroom(s) to which they were assigned and the curriculum they had to cover. In planning lessons, they also had to think about the ways in which they would forge a link between their goals for, and knowledge of, their students. Teachers' creativity in planning was often constrained by the degree of autonomy teachers had regarding a number of areas, including the recruitment and placement of students, approaches to instruction and grouping, and selection of curriculum materials.

Student Selection

The size and experimental nature of the program determined the degree of flexibility teachers had in selecting and placing students. In turn, the linguistic proficiency, the cultural profile, and the identities of these students, gleaned from the selection process, were the first sources of data teachers drew from as they planned for instruction. This information sometimes impacted on what was taught as well as on the materials that were used to teach.

The one-person program at the small experimental high school had the greatest degree of autonomy and, therefore, flexibility, in student selection. At this school, where the heritage language class consisted of a course on Caribbean History and Culture taught in Spanish, the teacher was responsible for recruitment and placement. Informal interviewing of students was the primary criterion used to determine student placement. The objective of the interview was to determine the student's degree of familiarity with spoken Spanish, focusing on their comprehension of it, irrespective of their willingness to use it.

In contrast, the comprehensive high schools were more diagnostic in their approach to placement because of the large number of students they served and the organizational structure of their schools. At the largest school, three separate tracks of Spanish were offered. Acceptance into the heritage language track was determined more formally and comprehensively than in the experimental school. It included a short writing sample, a recommendation from the feeder junior high school, and an interview with the coordinator of the program. The objective was to identify students who had both receptive and productive skills in the language, although they may have been unequally developed. While knowledge of grammar, tested formally, may not have been the forte of these students, many of them were able to write the language as they heard and spoke it. Teachers participating in this program saw this ability as a strength that could be nurtured in a heritage language class.

In interviews, heritage language students admitted that they did not always select the heritage class, feeling they would prefer the easy "A" they could get in a regular foreign language class. In all three schools the heritage language class was seen as more difficult, requiring more time and effort than the same level foreign language class. However, once placed, students could not easily opt out of these classes. Teachers sometimes cajoled students who were on the border between foreign language and heritage language placement into these classes.

Those who chose to study their heritage language did so for many, mostly personal, reasons. Some chose it to improve their communication skills noting, "I don't want to sound like an illiterate," or "I want to know how to speak Spanish correctly." Others wanted to improve their relations with their family. Yet others acknowledged more altruistic goals. As one student said: "I think if you're Hispanic you should learn our language and keep on speaking it and not forget about it." Another student stated: "If we have an Hispanic surname we should be able to represent it . . . never forget our roots."

The students' personal goals were not lost to these teachers. Nor were they oblivious to the ways in which the students were placed and their reasons for taking the class. In interviews, teachers acknowledged that this information was used in their planning. Recognizing their students' interest in speaking and representing the language, and of knowing their roots, teachers selected themes and literature to complement their students' goals. In many ways, the goals that teachers established for their students reflected their students' self-perception and lack of information about their culture and history. The personal and communicative goals of the students were also addressed by teachers' emphasizing communication in their planning.

Assessment and Planning

Data obtained from placement interviews, tests, and referrals were used to initiate instructional planning. However, once students were placed, teachers relied on their observation of students to better understand their relationship to their language and culture. Assessment, therefore, took the form of informal data collection, accomplished by listening to and observing their students in and out of class, even in their own neighborhoods or during extracurricular activities and events. One teacher, in visiting a relative in the section of the city from which many of his students had come, would see his students and chat with them. The other teachers volunteered their time to work with students on other projects in and out of school, using the opportunity to interact informally with them. All three agreed on the importance of knowing their students personally.

Once in class, student progress was monitored in a number of untraditional ways. In effect, teachers measured progress by monitoring engagement. They kept track of students' attentiveness during class, of the questions they asked, of their use of Spanish over time, and of the extent to which their work was shared with and/or involved others outside of class.

Placement tests made it clear that the ability to understand the more academic and literary forms of the language was a problem for many heritage language learners. However, not understanding literary forms was not held against them, but set as a goal for them to strive toward. Teachers saw their task as that of enhancing the forms of the language their students brought to school and adding the forms required to process academic text and literature. In order not to penalize students for what they needed to learn, initial assessment of written language focused on topics to which students could relate, and interviews allowed them to talk about topics of personal interest.

Also problematic was the students' resistance to using the language. This resistance came through not only in placement interviews but also through informal observations in class. However, even students who refused to use their heritage language when addressed in it, demonstrated a great deal of receptive knowledge. Teachers saw their responses in English as testimony to their comprehension. Often these students intuitively knew what sounded right or wrong, even if they could not explain why. Teachers felt that the inability to read and write in Spanish, French, or Haitian Créole should not prevent students with high degrees of receptive ability from hearing and working with literature, poetry, and text. This receptive knowledge was respected by the teachers as a resource in the classroom and a skill upon which to build. In their eyes, it made these students more capable of hearing the language spoken fluently, that is, embellished, paraphrased, and modified by the teacher.

All three teachers concurred on the limitations of formal testing, in particular with what it was unable to capture. They felt that the fluency of heritage language learners, that is, what these students knew and could do, could not be tapped by an instrument that decontextualized language, reducing it to a test of mastery over form. They recognized that heritage language learners fell between the cracks on scales of linguistic proficiency, simultaneously scoring high and low in some skills, with even greater discrepancy across skills. Teachers also felt that the knowledge of grammatical forms and of academic language should not totally guide the placement process, since it denied those with social skills in the language the opportunity to show what they knew and could do. In fact, knowledge of and respect for their students' receptive and productive ability in the target language (French, Haitian Créole, or Spanish) figured heavily into these teachers' plans. Realizing both the skills their students brought, as well as their resistance and their limitations, these teachers sought to teach to the strengths, goals, and interests of their students.

Setting up the Learning Environment

At the smaller experimental school, Riverside, the heritage language teacher was assigned a room for all of his classes, one he did not have to share with another teacher. This enabled him to turn the classroom into a second home for his students. The classroom contained cultural and personal artifacts reminding students of their heritage and their families. On a bulletin board in the room were pictures of the students and, in some cases, their children. In his interview, the teacher commented on how students coming into the room would go up to the class bulletin board and talk with pride about their babies. Students painted the ceiling of the classroom with the flags of the Spanish speaking countries from which their families had come. Posters representing literary figures of the Spanish speaking world and museums in Latin America adorned the walls.

In essence, the classroom was an extension of the home, the culture, and the students' countries of origin. The idea of the classroom as an extension of the home was evident in the teacher's comparing the classroom to the students' homes, in an attempt to elicit student pride in having it organized and clean. A sense of community was established by having students become owners of their own space, designing it, contributing to it, and maintaining it.

At the other schools, teachers displayed students' work, as well as inspirational posters, and travel posters from students' countries of origin. However, since rooms in these schools were shared with at least one other teacher, often from another discipline, it was not possible to personalize them in the same way as at Riverside. Personalization came through in other instructional forms.

Goals and Content of the Curriculum

Generally, the goals and content of a language class are defined and constrained by the textbook(s) a school adopts and the standardized tests the students are required to take at the end of a course of study. While the goals of a curriculum are prescribed, there is some flexibility in how those goals are attained. If the text uses a thematic focus, teachers can adapt/ extend the treatment of a theme. If the text is driven by grammatical form, or by the emphasis on a particular dialect variety, teachers may alter the means and the medium through which grammatical points are made and practiced.

In the heritage language classes that were observed, teachers found ways of going beyond what was prescribed without losing their focus on what was required. In fact, these teachers raised fundamental questions about the prescribed curriculum, questions that ultimately guided their instructional decisions. They took into account what students knew and could do with the language, including the dialect varieties with which their students were familiar. Teachers were guided more by what was relevant and interesting for this population, rather than by what was easy or difficult. They also considered the student's relationship with the language. What evolved in these classes was a coalescence of curricular goals. Teachers knew what had to be covered, thematically and grammatically, and they worked in and around what students could do and were interested in.

In planning instruction, all three teachers built their curriculum and literature studies, as much as possible, around students' cultural and ethnic identities, including readings that reflected the dialect voices of the people. They worked literature that reflected the student's backgrounds into their curriculum. At Uptown High School, the teacher included the study of the poems *"Danza Negra"* from Luis Pales Matos of Puerto Rico and *"Sensemaya"* from Nicolas Guillen of Cuba. The Dominican students, noting the absence of authors from their coun-

143

try, asked the teacher to be more inclusive. As she put it: "They wanted something for themselves." Without hesitation, the teacher sought out additional material for inclusion. She found *"Tengo"* by Blas Jimenez. This responsiveness to students' voices and concerns was characteristic of these teachers. In effect, it empowered students.

In planning, teachers also included reference to and/or the actual study of contemporary and folk music, history, geography, and culture of the Dominican Republic, Mexico, and Puerto Rico, among other Hispanic groups, and of Haiti and Africa—countries from which the students and their families had come. Relevant holidays were celebrated including *El Diá de los Muertos*, Dominican Independence, Puerto Rican Discovery Day, and Kwanzaa.

During the interviews, students expressed their resentment of studying only American history in school. It was for this reason that students at Riverside enjoyed the Caribbean History and Culture course taught in Spanish. The teachers at Midtown and Uptown, recognizing that students also wanted to learn about their culture, incorporated it into their language classes. Coincidentally, the French lesson that was observed at Midtown was on the African nations where French is spoken. Students proudly affirmed the impact that such studies were having on what they knew about their culture.

Current events related to local news coverage or to coverage in the foreign language media also figured into the teachers' instructional plans, either incidentally or by design. The plight of Cuban refugees en route to this country, or the border incidents affecting migration and the treatment of Hispanic and Haitian minorities were two such examples. Teachers did not shy away from controversial contemporary issues. In controversy they found greater student participation.

Teachers talked about their students in very personal ways, describing their journeys into this country, as well as their losses and the conflicts they faced while living here. Teachers also talked about the personal identities, ambivalence, and self-concepts of their students, all of which, they realized, impacted on the students' willingness to use their heritage language, and, by extension, on the nature of their relationship with family members. In order to ameliorate the personal problems and conflicts that their students face, teachers incorporated literary pieces dealing with migration, conflict, and adjustment into their courses. By including such themes, students were more likely to make personal connections to what was being read. This inclusion also enriched the level of dialogue and the contribution of students to the discussion.

Students, in turn, spoke about their connections to their home countries, cultures, parents, and language. Many spoke of language loss prior to formal study of their heritage language. But they also spoke of retrieval and of improved parental communication as a result of having participated in the heritage language class.

Realizing the impact of both language resistance and loss on family relationships, these teachers consciously drew students' families and community into the learning process. Assignments were planned that involved interviewing family members living in this country, writing personal letters to those living away, or reporting on issues from the point of view of community members. The impact of these assignments was not lost on the students. They commented on the new lines of communication that had been opened up with parents and grandparents as a result of sharing assignments with family members and involving family members in preparing them.

In terms of planning, it was obvious that the intimate knowledge these teachers had of their students' personal lives and the respect for their linguistic proficiency, including their dialect varieties, figured into the teachers' plans. In addition, teachers took into account their students' intuitive knowledge of what "sounds right," their comprehension of social language, their resistance to using the heritage language and their relationships with their parents. The teachers' approach to language development for heritage language learners was based on the philosophy that what students bring—linguistically, emotionally, and experientially—must serve as a point of departure and reference for language study.

Instructional Strategies

This section describes how teachers delivered instruction in the classroom. It focuses on the ways in which the teacher used the heritage language and encouraged its use by the students. It also addresses the ways teachers kept students engaged and motivated within the context of a lesson.

A Snapshot

Twenty-five inner-city high school students sat in a small windowless classroom discussing a video they had seen the day before on Ponce de Leon. The teacher addressed the students in fluent Spanish, often paraphrasing his own questions and adding information to students' responses and comments. Students comfortably contributed to the discussion in both English and Spanish. At one point, the teacher switched the discussion to grammar, focusing on verb conjugation.

This class, not unlike the other two classes that were observed for this study, encapsulates some of the critical dimensions of effective instruction for heritage language learners.

Language Use by Teacher

In the Spanish heritage classes, both teachers used Spanish almost exclusively. In all three heritage language classes, the teachers accepted English responses from their students, for reasons that will be discussed later. The teachers' rich, spontaneous, and fluid use of the heritage language emanated from their confidence, fluency, and the expectation that students would understand. Teachers did not slow down their speech, nor did they repeat utterances if students did not seem to understand. Rather they paraphrased, embellished responses, and used synonyms, metaphors, colloquialisms and regionalisms. This resulted in a language-rich environment, even in the absence of written language adorning the walls of some rooms. By using only the heritage language, teachers were enhancing their students' receptive ability and their passive vocabulary, while simultaneously modeling natural language.

Teachers also used humor to diffuse tension. When one student came late to the morning class, the teacher greeted the student with *"Buenas tardes"* (Good afternoon). Everyone laughed and the class just moved on without incident.

In addition, teachers acknowledged and used the dialect varieties of their students during instruction. This was done to illustrate a point, make an analogy, or to show their knowledge of the culture and their affinity with it. Students recognized and respected this in their teachers, making them feel a greater affinity for them.

Language Use by Students

The tenor of these classrooms emphasized communication. Student talk was encouraged in a variety of ways. A dialogue format was used extensively in all classes. Small cooperative groups promoted interaction among students, especially in the French class where native French ESL students were mixed with advanced level foreign language French students. In fact, in all classes, getting students to speak was more important than precision or even choice of language. The teacher, however, set the tone to promote heritage language use by consistently using it and gently encouraging students to use it as well.

Nevertheless, students were resistant to using the language, especially in Spanish classes and especially at the beginning of the school year. Teachers consciously attended to this resistance. Recognizing the students' fear of making mistakes, teachers allowed students to respond in their stronger language, with an eye toward getting them to feel comfortable using the target language and increasing its usage over time. While all teachers encouraged students to use the target language when contributing to class discussion, they did not insist on it. They accepted English responses from their students, but acknowledged students' attempts to integrate the target language, even when it was used within the context of an English response. Teachers saw this small step as a movement in the right direction. Rather than penalize students for it, they accepted its use without fanfare. Teachers consciously monitored the increase of use over time as a measure of progress.

Guidelines for written assignments were different. Students were expected to write in the heritage language, even though discussion among students in small groups might generate discussion in English.

What the teachers did not readily realize was that students were consciously taking the language out of the classroom into the cafeteria and into their homes, using it with friends and parents. They were talking more in Spanish and reading in it when it was not required. As one student noted: "Before, I wouldn't pay attention to the Spanish newspaper, and now I read it and understand it." Another student acknowledged "read [ing] stories to her parents."

Just as teachers sometimes used the dialect varieties of the students in class, they also accepted its use in the classroom. When students responded with a word or phrase with which the teacher was not familiar, teachers showed an interest in the students' use of language. Rather than dismiss or penalize students for its use, the teacher asked students more about it, seeking clarification to be sure they were talking about the same thing. By asking questions, teachers revealed their own lack of knowledge and their vulnerability. The focus was on meaning, mutual comprehensibility, and communication. Clearly, these teachers were not threatened by their students' proficiency in their heritage language; instead they embraced it, and were willing to learn from them.

Opportunities were created for students to teach many of the skills they had to their teachers. Students taught them the latest dances, shared recipes, music, idiomatic expressions, and vocabulary. What ensued was a community of learners, where respect and curiosity garnered respect and curiosity.

Use of Culture

During instruction, teachers made reference to their students' heritage cultures and dialect varieties to illustrate a point or to make a connection to the students.

One of the teachers shared with students his experience with *plátanos* (plantains), a food he knew his Dominican students knew well. In his own words:

> I told my students a little story about myself (to make the point that one has to accustom the body to new foods) when I went to the farm with my friends back in Colombia where they have *plátanos,* forget it, four, five times a day. And to me it was a new experience to eat *plátanos* so many times a day to the point that I got constipated by the second day. Everyone laughed. (At this point all the kids are contributing examples of foods from their cultures.) So one of the kids asks: "Is that why Sammy Sosa hit sixty-two home runs?" I said probably he ate *"compotas de plátano"* in the Dominican Republic. By this time the kids were on the floor.

This weaving of cultural information into the class was spontaneous. As such, it relied on a teacher's intimate knowledge of the student's cultures and of the realities of their lives in those cultures. Teachers were able to provide examples and draw analogies that would help their students make personal connections to the literature that they were expected to read. Teachers drew on their own knowledge of the music, dance forms, history, geography, baseball players, and foods that were connected to the students' cultural heritages. And they drew on it from a deep conviction that good learning must be personalized:

> I make it like this is one-on-one because that's how you learn better. Whatever I say, whatever we do, it's related to you somewhere, somehow. Perhaps to your family, to your ancestors, to what you do everyday at home or outside of the classroom.

Yearly, the students in Uptown High School produce a beautifully illustrated publication entitled, *Orgullo Hispano.* It is a compilation of their best work. Over the years it has grown to include poetry, responses to literature, short stories, plays, letters, interviews with teachers, biographies of famous public figures from the students' countries of origin, a love advice column, *"Querida Sabelotodo,"* a horoscope, and Spanish word puzzles. On the title page the following note appears:

> *Esperamos que por medio de estas obras los alumnos puedan comunicar lo que sienten por su cultura y su raza a otros de su generación. Esta revista es una muestra del talento literario y artístico de los estudiantes hispanos de la escuela superior de Uptown. El propósito de nuestra colección es y sera siempre inspirar el orgullo de todos los hispanoparlantes en nuestras clases.*

> We hope that through these writings the students will be able to communicate how they feel about their culture and their ethnicity to their peers.

> This magazine is a sample of the literary and artistic talent of the Hispanic students of Uptown High School. The objective of this compilation is to inspire the pride of all the Spanish-speaking students in our classes.

This inscription clearly expresses the respect that the teachers have for their students and the importance that they give to their voices, their language, and their culture.

Students discussed the importance of voice in class. When asked what they felt worked best for them, one student said, "More opinion-oriented lessons where you're able to bring in your background and your experiences and share them with the class." They wanted "stories they identify with."

Interpersonal Communication Strategies

In the effective heritage language classroom and outside of it, talk was intended by design or default to establish rapport with students. Teachers' interpersonal comments to their students upon entering the classroom spoke of the nature of the teacher-student relationship. This included informal communication with students before class, teasing them about the real reason for their absences and lateness, and the maintenance of their room. The camaraderie and respect teachers had for their students were evident in the way they interacted with them.

Students, in turn, spoke of the respect they had for their teachers. They respected the fact that these teachers "know the language" and "can explain it more easily." Students also recognized the language varieties understood and spoken by the teachers. As one student said: "It is easier if the teacher speaks the same Spanish as you." Clearly, in these classes language was a tool that fostered social cohesion: "Not so many teachers who teach a foreign language are from that culture, that environment, so I appreciate the fact that she was."

Teachers sought to get to know their students in a variety of ways, even outside of the school context. As one teacher pointed out:

> I think the first thing that I do and the main thing that I do is to get to them first, to get closer to them. I cannot teach history or foreign languages to these kids if I don't get next to them, if I don't get to know them.

The ultimate example of the impact of a teacher's knowing his students occurred when this same teacher visited the neighborhood where many of his students lived. The payoff was particularly high from one of those visits. He described his encounter with one of the new students in his class:

> Manny only came to this school three weeks ago. He seemed to be a little

149

rowdy and a little outspoken, ... so the first two weeks I had some difficulties with him. I tell him to calm down. I know he's excited. So last week when I went to see ... I always like to go uptown to Washington Heights because most of our population is from that area. Because I go to visit my mother-in-law and because I just like to go, just so I can keep an eye on the kids, just for them, to let them know that I'm there and that I do not live in this secluded area.... So I parked my car and I see Manny with his friend. I say, "Manny, how are you?" He says, "Chilling out," and, "What are you doing here?" (Not believing the teacher, Manny wants to know where his mother-in-law lives.) The minute I give him an address and directions, he realizes that I know the place. Believe me, when this kid came back on Monday he was a totally different person.

The other teachers got to know their students after school and on Saturdays as they coached students or supported them in other extracurricular activities. Their relationship with their students got them invited to parties, trips, and school dances. These were not nine to three teachers, but dedicated professionals.

The ways in which teachers interacted with students in and out of class were influenced by a teacher's self-identification, and in many cases by their own heritage language experiences. While they did not always come from the same countries as their students, nor did they all speak the same native language, they all shared some vestiges of the students' heritage language experience. The shared experiences of these teachers gave them the emotional language they needed to connect to their students. In interviews, teachers talked about their journeys into teaching, their identification with their students, their resistance and pride in their heritage languages (Spanish, Italian, and Haitian Créole) and their personal commitment to the success of these students. In one way or another, all three of the teachers in this study saw themselves in their students.

Attitudes Underlying Teaching

The goals that teachers held for their heritage language learners, the ways in which language was used and developed in class, and the ways in which teachers interacted with their students reflected the teacher's attitudes toward teaching and toward their students. In the next article, "Teachers' Belief Systems and the Heritage Language Classroom," Claire Sylvan discusses both in greater detail. However, since they figure heavily in the teaching paradigm to be proposed, they are synthesized here.

Attitude toward Teaching

The three teachers in this study perceived teaching as a dynamic process and the teacher as a reflective practitioner, one who re-invents teaching with each new group. They operated from the premise that "no two years were alike and no two students were alike." Of necessity, their approach to teaching was responsive rather than purely prescriptive. By continually reconceptualizing their teaching, they were able to maintain the dynamic nature of their classes. From one year to the next there were differences in the proficiency of their students, their attitudes and resistance to language, the countries their families came from, their goals, their experiences, and their cultural affinity, among many other differences. They recognized the fact that what motivates one group may not motivate another.

These teachers raised questions about their teaching. They tested new strategies, activities, and materials. When the usual icebreaker did not work with one group, the teacher immediately redesigned and tested out another activity. Teaching for them was constantly changing. It was a work in progress, emanating from the belief that there was no single solution to working effectively with these students. One teacher described her process: "Teaching for me is like learning from the students. It's like sharing."

These teachers were aware of the multiple roles they had assumed, as were their students. Teachers described themselves as social workers, guidance counselors, mentors, advocates, and surrogate parents. In turn, students described their teachers as "mother, role model, and friend." The African and Haitian students were especially vocal about the ways in which their teacher had taken them under her wing: giving them advice, actively supporting their pursuit of college, and generally making them feel that they could and would succeed. According to all students, the heritage language teachers were more available to them than most other teachers.

Attitude toward Students

One teacher described the heritage language population as "the kids who know more." This perspective allowed them to expect more and to aim higher.

Teachers spoke of the linguistic heterogeneity in their classroom and the attitudes of their students toward the heritage language as both a challenge and an opportunity. They saw the diversity in skills and in dialect varieties brought by the students as a strength and a resource. The focus for them was on the receptive abilities that their students brought with them and what they could do with the language, rather than on what they could not do. These teachers approached teaching with high expectations for students, and a recognition that their students were capable of understanding and using the language. The respect these teachers had for their students and the rapport they developed with them enabled them to be effective.

Summary and Conclusions

It is impossible to discuss strategies in a vacuum. Throughout this process it was evident that the strategies used by effective heritage language teachers reflected their philosophy about the teaching and learning process and their belief systems about, knowledge of, and goals for their students. In fact, these were inseparable. The premise is that a teacher's instructional response to this population takes into account what they know about their students, at the same time that it is consistent with a particular set of beliefs (Figure 1). In turn, what they know about their students impacts on their instructional planning and their delivery of instruction. The interface of these three components was evident as the teachers' instructional practices were analyzed.

Figure 1.

The measure of success of a heritage language class was, in the case of this study, the student's response to their teachers and their class. In each of these cases, we observed a change of attitudes, a receptivity and interest in the language, and a willingness to use it outside of school. While these behaviors are not objective measures of the effectiveness of these classes, they are indicators of success.

In addition, students acknowledged the positive impact of the program, as well as the personal impact of their teachers in spite of some resistance to the additional work that was expected of them. For some, the result was a change in their career goals to include the use and continued study of the heritage language beyond high school. Others felt the heritage class forced them to use skills they had, and for that they were grateful.

Teachers in this study were driven less by a prescriptive curriculum, than by the desire to make content both intrinsically interesting and personally relevant to the students. They did this by building on a student's knowledge base formally and informally. They were propelled by deeply held beliefs in their students' abilities and respect for what the students knew and brought to the classroom, in terms of language, culture, and prior knowledge and experience. They were convinced that their students would "make it" and contribute to society.

For heritage language teachers, this approach to teaching and learning requires a shift in paradigm (see Figure 2, below) from traditional foreign language instruction. It involves using the student rather than the text as the point of departure for the curriculum. While the text and the objective performance standards must be utilized for effective heritage language learners' instruction, they must remain in the background. The student must occupy the foreground. More specifically, what the student knows and brings to class is what needs to drive the curriculum. Effective heritage language instruction is a marriage between a focus on content and structure, with meaning and relevance leading the way, and form following the dynamics of the class.

In terms of planning, teachers must first get to know their students' cultural and linguistic realities. This involves data collection even before classes begin, when rosters are distributed. Some of this data is accessible during the first weeks of class as teachers set up the learning environment with their students, establish routines, and personally get to know their students. Library research on the countries of origin of students' families can also provide fodder for curriculum.

Figure 2.

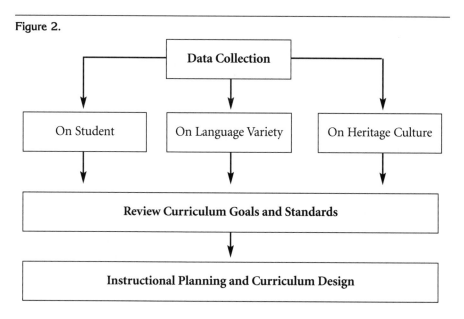

The goal during this part of the year is for teacher and students to learn about each other and from each other. Teachers must show in their actions, not just their words, that they respect their students' diversity; their receptive knowledge of the language, in spite of their resistance to use it; and their students' intimate knowledge of their own cultures.

In such a curriculum, teachers build on students' intuitive knowledge of what sounds right and the ability of many to comprehend much more than they are able to produce. At the same time, teachers accommodate students' resistance to use the language in formal settings, while simultaneously supporting its use informally.

In terms of instruction, this means that grammar is taught in context, with language growth emerging from interesting content. The teaching of grammatical form becomes both an implicit and an explicit goal, and language becomes a tool, and the means to an end. This type of teaching requires an intimate and comprehensive knowledge of curriculum and standards, a degree of fluency in the language, and an ability to "seize the moment," thereby promoting incidental learning. It also requires that teachers know what is intrinsically interesting to their students and the personal goals that students have established for themselves.

The challenge and the opportunities that this population affords foreign language teachers are enormous. The challenge is greater for those responsible for preparing teachers to work with heritage languages. They must help those teachers explore and cultivate their belief system, expand their knowledge of diverse cultural groups, and foster respect for dialect varieties of the language under study. All of this is essential to effective instruction of this student population. The question that remains unanswered is how teachers can develop both the belief system and the linguistic competencies that drive this model of instruction.

References

Kauchak, D.P. and P.D. Eggen. 1993. *Learning and Teaching: Research Based Methods. Second Edition.* Boston, MA: Allyn & Bacon.

Valdés, G. 1995. *The Modern Language Journal,* Vol.79, pp. iii, 299-328.

Appendix 1

CLASSROOM OBSERVATION CHECKLIST
Developed by
Drs. Migdalia Romero and Claire Elaine Sylvan

I. CLASSROOM ENVIRONMENT
•Seating arrangement
•Displays

II. STRUCTURE OF LESSON
•Routines
•Homework
•Use of down time

III. FOCUS/ EXPECTATIONS OF CLASS
•Form vs. content
•Theme

IV. INSTRUCTIONAL TECHNIQUES
•Use of board
•Materials
•Handling code switching/ dialect varieties
•Handling discipline

V. CLASSROOM LANGUAGE USE
1. Teacher talk
•Quantity and quality?
•Distributive use of HL/English by teacher?
2. Student talk
•Distributive use of HL/ English by student?
•Opportunity for?
•Quantity and quality? (Extent of? With whom used? Nature?)
3. Interaction
•Between students
•Between teacher and student
•Between student and text

Appendix 2

FIPSE Research Project
Sponsored by ACTFL and Hunter College

Teacher Interview Protocol Areas of Inquiry

Baseline Data on Teacher: _____

Place of birth? _____

Years living in U.S.? _____Spanish speaking country? _____

Years teaching FL? _____Years teaching HLL? _____

I. Best class scenario (projects/ activities/ materials/ themes/ books/ strategies)

II. Student awareness (monitoring progress/ assessing growth; goals)

III. Dealing with diversity in skills and levels of competence among HLLs

IV. Idealized program—If there were no constraints on organization or implementation, how would you set up your class, who would be in it, and what would you do?

V. Teacher Preparation—What would have prepared you better for teaching HLLs?

Return completed responses to: Dr. Migdalia Romero, Dept. of Curriculum & Teaching, Hunter College, 695 Park Ave., New York, NY 10021

Appendix 3

FIPSE Research Project
Sponsored by ACTFL and Hunter College

Student Interview Protocol Areas of Inquiry

I. Purpose for taking course

II. "Good" language learning experiences in school (activities, projects, teachers that had an impact/ made a difference).

III. "Bad" language learning experiences in school.

IV. Recommendations for improving language learning in school.

V. Personal impact (outside of school) of studying your heritage language.

Return completed responses to: Dr. Migdalia Romero, Dept. of Curriculum &
Teaching, Hunter College, 695 Park Ave., New York, NY 10021

Appendix 4

Coordinator Interview Protocol
Developed by:
Drs. Migdalia Romero and Claire Elaine Sylvan

I. **School Level Information**
    • Student population (ethnic distribution, SES, age range, grades)

II. **Foreign Language Program Information**
    • History of program
    • Structure of program (size, languages offered, levels, enrollment profiles)
    • Advanced placement options and enrollment profile
    • Profile of teachers

III. **HLL Program Information**
    • History (age, evolution)
    • Organization (structure)
    • Placement of students (criteria, procedures, and structure)
    • Classroom space (dedicated, # rooms, laboratory)
    • Teachers (experience, heritage language proficiency, ethnic affiliation, criteria for selection)
    • Materials (text, curriculum guides)
    • Written goals; mission statement for program
    • In-service training
    • Support (leadership, fiscal)
    • Nature of services provided
    • Unique characteristics of program

IV. **HLL Student Information**
    • Profile of students (linguistic competence, proficiency, literacy skills, countries of origin, time in U.S., SES)

Teachers' Belief Systems in Exemplary Heritage Language Classes

Claire Elaine Sylvan ❋

*"At the beginning, I noticed the population and I said to myself, well, I need
a class for native speakers. So I grabbed whatever I had from AP classes, like
grammar and vocabulary and advanced literature...but I was not satisfied
because I felt that the kids could have learned more and I could have taken
a different approach towards teaching the class...So I said, wait a minute,
I have the information...I ask the kids, what do you know about history,
their history, about literature...I put all that together and really created my
own curriculum. And the minute I started, I thought that I was very successful and I continued."*

—Taken from an interview with the classroom teacher.

One of the major themes that emerged from the research described in the
previous article, "Instructional Practice in Heritage Language Classrooms," was the fact that highly successful and exemplary heritage language teachers share a common philosophy that they are able to articulate fairly
clearly. Although the three teachers in the study shared many common instructional strategies, which the researchers noted during lesson observations, they

were generally less able to articulate these strategies. It became clear that their daily planning, their delivery of instruction, and their creation and control of the classroom environment were all guided by their underlying philosophy. This article, therefore, is focused specifically on the teachers' belief systems, bringing together and revealing the philosophical foundations upon which they based their work. It also contains a review of the literature on teacher thinking and beliefs that suggest that belief systems are central to all effective teachers' practice.

The Impact of Teacher Thinking and Beliefs: A Review of the Literature

Descartes' famous statement regarding humans was "I think, therefore I am." In the case of teaching, some researchers suggest that what a teacher thinks or believes is the single most important factor determining who he or she is as a teacher. P.J. Palmer (1998) in a book that examines "who is the self that teaches?" describes how "teaching ... emerges from one's inwardness." Noting that techniques and methods are important, he nonetheless argues that only by focusing on the inner soul of the teacher can real reform be achieved.

Earlier research by others, such as Popkewitz, Tabachnick, and Wehlage (1982) also supports this idea. Popkewitz, and others, found that schools implemented the same reform program in widely differing ways, dependent on differing assumptions and values concerning schooling, social relations, and authority that were held by the teachers and administrators in each school.

More recent research by Millies (1992) describes three domains of a teacher's mental life: the pedagogical personality, the pedagogical assumptions, and the pedagogical repertoire. The domain of pedagogical assumptions are "the givens of one's cognitive world in regard to how one should function in one's practice ... consist[ing] of values, beliefs, principles and strategies."

Teachers' philosophies impact on how they create classroom environments, how they plan instruction, and how they deliver it. In an anthology of writings of teachers examining their own practices, Coughlan (1985) writes: "I really had some underlying theory lurking around in my head, affecting the way I functioned in my classroom.... Yes, I possessed a theory of learning— every teacher does."

Others have suggested that teachers' philosophies must be taken into account in designing staff development. Newman (1998) argues that teachers must uncover their underlying philosophies. She notes that it is not enough to teach specific strategies or techniques since they cannot fundamentally alter how teachers teach. That is because how they teach is based on their deeper belief system.

Popkewitz, and others (1982), points out that strategies can be transformed to fit philosophies.

In conducting this research to identify the successful strategies used by teachers of heritage language learners, we discovered that, for the most part, teachers were unaware of the specific strategies that they used. They were, however, much more cognizant of their outlook, or philosophy, of teaching. More significantly, the exemplary teachers interviewed for this research project shared major philosophical beliefs.

Respect for Student's Prior Knowledge

Exemplary teachers of heritage language learners believe that their students come to them with important knowledge about their heritage language. The Riverside High School teacher describes his attitude toward his students: "Okay, you know Spanish and that's good and that's great. Okay, let's take advantage of that. And let's use that to learn even more."

Both the exemplary heritage language teachers and their students point out the contrast between this attitude and the one that heritage language learners face in more typical foreign language classes: lack of respect or overt denigration for prior language knowledge. The Riverside teacher notes this negative attitude in Advanced Placement foreign language classes when he said, "And with the AP classes, there's the assumption that you are a native speaker, but hey, how much do you know?"

Students were also aware that their prior knowledge was not respected in other language classes. In one case, a student pointed out that her previous foreign language teachers "used to teach me words I already knew as if I'd never learned anything."

Heterogeneity of Heritage Language Learners

Another characteristic belief of exemplary heritage language teachers is that all heritage language learners come in with prior knowledge, and that this knowledge is manifested in different ways by different students. Thus, each student intrinsically has something to offer to others in the class and to enrich within him or herself.

The teacher at Riverside High School notes that "some of the kids have more knowledge and more skills than other kids in the language and that's already an advantage." The teacher at Midtown High School tells her students, "If people are making mistakes (speaking French), then if you know it better than they do, it is

161

your responsibility to teach them." The concept of peer teaching is integral to the class, because the teachers' conceptualization of prior student knowledge is not linear in nature. Students have complex patterns of linguistic strengths. As a result, the traditional methodology of measuring student knowledge along a 1 to 5 scale of fluency developed by the U.S. Defense Department is ineffective in designing and assessing instruction for heritage language learners.

The teachers' awareness of the diverse pre-existing knowledge base of their students leads them to individualize instruction. Some students may write better, others may speak better, while still others may have mainly a receptive knowledge of the language. The Midtown teacher pointed out that she "assigns work for them to do" when she "sees the different levels." The Riverside teacher chooses to assign books from Julia de Alvarez to more advanced students to "sharpen [their] skills in writing or reading."

The teachers' respect for students' prior knowledge and their acceptance of the diverse nature of that knowledge encourages them to individualize instruction. It also leads them to develop multiple standards for assessing student learning. In evaluating students, the teachers seem to automatically take into account their students' abilities. The Midtown teacher, who makes herself available to students individually, says, "That's how I monitor them, individually and gradually." The Riverside teacher describes the differences in how he will evaluate written examinations from two students. With one student, who speaks very good Spanish, he "makes sure that she writes the test in Spanish, because I know she has the ability to write in Spanish, so I don't expect less from her in that sense. From another student, I know he's going to write most of the stuff in English, a few words in Spanish."

Locus of Control of Language and Learning

This sensitivity to the diversity of student's prior knowledge is linked to an instructional approach that allows students to maintain the locus of control over their own learning and language use. At the same time, the Riverside teacher chooses to use Spanish almost exclusively as the classroom medium of communication. By example, and through praise, the teacher strongly encourages students to use the heritage language both inside of the classroom and out.

During a classroom observation at Riverside, the teacher became quite animated in response to a student's comment in Spanish. When asked about this later on during the interview, the teacher noted that it was the first time that the student had ever spoken in Spanish during class. The teacher noted his desire "to reward (the student) for what he said ... a couple of times during the class," adding, "Hopefully, tomorrow, he'll come out with something else. That's one of my little goals."

Although the teacher's goal is clearly to have students increase their use of the heritage language, he consciously gives them the ultimate decision-making power of the language in which they choose to communicate:

> "I try sometimes ...to really reinforce it but I don't push it. 'Oh, D. you have to talk to me in Spanish, I know you speak Spanish.' No, I don't force it. And if I see the second time that she doesn't want to do it in Spanish today, I back up a little bit and I say, okay. Because I probably won't get any more Spanish from her, and I'm the one who loses. If I work with them, they work with me. But, if I want it always my way, I probably don't get anything."

The teachers realize that language use by their students involves much more than an academic exercise of intellectually acquired material. Recognizing the complexity of their students' efforts to improve their knowledge of their heritage language, they leave the final locus of control of language use in their students' hands.

The Riverside teacher notes that, in fact, students have a choice to say, "I'd rather flunk the course than learn all that crap." If teachers can understanding the complexity of learning in school a language with which a person grew up, they can consciously set up situations that empower students to make choices about their learning. For example, in teaching students the fine points of grammar, in this case, definite articles in Spanish, students may respond that they "know" it. So the teacher writes ten words on the board, asks the students to choose the correct articles, and tells them that he "won't teach definite articles any more" if they are able to respond correctly. Students start out saying, "Why should I learn about definite articles?" But, they soon "see themselves that they don't know it all, and they say, 'Oh, I know most of this stuff but there are some exceptions and some things that I need to learn.' " The teacher notes the dissimilarity between this approach and saying to students, "Okay, here we are. Definite articles. Learn! And here are some examples. Read about it; do it."

In essence, the teacher is validating his students' knowledge of the heritage language, and putting them in a position to make positive choices to increase their knowledge. They make decisions to learn grammar and to use, and thus learn the language.

This teacher recognizes that students may have learned about things that he did not teach, or at least did not teach consciously, by allowing them to construct their own questions in addition to responding to the teacher-constructed items on tests. For example, if the teacher "didn't talk about Juan Ponce de Leon, but I study a lot about Juan Ponce de Leon, I can write my own question about Juan Ponce de Leon." In this way, the teacher shares the locus of control in assessment with his students.

The Midtown teacher says her philosophy of teaching "is like learning from the students." She says she "shares with (the students) the notion that they are cheating themselves by not doing what they're supposed to do." By doing this, she gives students the incentive, and also the option of deciding to take control of their own learning.

Classroom as Family

Perhaps linked to their awareness of the complexity of teaching heritage language learners, exemplary heritage language teachers believe that a classroom is in some ways like a family. There are diverse members of the group, but the group must support and help each other, and the role of the teacher is to guide, to lead by example, and to encourage the students to make decisions, such as using the heritage language, within class and outside of it. The Riverside teacher explicitly describes his classroom as "our second home," and later notes that he wants the students to "feel comfortable."

This same teacher has a bulletin board with baby pictures—pictures of his students' children—because this engages them. Connections are created among his students as classmates, who upon seeing the pictures ask, "Who is that little beautiful baby?" The student-parent will respond, "It's my baby."

The Midtown teacher describes the struggle she encounters to ensure that the students are supportive of each other in attempting to create a warm, safe environment, where classmates, like members of a family, take responsibility for each other. She explains:

> "They do not want to speak even when they know how to write. They have this phobia of mistakes. They don't want to make mistakes so that people won't make fun of them. And this is the thing that I'm still fighting in class. Because any time people make mistakes, the others, they'll react.... If you don't correct their habit, then I tell them if people are making mistakes, then if you know it, and you know better than they do, it is your responsibility to teach them ... and gradually when I do that, the others who don't want to speak, they come out and they speak."

Family members tend to speak the same language. Thus, teachers' consistent use of the heritage language serves as an example and a stimulant to the students to use the language. As discussed above, the decision of how to speak it, when to speak it, and whether or not to speak it is left to students. That is to say, the students retain the locus of control of language use, akin to what happens in a family.

Language: A Medium for High Interest, Culturally Relevant Content

In a family, language is used principally to communicate ideas that are of interest to the members of that family. In these classes, therefore, the focus is on material of intrinsic interest to the students. The Midtown teacher described it this way:

> "I think that is the best way to learn. Whatever we do, it's related to you somewhere, somehow. Perhaps to your family, to your ancestors, to what you do everyday at home or outside of the classroom. Moreover, I think that's always going to stay with them if I do that."

The teachers have made their curricular choices based on their understanding that their students need to have not only a fuller comprehension of their heritage language, but, in fact, of the heritage itself. The Midtown teacher made this point, saying:

> "To me, when I see heritage language, I see the whole heritage—food, music, politics, society and the language itself. ... The language is used to express these other ideas."

The Riverside teacher expresses concerns about his students' knowledge of their own heritage:

> "They don't know anything about history or their culture, about their literature. ...They don't even know who Julia Alvarez is, or Albizu Campos, probably one out of twenty knows Luis Munoz Marin."

This teacher uses a chapter from Julia Alvarez's powerful novel, *The Time of the Butterflies,* because in it, Alvarez "talks about the history, the customs, the traditions and (about) Dominican people." The teacher chooses high interest content. Still, he allows student choice in their reading of the content. He gives students "who have great skills in Spanish the chapter in Spanish. But those who have difficulties in Spanish, I will give it to them in English so they feel comfortable. So when it comes to the discussion in class, they can participate." The class discussion is held in Spanish, although no one is excluded from commenting in English, if necessary.

While aware of students' limited knowledge of their history and culture, these exemplary teachers respect the cultural knowledge that students have, and actively seek to incorporate it into the classes. In this context, the somewhat trite approach to culture, of sharing food, for example, takes on a deeper and more profound meaning. It becomes a way for students to learn about the diversity of speakers of their heritage language and to be the experts sharing their own cultural knowledge.

"They have to bring something from home," says the Riverside teacher. The Midtown teacher feels that she and her students "should learn a little bit about each other." The knowledge they learn about each other is consistently deepened by extending it linguistically, for example, by learning a variety of names of similar foods, and locating foods within the cultural and historical context of different nations.

Teachers' Roles

The broad curricular emphasis on content rather than a narrow focus on language is paralleled by the broad conception that teachers have of their responsibilities to their students. They do not limit themselves to one role as a teacher of a target language. Like parents in a family, they take on many roles in order to shepherd their charges. Certainly, a major role is the planning and delivery of instruction. Yet, even this is multifaceted. As noted above, although they are nominally language teachers, they do not plan instruction around language. They plan instruction of high interest content to heritage language learners, focusing on the history, geography, and culture of the people who speak the heritage languages, or on specific skills needed to advance academically, such as the ability to carry out research and write a research paper.

Other teacher roles emerge, such as guidance counselor, mentor, and advocate. The Midtown teacher points out that her approach to teaching "is more like sharing of knowledge.... I share everything that they can absorb." This teacher talks about sharing "not just things in class, but how to plan, how to look ahead, how to go to college."

These teachers view the teaching of their subject as part of a process of preparing the student to succeed in secondary and post-secondary school, as well as in life, particularly life in the United States. Says the Midtown teacher, "They are not extra. I consider them to be regular things that one should do when teaching." These other areas that impact on their students' success are considered part of the teachers' domain—living in a diverse society, preparing for college, what courses are needed, and so forth.

These things may be discussed explicitly. Students at Midtown note that "Ms. D., when talking about the class, she's not only talking about the French class. She talks about the whole school classes that we're taking." Their teacher is explicit in explaining college to them. "She talks a lot about it; she talks almost every day ... before she starts, she always talks about college."

The teacher does not limit herself to academic concerns. A Midtown student says that she's like a mother. They say, "She's friendly," and that though "she seems to be tough, it's for our own good.... She's giving us the good things. She wants to help us." Another Midtown student points out, "She teaches me to not get in trouble and [not to] get suspended in this school. That's why I like her."

The Midtown teacher herself points out that having a mixed class of heritage and foreign language learners together is a major benefit for her. It enables her to teach "the lesson of tolerance [which] helps them become better citizens in the United States." Again, she chooses not to focus merely on the linguistic benefits, but rather broadens her perspective to include preparing her students, in a full sense, for life in the diverse society of the United States.

The Riverside teacher talks about how he "cannot teach history or foreign languages to these kids if I don't get to know them." He gives an example of a new student in class who was resistant until the teacher and student met by happenstance outside of school in the student's neighborhood. The teacher shared his knowledge of the student's neighborhood, mentioning a relative he would be visiting and the address and, as a result, the student was "a totally different person" in class. The teacher attributed the change in the student's attitude to the fact that he, the teacher, had stepped outside the narrow role of foreign language teacher.

Reflective Teaching

Stepping outside of narrow roles is endemic to the philosophy of the exemplary heritage language teacher. Equally endemic to their approaches is their reflective thinking on their own teaching. The Riverside teacher makes this point, saying, "You find different ways ...somehow, to [reach] your target, and that's how you're going to be successful." As quoted at the beginning of this article, this teacher indicates that he thought about his teaching and his students, about what worked and what did not, and he used his observations and reflections to change the nature of his teaching. When asked about whether his pre-service professional education in college had prepared him for teaching heritage language learners, he replied, "There is not one school, there's not one textbook that you read that tells you that these are the kids you're going to deal with and that this is the type of practice you're going to have in front of you." In reflecting on individual students who totally refused to learn, this teacher feels that with a "different approach, I probably could have reached that kid. That's my approach." He makes clear that he does not blame the student, but rather, learns from the experience to expand his own teaching repertoire.

Conclusion

The researchers found that successful teachers of heritage language students share a philosophical approach. This approach may have, in fact, developed from their reflections on their own classes, as they have observed their students at work and as they have watched their students' reactions to what is being taught and how. The fact that these successful teachers are so unaware of the strategies that they employ suggests that attempts to summarize and train other teachers in specific strategies may not lead to success. What holds more promise for disseminating these successful practices is clarifying the educational beliefs and philosophies that guide successful educators of heritage language learners.

References

Coughlan, M. 1990. "A Belief System Under Siege." In J. M. Newman (ed.), *Finding Our Way: Teachers Exploring Their Own Assumptions*, pp. 123-126. Portsmouth, NH: Heinemann Educational Books.

Millies, P.S.G. 1992. "The Relationship between a Teacher's Life and Teaching. In W.H. Schubert and W.C. Ayers (eds.), *Teacher Lore: Learning from Our Own Experience*, pp.25-43. New York: Longman.

Newman, J.M. (ed.) 1998. *Tensions of Teaching: Beyond Tips to Critical Reflection*. New York: Teachers College Press.

Palmer, P.J. 1998. *The Courage to Teach*. San Francisco: Jossey-Bass.

Popkewitz, T.S., B. R. Tabachnick, and G. Wehlange. 1982. *The Myth of Educational Reform: A Study of School Responses to a Program of Change*. Madison: University of Wisconsin Press.

Teachers' Stories

Student Achievements:
A Story of Challenges, Caring, and Mutual Respect

John Figueroa

As a Spanish teacher in my New York City high school, my Latino students constantly speak the following words to me:

> "Coming to this school was my last opportunity to obtain a high school diploma. At the time, my priorities were to take the major subjects, such as English, Social Studies, Math and Science. I needed Foreign Language credits and I thought about taking Spanish 1 and 2 in order to get good grades and speed up my graduation."

As the years go by, this has not changed, and it saddens me to hear them say this. Most of the students who attend this high school have previously gone to two or three schools already. They come to this school to graduate as soon as possible. Obviously the Latino students want to avoid taking heritage language classes, because they consider them "too boring and too difficult" based on what they have experienced in other schools. Therefore, they would rather take elementary Spanish classes to meet the requirements.

I decided that I would assign the native students to the appropriate level in the foreign classes. I needed to develop a method of teaching that students would find interesting and that they would be willing to take as part of their curriculum; this was my initial goal. I thought that once the students were signed up for my class, I would handle the rest. I felt that many language arts classes are based on grammar and vocabulary, and this is the reason why many students find these classes boring.

The majority of the Latino students at this high school are from the Caribbean islands. With this in mind, I created a curriculum that involved the usual grammar, vocabulary, and literature, but with the main focus being on the history and culture of the Caribbean islands. The class was related directly to the students, especially who they were and from where they came. I called this class, "Caribbean History for Native Spanish Speakers." Five years later, I still have the same success that I had the first time that I taught the class. I believe that the name of the class is appealing enough to the students, because it does not sound or appear to be a typical Heritage Language class, but rather an encounter with their history, literature, and ancestors. They come to the class knowing little or nothing about their culture, but now they have a great interest and curiosity to learn more. When students are motivated, this is the time when learning takes place.

Two years ago in late May, a student named José came to speak with me. He was very anxious to graduate and join the Navy:

José: Hey John, two weeks is the Puerto Rican parade and I am going. Are you?
John: No, I can't. I have to study and do some work.
José: You know, I am so proud of being Puerto Rican.
John: Is the only reason you are proud to be Puerto Rican is because of the parade?
José: Well, yes, and because I have to represent my country. You know the islands, the colors, and my people.
John: That is okay, José, but you can also feel proud being a Puerto Rican, without participating in the parade. There are other ways of representing your native country and people.
José: Well, John, I don't know much about Puerto Rico and I feel embarrassed about this since my parents were born there.
John: But José, you can learn all about Puerto Rico in your history classes.
José: Not true, only the fact that we are part of the United States and that we are citizens of this country. Personally, I find it confusing that we are.
John: I understand what you are saying. An alternative would be for you to

read a book about Puerto Rico. I can recommend a couple of books that would be very informative. Better yet why don't you take the class I teach for native speakers?

I paused for a few seconds, and proceeded to talk to José.

John: I know you have been trying to take Spanish 1 and 2, and I have not let you take them, because I feel you have a lot more potential than just to take a class to pass.

At that point José got very defensive and quite upset.

José: Look, just because my Pops speaks to me in Spanish does not mean I know or speak Spanish.

I stepped back and let him say his piece.

John: *Mira*, José, I know you have one more year, and I want you to graduate next June as much as you do. Therefore, I am going to make you a deal. You will take my Caribbean History class for native speakers, and you will improve your Spanish skills (reading, writing, and speaking), since I know you already understand it perfectly. Besides, you will learn a lot about Puerto Rico and the other islands. In this class we can discuss more in-depth why you are so proud to be a Puerto Rican. *¿Qué te parece?*

José: Only because I need the credit, I guess I'll do it. Also, my girlfriend told me you were a good teacher, and she learned a lot. Now she is teaching her son the material you taught her. She felt bad because you made her feel guilty.

John: Did I? And who are you talking about anyway?

José: Oh man! I am sorry I did not tell you. Her name is Teresa.

John: Who is Teresa?

José: Teresa Martinez. We've been going out for the past six months.

John: Okay José, going back to what you said before, how did I make Teresa feel guilty?

José: Well, when she told you she was Puerto Rican, she felt bad she did not speak any Spanish. Then she realized she had to do something about it. That is why she made the decision to teach Spanish to her son while he

171

	is still young so as not to make the mistake her parents made with her.
John:	*Mira*, José, I only asked her why she never learned Spanish, or why her parents did not teach her. But I am glad she took it that seriously. *Bien*, José, we will talk more. Say hello to Teresa for me, and tell her I am proud of her achievement. Am I going to see you in September?
José:	*Ta to, Te veo!*

School opened the following September, and for two weeks there was no sign of José. For a minute I thought he had dedicated himself full time to his number one passion: boxing. One week later, during my prep-period, I saw him wandering the halls.

I approached him and asked, "*José, Qué te pasó* brother? I thought we had a deal."

He looked surprised to see me and answered, "Look, John, a lot of things are going on, and right now I am trying to get a job."

I turned around and told him that I understood his dilemma, but at the moment, he was not setting his priorities correctly. I told him that I expected him in class the next day and that we would discuss his situation a bit more. The following week, José did not attend my class every day. As soon as I started teaching about Puerto Rico, its history, and culture, reading poetry, and short stories by Puerto Rican authors, José started to come to class every day. He became more involved in the class activities than he ever did before.

Unfortunately, it was toward the end of the cycle and, even though he passed the final, he did not pass the class. He had done very poorly in the two previous tests and assignments. It did not bother José that he had failed the class. A couple of days before the end of the cycle, José approached me one day before the class started and told me: "I did not know anything about Puerto Rico until I took your class. Did you discuss other things, like politics and economic aspects of the island?"

I replied, "Certainly. Unfortunately you were absent during those days."

"That is messed up. Did you discuss the same things about the other islands, like the Dominican Republic, Cuba, Haiti, and the bunch of islands around?"

"Oh *sí*, José, I tried to cover as much material, in particular of *Las Antillas Mayores*."

"What? *Qué es éso?*" he asked with his eyes wide open.

I calmly responded that if he had attended my class, he would know what I was talking about.

"Wait, wait, I want to take this class again, I am serious about it. I mean it."

"José, you can take my class again and I assure you that you will learn many other interesting things about Caribbean history."

The following cycle, I had José in my class again, and this time he was ready and willing to learn. He progressed slowly, but he became one of the best students in the class. After I finished the class, he asked me to lend him more "stuff" to learn about Puerto Rico, because he wanted to learn more. I let him borrow two of my precious books to be returned: *Puerto Rico: A Colonial Experiment* and *Literatura Puertorriqueña*. It has been two years since, and I am still waiting for the books. I guess they are in good hands.

There were other students doing as well as José in the class. However, there was another student that was even more challenging, and his name was Jaime Lora. His passion was soccer. He invited me to see him play, but shortly after, he was forced to quit the team due to school responsibilities and personal problems at home.

Jaime had emigrated with his family from Chile. He completed his elementary education in Chile and came to the United States when he was ten years old. He continued his education in New York and always excelled in all his classes and made the honor roll every year. His parents, in particular his mother, pressured him to be "*el primero y el mejor.*" That is what he once told me. She was definitely right; he was the most intelligent student I ever had in my native speakers' class. He was sixteen and so eloquent and knowledgeable that it really surprised me. One class period of forty minutes was never enough for him. Discussions and questions would continue at lunchtime, after school, and even via e-mail.

Jaime's conversations with me ranged from politics to literature to simple sports. Often, he would send me e-mail messages or, by chance, we would be on the internet at the same time. This gave him the opportunity to discuss the history of his country and his point of view. He would go on to ask me questions about the homework I had assigned for that day. Without any encouragement from me, he once told me he had no friends. Even though he lived with his parents and siblings, he always felt alone.

When a student comes to me with their thoughts and feelings, I often feel overwhelmed because they trust me enough to open up to me. I have boundaries and rules that I have previously set, and my students know and understand why they are there. Once we have that clear, we go from there and work together as a team both inside of the classroom and outside when I am coaching them in volleyball and softball. When I find myself in their neighborhood, I say hello to them.

I have been chastised by many of my colleagues for taking such an interest in what my students think. They feel the students will not respect me or respond in the classroom if I permit them to get close to me, but in actuality, I get an entirely different response. The students amaze me when I see how well they assimilate the topic that I am teaching and how much they want to learn from me.

This past semester, I provided my heritage language class with a list of books. From this list, they were allowed to choose what they wanted to read. The following week, I took them on a little field trip to the Midtown Manhattan Research Library on Forty-Second Street and Fifth Avenue. I explained the concept of doing research and answered as many questions as possible without giving away everything. In order to complete the assignment, the students would have to gain access to journals, books, and magazines to help them answer the questions that I had given them.

Many of the students did not want to read the book. "I have never read a whole book in my life," a student said.

"There is always a first time bro... ," I replied.

That particular day was Thursday. The following weekend, I went to visit a friend uptown. As I was looking for parking, I saw Manny, one of my students, coming down the street with one of his friends. As soon as he saw me, he started to walk in the opposite direction from where I was parked. As I got out of the car, I decided not to walk toward him, but to pass him. I spoke to him softly. "Hey, what's up? Going to play ball?"

"Hey what's up?" Manny responded, "My friends and I are going to play with other guys, but what are you doing around here?"

"Nothing much, just visiting a relative and a couple of friends."

"For real! That's cool!"

"I will see you on Monday?"

"Okay!"

The following Monday, Manny told me the book he was going to read was *In the Time of the Butterflies*. His aunt was coming from the Dominican Republic and bringing it to him. I suggested to Manny that the book was easy to find in certain bookstores, and he did not have to go out of his way to get it.

"No, no, John you don't understand," Manny said, "This is my the first book that I am going to read, and I want it to be special, you know. Brought from D.R. and all that."

"Well, dear Manny, as long as you start reading it as soon as you get it!"

"Fine, with me," he said.

The first time we went to the library, the whole class was uptight. They looked as if they did not want to go. This was an indication to me that they really had not ventured into a library of this magnitude. In order to make them feel comfortable, I made sure they knew I was there to help them and guide them through the steps needed to reach their goal.

On the way to the library, I had conversations with some of the students to take their minds off the new venture. I set up this trip to the library because many of the students are between the ages of sixteen and twenty and have never had a field trip quite like this. I wanted to give them the knowledge needed to do research for whatever they would need in the future.

As soon as we got to the library, I gave them a quick tour. I explained to them, step-by-step, how to start a research project. First I showed them the catalog and indicated that the computer was a more effective method of research. We looked for some of the journals, and some were on microfilm or microfiche. After this, I sat back and watched in amazement at how they were enjoying and learning at the same time. Manny dropped the film three times. Ernesto passed the shelf where the journal he was looking for was located. He looked exasperated and turned to me for help and said, "John I can't find the journal." I was certain that the journal was there and that, regardless, I was not going to help him to look for it, so I told him: "Ernesto, the name is *Hispanic Review* and the year 1996."

Moments later he came running back. "John, here it is, 1996."

"Oh, no Ernesto, this one is *Latin American Hispanic Review*, and you are looking for *Hispanic Review*. They are two different journals."

"You probably made a mistake, John!"

"No Ernesto, if you look closely, you will find the journal. It should be before the one you brought me. Try again, and I am sure you will find it."

After five minutes, Ernesto came back with the correct journal. What Ernesto did may look insignificant to others. However, to someone who has never done anything like this, it is a major accomplishment. I would bet that he will never forget how to look for a journal again. Three hours went by, and the students looked exhausted and angry, because after all the time spent, they had only found a couple of sources.

I grouped them at a table and told them, "This was a good day. All of you learned a lot about things you did not know. Don't think for a minute that you will find all the information you need at one time and in one place. That is what research is all about. What you did not find today in a particular place, you might find somewhere else." I gathered them all and headed back to the school, explaining that the following day, we were going to continue our work in the research library.

After that afternoon, the students were not too happy; many of them did not want to continue with the class. Once again I reminded them that I was there to help them. But they should not expect me to do their jobs.

The experience in the research library was indeed unforgettable. During that cycle, eight of my students out of twenty-five handed in the final assignment. Four students dropped the class after the first trip to the library. I still felt that it was a success. I felt that every student had learned something new. Some went on with the whole project, and with the kind of students we have, this was a big victory for me. I hope to get the students that dropped out on the next cycle. I know I will persuade them to come back when the time comes. For now, I have to make sure this group finishes their research.

As a teacher, my job is to educate and to help, and for these students in my classrooms, I feel that learning has become a challenge. The fact that they all are at risk, makes me work harder for them, and makes their achievement all the more important.

----·•·----

Speak My Language: Open the Window to My Heart, to My Conscience, to My Intelligence

Jocelyne Daniel

This September makes it two years since Créole was classified as one of the official languages of Haiti. The question of French versus Créole is still hotly debated. The people of Haiti, just as the Haitians who live in New York, are divided over this issue.

For outside observers, there does not appear to be any language problem at all. They simply assume that all Haitians in Haiti speak Créole, or that they all speak French. Well not so fast. The truth is that they all speak Créole, but not everyone speaks French.

For language experts, this language controversy is not that simple. For the Haitians, whether they are living in Haiti or not, the Haitian Créole language, or as some prefer to call it, "the Haitian issue" (as in Haitian language), is not easy or simple. The decision to make Créole one of the official languages of Haiti is considered by some to be a democratic move, a move that gives voice to most of the Haitians. Others see it as a backward move, which could cause the country to be more isolated. Some question the usefulness of the language, since it is spoken by very few people in the world. A large segment of the Haitian population still resists making Créole an official language of Haiti. Most of them desire to speak or to have their children speak French, which is given more value and prestige in Haitian society, whether they are living in Haiti or in the United States.

So, on the first day of school that September afternoon, as I walked to meet my eighth period Créole class for the first time. I thought about the real possibility of my Haitian students being a true representation of their parents' views and perceptions of the language that they were about to study. I wondered whether the first day's lesson that I had used in my four previous classes would work. The first day of school is usually an administrative day. There are a lot of freshmen in the building who do not know where to go or what to do. So on the first day of school, I often introduce myself to the students and then ask them to do the same. Then the students are asked to fill out their official attendance cards, and we discuss briefly the school regulations and my rules for conduct in class. If time permits, I go over the first homework assignment. "Can I do that today?" I wondered.

My mind was running ten miles a minute. As I reached the fourth floor, I walked a little faster in order not to arrive late. I forgot that everyone, students as well as teachers, have five minutes to move from one room to the next. When I made the right turn to walk toward my room, students were standing in the hallway. I immediately asked them to come inside. Most responded quickly. They walked into the room and found a seat. Others moved as slowly as molasses on flat ground. I took a mental note of that as I encouraged them to find a seat. Then, without a second thought, I began my first day of class routine. As I finished reviewing both the school and class rules, some of the students started to complain about their placement in Créole, a language they spoke already. They were talking loudly so that I could hear them, but they were not talking directly to me. They were simply letting everyone who wanted to hear know that they did not want to be in "any Créole class."

I did not like it, but I did not want to single out students simply because they were voicing their opinions. I quickly reminded myself that this class was going to be a place where every student would have the opportunity to speak up and share ideas. I asked everyone to fill out an attendance card. The students who were complaining did not want to complete the form, because they said they were not going to be in the class for long anyway. I told them that their attendance must be recorded on the card. Otherwise, they would be marked absent. They quickly complied and filled out the card. Now, they knew that I was aware of the kind of problem an official notice of absence from school could cause them.

Their reactions to this little bit of cultural information were immediate. Everyone was talking about how strict their parents were. After a few minutes, they were refocused and back to the task at hand. When I finished, I asked if anyone had any questions. No one did. That was the first time in my career of teaching that no one had any questions about the rules, school-wise or otherwise. That surprised me because as a Haitian myself, I know that "everyone always has an opinion on everything." So I told the class that if anyone had any questions later on, they should not hesitate to ask. I introduced myself and briefly shared with them the purpose of the course. Afterward, I asked everyone to introduce themselves and to share with the class their experience with Créole, not just as a spoken language but as a written language as well.

Many students had some positive things to say, but one student, Will, was very, very upset to be in the Créole class. Will was very angry with his grade advisor for not placing him in the French class as he had requested. He felt that he had been treated unjustly, that nobody was going to force him to come to "this class." When Will finished making his point, I asked the class if there was anyone else who felt the same way. There were a couple of hands raised. I explained to them the process "of program change" and the procedure to follow to get any class changed on their program, and I promised to bring the forms for them the next day.

Meanwhile, the rest of the class appeared to be very stressed by the discussion. How dare a student question the decision of a school advisor and openly disagree with a teacher? That was rare in Haitian culture, and many students who were recent immigrants to New York seemed puzzled by the whole discussion. They did not know how to react. I again took a mental note and continued with the lesson.

I must confess that, at that time, the school had only recently started to offer Créole. So, there wasn't any long history or tradition to go back to for reference. Anyone who takes on the task of teaching Haitian Créole must be prepared for some challenges. But, let's get back to the classroom. I checked the time. There still was enough time left to explain to them their first homework assignment. This was to write a paragraph, a short composition, or a two-page essay on their opinion about the Créole class, what they would like to learn, any project that they would like to work on, any suggestions that they might have. I further explained that the homework could be written in any one of the three languages—Créole, French, or English. I would accept that, because I valued their input and participation in the class.

I thought that I should start with what they feared most, which was to publicly express their opinions and write them down on paper. Also, since it was a very diverse group in terms of language levels and development, I gave them a wide range of possibilities so there could be room for everyone. I explained to the class that they and I would sit together to evaluate and explore the possibilities and to decide the direction for the class. All of a sudden, everyone was talking at the same time. Some were asking: Will we be able to read Haitian literature in Créole? Will we be able to read our poems in class? Can we put on a Haitian show? (Their teachers in junior high school had done it once.) Others said that they did not know how to write Créole and that they would not be able to write their suggestions to the class. So I told them again to write in the language they felt most comfortable.

"Oh! Mrs.," said a student, "do you want me to go to my old school to ask my teachers for the name of some of the books that we can use in this class?"

The questions were coming to me at such a speed that I could not answer any of them. In fact, when I thought about them, I didn't think that the students wanted an answer right away. I thought and felt that they wanted to share and contribute something, anything, because they suddenly had become partners in learning. They were about to take part in the selection of topics and materials to be used in the class. That was exciting.

The bell rang, but before Will and the others disappeared into the crowd, I encouraged them to write their work in any language in which they felt comfortable. I told Will in particular not to worry, that his remarks and comments were very important to the class and to me. As he was leaving, he said, "See you tomorrow, Miss." That meant a lot to me. I said to myself, "Tomorrow is another day. I am hopeful."

When the classroom was empty, I allowed myself to droop onto the chair. "My God!" I said, "that was the longest forty-two minutes ever." What was I going to do with a class of thirty-five students? Some of them had known each other since they were in junior high school. Some had come to the United States when they were so young that they only wanted to speak English. Some were recent immigrants who wrote French as well as Créole, but who wanted to be in the Créole class so that they could continue to read and write in the language and become ready for the native language examination. Then there was the book issue. What book could I use in the class?

As I thought about the difficulties that lay ahead, one issue dominated: The problem of the students who did not want to take the course. I could not force them to stay, but I was not going to give them up without a fight. I knew that I had to devise some strategies to keep all of them, but the plan was not in my head yet. The entire class was important to me, but the few who felt that they did not belong to the Créole class were like "a precious cargo" to me. I had to protect and guide them during this oceanic voyage full of rough waves. I thought that if I could not come up with a particular plan, then I would structure the class in a way that would eventually make them want to join. My work was cut out for me, but I was looking forward to tomorrow.

The next day, when I went to the Foreign Language Department before going to lunch, I found a group of students waiting to see me, and one of them was Will. They all wanted to talk at the same time. Before I could ask a question, one of my colleagues told me that she thought they all wanted to be in the Créole class, but that the class was closed. Technically, a class should not have more than thirty-four students. It had thirty-five already. Now, more students wanted to take Haitian Créole, but the school was only offering one section of the subject. In order for any more students to be added to the class list, I, the teacher, must actually sign the program form giving my permission to the grade advisor to add an extra student to my class list.

I set up shop right away. I spoke to each student individually in an effort to establish criteria for selection. There were about ten more students, including Will. I knew that I wanted Will to take the Haitian Créole class, especially after he had complained about being enrolled in the class in the first place. I spoke to everyone before I spoke to him. As he waited his turn to speak, he seemed worried, but I was not sure that it was simply because he wanted to take a Créole class. My entire lunch period was spent talking to students.

When I finally talked to Will, the first question he asked was, "Mrs. did you ask my grade advisor to take me out of your Créole class?"

I told him no, of course, because I wanted him to be in my class. But then I asked him why he was fighting now to get back into the class that he had not wanted to be in only yesterday. What had made him change his mind? His answer was not surprising, but frank. Will said that his friends who had complained yesterday came this morning "showing off" their homework written in Créole. I asked him if he had done his homework. He said he had, but that it was written in English. I said that was not a problem. I asked him again if there were any other reasons why he did not want to change his class schedule. He said, with a little bit of embarrassment, that he did not want to change his math class, that he loves math, that the other students in the class like the subject too, and most of all, that he really liked his teacher and did not want to change.

I thought about what he said for a few minutes. Will sat across the desk waiting for my answer. During these few minutes, I was envious of the teacher who had captivated my student's mind. I was thinking about what I could do to "zap" their imaginations too. How lucky, I thought. The bell rang and brought me to reality. Will asked me, "So what do you think, Mrs.? Are you going to let me stay in your class, Mrs.? Please!"

I looked him straight in the eye and said, "Under one condition."

He said, "Anything."

I said, "You must promise to come to class and participate in the various activities that will be planned. Thank you very much! I'll see you later."

There were forty students in the class that year, and Will was one of them. The students and I had a very laborious year. Since it was in the early years of teaching Créole in my school, there was no budget for books. The students and I had to improvise. I bought books with my own funds. The students were more imaginative. Some went back to their old schools to gather information and to get resources from their previous teachers who had been teaching in bilingual settings. Others asked their parents for information such as titles of plays, songs, and poems. A few even wrote to Haiti to ask friends to send them copies of classic plays translated by Haitian playwrights. Before the year ended, we had plenty of material, and we got involved in many school activities. That year we had the first celebration of Haitian Flag Day at school. Everyone in the school community was invited, and many came. We had a poetry writing competition, and Will was among the contenders. He did not win any prizes, but he won for just being in the Créole class for a whole year.

In fact we all won. My students and I, we all won, because that year, since we did not have a strict curriculum to follow, we studied and discussed anything that we thought was interesting, from politics to comedy, from the best Haitian dishes to regional food. The newly arrived students, who were not so new anymore, had many opportunities to talk to those students who had been living in New York for many years and who apparently felt that they had nothing in common with them. In June, they were all laughing at the same silly jokes, and none seemed to remember how strange they had felt sitting in the same class.

As for Will, he was in my classes during the next three years. Upon completing the Créole class, he studied French until he took and passed the New York State Regents Examination.

I said that my students learned a lot that year, but I think that I benefited even more then they. The fact that they came from diverse backgrounds, including length of time in New York, education, and geographic/regional parentage, required me to approach tasks in many different ways. This variation both prepared me as well as challenged me. I taught Créole in the school for many years after that, and each year brought in a group of students who had the same initial reaction as Will. That is to be expected. Children learn their values from the adults. As long as there are people who think that learning to read and write Créole is not useful, students will continue to reject it. The hope remains with those Haitians who, after learning to read and write Créole, make the connection to self-discovery and increase of self-esteem. I have witnessed the effects of a boosted self- esteem. Those affected take charge of their lives and become whole again. Meanwhile, I will continue to teach, to share, and to learn from my students whom I hope will eventually help to turn the tide of heritage language instruction.

El Día de los Muertos

Dora Villani

Throughout the years that I have taught various classes of heritage language learners we have had a lack of materials, mainly textbooks. This inspired me to develop activities that would make the students' language experience rewarding. I wanted some of these activities to be ones in which the students would be able to share their ideas and their traditions. During one of the activities in which my classes participated this fall, I received the following poem from Salid García:

La muerte

Es difícil de entender
No se puede creer
¿Qué es la muerte?
Da tanto dolor
Pero es parte de la vida
¿Qué es la muerte?

Death

It is difficult to understand.
It is unbelievable.
What is death?
It gives us so much pain,
but it's part of life.
What is death?

Salid García is a student in my Level 3 Heritage Language class. She is of Dominican descent and was brought up in New York; thus she is very assimilated. When I asked her why she wrote this poem, Salid said, "The poem I wrote came straight from the pain that I felt when I lost my dear great grandmother. She was someone whom I treasured and loved deeply and it hurt me when I lost her. This gave me the ideas and the feelings I needed to write this poem."

Although death is an inevitable occurrence during a person's lifetime, its acceptance is often difficult. We live in a time when so many are afflicted by diseases, such as cancer and AIDS, by violence, and by natural disasters. As adults we have learned to accept death, although we are saddened by the loss of a close family member or friend. However, how does a younger person accept death mentally and emotionally?

I have had several students who have lost family members due to AIDS and violence. I have been inspired by the Mexican beliefs concerning death to turn my classroom into a support system by celebrating *El día de los muertos*. I want the students to see that there might be a different way of looking at death. Salid offered the following comment concerning our celebration:

> "I learned a lot during the celebration of *El día de los muertos*. I never understood why it was celebrated but now I do. This is the day to remember your loved ones and to cherish their memory. Throughout the celebration a person learns to feel less afraid about death, a nice idea, since as a result you can be prepared to face death, but you can still enjoy the most of life."

Evelina Martinez, in the same class and also Dominican, discusses the inevitability of death in her poem:

> *La noche oscura*
> *como el bosque.*
> *El cielo azul*
> *como el mar.*
> *La muerte siempre nos rodea*
> *y no nos podemos escapar.*

The night is dark
like a forest.
The sky is blue
like the sea.
Death always surrounds us
and we cannot escape it.

Mexican beliefs concerning death are a combination of the Pre-Columbian indigenous beliefs and the Catholic beliefs brought by the Spaniards. Indigenous people of Mexico honored and remembered their deceased ancestors during the entire month of October. They believed that when people died, they went to another world in the underground, a resting place; thus it was a continuance and an end. The Spanish missionaries brought in the celebration of All Saints Day on November 1st and All Soul's Day on November 2nd. Thus evolved *El día de los muertos,* which combines the indigenous beliefs and time of remembrance and the Catholic celebrations.

Linda Diaz, also a student in the Level 3 class and from El Salvador, shares the idea of an afterlife in her poem:

Después de la muerte comenzará una nueva vida.
Donde uno entra en la luz
escogiendo uno de dos lados.
Uno donde todo es felicidad,
donde se quedan las flores,
y donde los suenos se hacen realidad,
o en el lado en que no hay día,
donde es un mundo de locura,
oscuro y misterioso.
La puerta que te escoge Dios,
Será adonde desaparecerás,
donde tu nueva vida comenzará,
hasta el día que regresarás.

After death a new life begins.
Where one enters the light,
and chooses one of two sides.
On one side there is happiness,
we find flowers,
and dreams become reality.
The other is the side without daylight,

and it's a world of insanity,
dark and mysterious.
The door that God chooses for you,
will be the one into which you'll disappear,
where your new life will begin,
until the day you return.

Linda Diaz explained how she felt in writing this poem in the comment, "Writing a poem about death was a new experience for me because I write poems about life. I did feel good to be able to express my feelings concerning death."

Melany Rodriguez, a student in the Level 2 Heritage Language class, wrote the following letters as a result of our class activities:

Querido Abuelito,

    No sé cómo empezar. Bueno, primero te quiero decir que me haces falta que todo es muy diferente sin ti. Cada vez que la familia se reúne yo siento un vacío que nadie mas que tú puedes llenar. Yo siempre pienso en los chistes que siempre contabas y lo cariñoso que eras. A mí me hubiera gustado conocerte más haber tenido más tiempo contigo, pero te fuiste. Llegará el día cuando te voy a volver a ver. Siempre estarás en mi corazón, abuelito.

          Con mucho amor,
          Melany Rodriguez

Dear Grandfather,

    I don't know how to begin. First, I would like to tell you that I miss you and that everything seems different without you. Each time that the family gets together, I feel an emptiness that no one but you can fill. I always think about the jokes that you used to tell, and about how kind you were. I would have liked to know you better, and to have had more time with you, but you left. The day will come when I will see you again. You will always be in my heart.

Melany expressed the following thoughts concerning this assignment:

"When I wrote this letter for my grandfather, I felt very sad. He died during the summer of 1996. I felt very sad since it was the first time that someone so close to me had died. The sadness lasted for a long time. Being able to write this letter has helped me to feel better and although the sadness is there, I know that it will get better."

Venus Johnson, a student in the same class, wrote the letter:

Querido Tío Chino,

    Te estoy escribiendo esta carta porque quiero que sepas todo lo que estoy pensando. Quiero que sepas cuanto te amo y cuanto me haces falta. Ya que no vives, no puedo hablarte de mis problemas. Yo no puedo jugar con tu pelo negro. Lo único que me falta en la vida es ver tu sonrisa y sentir tu amor. Siempre voy a tenerte en mi corazón. Espero el día cuando pueda abrazarte y decirte que te amo y te recuerdo mucho.

Con cariño,
Tu sobrina,
Venus Johnson

Dear Uncle Chino,

I am writing this letter because I want you to know what I'm thinking. I want you to know how much I love you and how much I miss you. Since you are not here, I cannot tell you my problems. I cannot stroke your dark hair. I miss seeing your smile and feeling your love. I will always have you in my heart. I await the day when I will be able to embrace you, and tell you that I love you and remember you.

Affectionately,
Your niece,
Venus Johnson

As part of the unit on *El día de los muertos*, I ask the students to write letters to deceased family members. The students are very expressive in these letters and relate what they would have liked to say to the person when he/she was alive but did not have the opportunity to do so. Some students wrote to a pet or a celebrity. Stephanie Pratt, in the same class as Venus and Melany, resisted writing to anyone. She felt that it was silly and refused to do the assignment. Perhaps there was another reason for the resistance, but since it was an emotional experience, I did not want to intrude on her privacy. After having written these letters, students said that it was a difficult assignment, because their work was interrupted by tears. Reading these letters is always an emotional experience for me, and one with which I can identify.

In Mexico, *El día de los muertos* is a celebration since the people joyously prepare to honor their deceased ancestors. There are many aspects of this celebration that are not sad. For the Mexican people, death is not an end. They embrace death and know that it is something that will occur. According to the Mexican writer, Octavio Paz, Mexicans embrace death and they delight in it. Therefore, once it is accepted in this way, there is no reason to be afraid or to be saddened. The souls of their ancestors are somewhere else, and the spirits will return to be with family members during the celebration. Salid García said, "I love the thought of their souls coming back home and enjoying the *ofrendas* that are placed for them. It is a very nice thought but also a spooky one." This celebration is an important Mexican tradition, one that they want to hold on to and to pass from generation to generation.

El día de los muertos is celebrated in various parts of the United States, although most prominently in areas with a large Mexican population. *El día de los muertos* indeed comes to life in the United States perhaps to give us a feeling about death.

This has certainly become a yearly celebration in my classroom. I feel that it is a way to help the students to accept death, and at the same time, it is an exposure to the culture of a country where Spanish is spoken. The students have delighted in this celebration every year. Venus Johnson said:

> "As *El día de los muertos* came near, my teacher, Ms. Villani, prepared many activities for us. I liked all the readings because they helped me to learn more about this wonderful holiday that many people celebrate. As the days went by, I understood more and more about why it is celebrated and how. I loved it when we all had to bring in food for the *ofrenda*. It was also fun to make the rising skeleton project."

The unit on *El dia de los muertos* usually takes three to five days. We start with an introduction by reading articles concerning the celebration. We continue with a video that shows how it is celebrated in Mexico, so that students actually see what is described in the articles. This year we devoted one day to work on our rising skeleton project. This is like a toy in the shape of a casket that has a little skull peeking out from a hole when a string is pulled. The students really enjoyed taking part in this project and were able to display their artistic talents in decorating the casket. The culmination of the celebration is to actually set up an *ofrenda* table to which the students contribute cakes, cookies, and juice, later to be shared by everyone in the class. Written activities follow each of the class activities such as the ones that have been presented in this story. The students' work is published in our yearly literary magazine, *Orgullo Hispano*.

Ysaura Torres expressed what learned about the *ofrenda* in the following poem:

> *El día de los muertos*
> *Es un día especial,*
> *porque se recuerdan*
> *los que estan en el más allá.*
> *Las personas que mueren,*

algún diá resucitarán
para buscar el olor y la comida
que en la ofrenda les guardarán.

The day of the dead
is a special day,
because you remember
the ones who are not here with us.
The people who die,
will one day rise again
to follow the aroma and search for the food
that will be there for them at the *ofrenda*.

My heritage language learners usually partake in some celebration in their homes, but usually it is to celebrate All Soul's Day. They like to share what they do and, as a result, the students also learn what happens in other Hispanic countries. Ysaura Torres said:

> "I felt a little strange because I'm not used to celebrating it in this way. In the Dominican Republic we just light a candle in the name of the person who died or we go to church and listen to the ceremony. When our teacher told us that we were going to celebrate *El día de los muertos*, I thought that we were going to light a candle and say something about a person who had died. I was surprised to see how it is celebrated in Mexico. When she asked us to write a poem, the words came to my mind easily while I was writing."

I feel that the unit on *El día de los muertos* presents a very rewarding cultural experience for the students as well as giving them the opportunity to express themselves in writing. Each year it has new dimensions and positive effects. It is both a learning experience and a personal experience since everyone is touched by death. The students' reactions have always been positive. Idalis Diaz said:

> *"En realidad a mí me encantó mucho que celebramos El día de los muertos. Me divertí mucho al participar en las diferentes actividades. Me parece muy importante que haya un día cuando se recuerdan los seres queridos que ya no están con nosotros. En mi opinión, esta celebración debería ser una celebración mundial. Aunque en mí familia no se celebra, a mi me gusta la idea."*

> "I was truly delighted that we celebrated the Day of the Dead. I enjoyed myself very much participating in the different activities. It seems important that there be a day when one remembers the loved ones who are no longer with us. In my opinion, this celebration should take place all over the world. Although it is not celebrated in my family, I like the idea."

Linda Diaz said:

> "During the celebration of the Day of the Dead, I felt weird because I never experienced leaving food for someone who had passed away. My favorite part was watching the video and seeing how people celebrate it. The food at the *ofrenda* was really good. My favorite was *el pan de muerto* that my teacher made. It was good and sweet and something that I had never tasted before."

Melany Rodriguez said that she learned a lot from the celebration and that it was something that she had never experienced before. My students' comments and written contributions always assure me that this activity is indeed an enriching and positive experience.

Spotlight on Haitian Students in New York City

Jean Mirvil

In the back of my eighth grade class was Jean Jasmin, a student from Haiti. He had been living in America for almost three months when he was first placed in my foreign language class.

I remember the day when Jean and I first met. Jean was not displaying the reactions that I usually got from the other students in my class. My routine way to attract my students to this class was to begin with my list of cognates of French and English sentences. To give you an example using the topic — food; this is what we talked about:

> *voulez-vous le fruit?*
> *le melon*
> *l'orange*
> *le raisin*
> *la prune*
> *donnez-moi la prune*

My English speakers were motivated by their participation in the lesson. They were generally amazed to realize how many French words they knew. I was always stunned by the reactions that I used to get from students like Jean. Usually, he would focus on what was happening, copying as much as he could off the board and answering some questions. The dilemma for Jean was always shown in

189

his blank-faced statements, which read that I was probably wrong, or that he did not know what was being taught. Being with Jean was a daily challenge. I developed a guessing habit each time he looked at me. What did he surmise? What's wrong? Did he understand?

Jean was always so courteous and so well-mannered that he would not have the temerity to act beyond a facial grin. I knew my work was not challenging Jean, though the remaining students in my class were jumping out of their seats to catch my attention to let me know that they understood the lesson.

I was intrigued by the possibility of bringing Jean into the full lesson that I used to carefully plan. In retrospect, the adjustments that I made in my teaching methods were those of basic sociological understanding. It behooved me to accept Jean as a student with minimal knowledge of French.

Jean was not a French student. His level of proficiency in both French and English was minimal. In those days, we did not speak Haitian in any French class. I simply assumed that Jean was fluent only in Haitian.

In order to meet the needs of students like Jean, I planned my lessons by following the first year foreign language curriculum and text. I began to integrate additional materials with a zest of higher proficiency in the lesson. As a result, my basic conversation always included many levels of responses.

As my questioning techniques became more sophisticated for the students, I began to challenge Jean to get him involved. Most of the time, he was able to comprehend and respond appropriately. Sometimes the students came to Jean's defense by saying that Jean's questions were "too complex."

While I was making adjustments in my lessons in order to address Jean's needs, I carefully planned for all the students to work in groups so that they could become more familiar with each other. Hence providing a greater opportunity for group reports during various class activities.

I recalled some of the materials that I used in my class. *Les Petites Contes Sympathiques*, published by Houghton Mifflin, were a great help. The context was light, but the follow-up group activities were quite appropriate for my challenged learners. I was determined that no one was going to waste a moment in my language class. Moreover, heritage language learners were too precious to permit them to waste time in my class. By creating an appropriate environment for Jean, together with the support of Jean's new friends in my class, my room soon became a safe haven for many students like Jean.

I brought in elements of the Haitian culture in proverbs, stories, myths, jokes, rituals, and real conversation. It was there, too, that I started to introduce Jean to this culture. I would remind him how people actually behave, what is accepted, and what people complain about. I built his self-esteem by helping him to recognize styles of dress, speech, and very concrete behavior. We discussed American culture through reading selections dealing with attitudes, fears, spiritual beliefs, and values.

The support Jean received from his friends did not manifest itself the same way for all students. Many times, my new students were targets of verbal abuse by their peers. Sometimes, Jean was harassed for demonstrating how much or how little he knew about French. Being silent was Jean's way of coping with the situation. Teaching in those conditions became unbearable. On the one hand, my time to challenge Jean was limited. On the other hand, my foreign language learners were not getting their instruction in a stress free environment. Many times, these learners showed practically no motivation to handle the work and to remain in that setting.

By the end of the second marking period, I brought my concerns to my assistant principal. After hearing me plead my case, he responded by creating a separate class for my heritage language learners, and I became their teacher. A colleague was given additional foreign language hours so that she could take over my foreign language class for English-speaking students.

To date, when I reflect on my past experiences as a language teacher, I often do not mention how I remained flexible throughout those years in order to provide for all students in the heritage language setting. I am most grateful for having worked with an extremely supportive supervisor of my department and some great friends that I made along the journey. Without these people, I would not have been able to transform the difficulty that I had in the beginning into a positive experience, worthy of sharing with people in the field. We must carry this legacy further for the sake of educating all students in our school and our nation.

Those days were exciting. The search for ways to address Jean's needs has helped me to become a resourceful person and teacher. Before I met Jean, I had not yet begun my degree in bilingual education. Today, I am pleased to see the outcome of that endeavor. Concurrently, there has been a positive transformation of issues related to the Haitian language as we enter the new millennium:

- It has finally been recognized that Haiti is in essence a monolingual country where only a small proportion of the population (10 percent) can be considered as balanced bilingual speakers of French. The majority speaks only Haitian.

- Some prefer to call the language of the country Haitian rather than Haitian Créole.
- The publication of materials in Haiti multiplied by the end of the 20th century. Years ago, a language was official if it had a Bible, a grammar, and scientific terminology. All of these things now exist in Haitian. The Haitian constitution and President's speeches are also available in Haitian.
- The New York City Board of Education supported the publication of materials in Haitian that are now being used by Haitians who must catch up with the evolution of the Haitian language worldwide.

The Haitian conditions have improved both in Haiti and in the United States. Though improvements are still needed to support students and parents, we are certainly not where we started fifteen years ago.

An Academic Journey with Pablo Neruda on Board

Maria Hahn-Thomson

It is June, a drab, warm and what feels to me like a semi-empty day in a classroom where the chalk dust settles. I am returning their projects to the few students of third-year Native Language Arts Spanish who showed up today. I am bemused that the most resistant, nonstudious types are claiming the fruits of their labor. Flashes of thought dash through my mind with one word echoing, "Why?" The bell rings; I return to reality. The period ends, and "Have a nice summer" lingers in the air. Just like the chalk dust, I, too, settle numbly into my seat, taken by the flashbacks to the beginning of that year's academic journey with the Latino students—Pablo Neruda on board.

For years, I wearily continued the tedious process of rote learning, having students read books on their own during class. As for me, well, it was the usual show time with chalk and talk. On an ordinary day in May of that year, in my semi-comatose, burned-out teacher stupor, I saw my students leaning at a forty-five degree angle at their seats. I was glazed over— barely peering from the edge of my desk. I couldn't take it any more. I blurted, "How many of you find this textbook boring?" Hands went up faster than I could exhale. If I was bored, these hormonal beings must have been undergoing academic *rigor mortis*. So, the remainder of the class period was a purgative to rid ourselves of the dead film of words and nothingness.

"Ms. Hahn," stated an incredulous Natalia, "I don't know what happened. You seemed to enjoy the book. You were so into it!" Poor dear. Her rolling eyes truly left an imprint in my mind. I prayed assiduously. "Grant me the serenity ... help me find the way ... I want to do my best ... I really care ... guide me."

That afternoon, as I was cleaning my desk and filing cabinet in anticipation of the coming summer vacation, I came across Pablo Neruda's "Ode to the Tomato." I smiled, relieved yet hesitant. After all, I did pray. The moment was appropriate; my prayers were answered. A friend told me once, "Magic is changing consciousness, and consciousness is the magic."

My change of consciousness from omnipotent-teacher-in-charge to co-conspirator in the classroom was about to begin.

Day One

"What is your favorite fruit?" was scrawled on the board. The students took three minutes to discuss fruits. Students in the first period class often have slits for eyes, barely recognizing what goes on, still asleep. Within a three-minute time span, they blossomed like lotus flowers, opening their energies to their favorite fruits and their stories that went with the luscious edibles. Each student went to the board listing mango, papaya, *patilla* (watermelon), *pera, guineo* (banana), *cereza* (cherry), *zapote* (one has to experience its fleshiness), *sandia* (watermelon), *frambuesa* (raspberry), *maraculla* (a delectable with a life of its own in another country).

The *tabula rasa* came to life, with the teacher, in the back of the classroom listening, observing and enjoying the moment. She was a co-conspirator at work with the students, allowing them to inspire her to teach each other. They were in charge. They harvested from their memories their favorite fruits and recollections of their childhood: fun, refreshing, and sad.

Homework: Tomorrow bring in a list of adjectives describing your favorite fruit and your favorite eating delight, a drawing or photograph if the actual fruit is not available at the market.

Day Two

Fruits colored the students' desks, and the air was abundant with freshness, sweetness, and the proximity of summer. The kids were still asleep. My suggestion:

Smell the fruit. What concept or idea do you have of its fragrance? The answers varied: sweet, fresh, recently mowed grass, the beach, the warmth of my country. Blink! Blink! Sleepy eyes were rounded. "Hungry." "*Sí, claro.*" "Bite into the fruit. What do you taste? What do you feel?" The words flashed in Spanish across the classroom: crunchiness, soft, sweet, tart, sour, burst of flavor. Again they wrote on the board in colored chalk, on newsprint with colored markers.

Homework: Go home and write a list of twenty fruits and the adjectives, the words that describe them. They needed reminders of what an adjective is. I didn't expect them to remember. Those who did would remind them and teach them. I would stand aside and smile.

Day Three

While I collected their homework, I asked the students to tell their partners about their favorite fruit and the memories they had or the experiences that came to mind. The listener would relay to the class his partner's experience. Mini-videos of the imagination played for thirty-five minutes in the classroom: childhood with grandpa, the country left behind, family, hiding in a tree while biting into the fruit.

Homework: Write an essay of no less than ten sentences and no more than fifteen. Include your experience with fruit, its smell, taste, texture, shape and size.

Each of the homework assignments was placed in folders that each student had. The fruit was the center of attention. Their favorite fruits motivated and inspired them. Students taught each other and learned. The teacher sat, walked, listened, and was happy.

Day Four

On the board:"Do Now." Work in groups of three or four and read their essays to each other. "Guess what the fruit is." On the board, the instructor had written two columns: *Aspectos físicos* and *Aspectos abstractos*, leading to the concepts of simile and metaphor. Homework: write three columns: (1) fruit, (2) prosaic description, (3) abstract or poetic description.

Day Five

Students read their homework to each other. A handful of students were lost. They looked to me, but I advised them, "Look to your fellow students for help, then consult with me." Reluctantly, they did. "Quiet time" is what told them. They put away their books, cleared their desks and listened. The teacher read, *Oda al tomate.* The audience was a group of kindergarten children ready for milk and graham crackers. They were big and cool, but they loved to be read to.

A second reading was in order with such questions as, *"¿Donde estan los tomates?" "¿Que hora es?"* They had to think and answer. Homework: Read *Oda al tomate.* Answer questions on Pablo Neruda, the analysis and characteristics of the poem. The *desatarse* and *oda.*

Day Six

"Do Now." Discuss among yourselves: metaphor, simile, the prosaic, poetic, or abstract description of the fruit. Review *personificación.*

Homework: Study for a quiz based on the homework and the "Do Now" in class.

The instructor dictated the quiz questions that the students wrote on their papers. *Por cada respuesta a las siguientes preguntas, de un ejemplo:* (1) *¿Qué es un adjetivo?* (2) *¿Qué es un verso?* (3) *¿Qué es una oda?* (4) *¿Qué es una descripción abstracta?* (5) *¿Qué es una descripción prosaica?* (6) *¿Qué es personificación?* (7) *¿Qué es simil?* (8) *¿Qué es una metáfora?* (9) *¿Quién era Pablo Neruda?* (10) *La flor blanca el color del alma pura: es un ejemplo de?*

Day Seven

After the quiz, students were somewhat dazed. My objective was not for them to memorize but to determine how well they knew what they were learning. Not very many knew how to study, only how to memorize for a test. They were not used to discussing with each other or consulting with their teacher. It was time to instruct them. Instruction serves to clarify and direct, and it helps the student to focus.

Homework: Write a list of ingredients for making a salad using Neruda's description. Make up a menu that includes the entrée from Neruda's ode.

Day Eight

Homework assignments were collected and students were asked to identify their favorite item, person, or experience, and to celebrate it in an ode. As students wrote or tried to, their teacher supplied them with dictionaries, ideas, suggestions, and her presence. They worked on their odes for four days, all homework, notes, and corrected quizzes were in their folders for reference. Their odes varied: to Sammy Sosa, summer, love, a favorite pet, mother, grandma, grandpa, a person, thing or concept. Some were funny; others were bittersweet. Quite a few rhymed beautifully; others needed to be revised. One or two were salty. I steered them toward something that was more appropriate. I helped them to stay focused.

"Is this right, Miss?" "What do you want?" "What do you think?"

They were not used to making their own choices. They needed to begin now. Their project was due on June 7. The objective of the project was for them to identify, analyze, and interpret an ode. Their work had to be neatly and legibly written, and it was supposed to reflect the care, the effort and the comprehension that the student had gained during the study of an "Ode." In their portfolios, they were required to include: A list of the fruits discussed in class, the essay about their favorite fruit, their gastronomic topics, and their ode to an object, a person, an experience, a concept or a place. The odes were to be made up of between fifteen and twenty verses, and they were to have prosaic poetic or abstract aspects as well as simile, metaphor, and personification. I informed them that this project would comprise 50 percent of the work.

I was nervous. What in heaven's name had I gotten myself into, and how was I to correct their portfolios? Here I was an ingenue, a gutsy one taking on five classes of portfolios. I slept at night. Breakfasts were rich. Lunches were gulp feasts, and dinners were meant for two. I gained weight. I lacked faith in my students. However, I lacked faith in myself as a teacher. Soooo, on with mantras …

Those students who put in the work and cared took back their portfolios. I kept the portfolios of the students who did not show up to claim theirs. In hindsight, they succeeded and I learned. A few of them learned to think critically while opining and communicating with other students. Those who hardly knew, or never attempted, needed to make their voices heard. They need to be empowered more. They were not allowed to express their thoughts at home. I reassured them that the classroom was a safe and nurturing space, their very own.

From then on, I knew that I would confer with my students. I would take my time, be patient with myself and with each youngster. If I want them to exercise boldness, then I too need to be bold as a human being, a woman, and a teacher.

Johann Wolfgang von Goethe said it best: "Until one is committed, there is hesitancy; the change to draw back always is ineffectiveness. There is one elementary truth when it comes to acts of initiative [and creation].... Whatever you can do or dream you can do, begin it."

Boldness has genius, power, and magic in it. Begin it now.

Students Share the Voices of their Cultures

Adriana L. Macera-Aloia

As an upper level Spanish teacher for juniors in the fourth year of their language study, I have specific student goals to accomplish. With New York State's Spanish Regents Examination behind them and the Spanish Advanced Placement Language course available to them the following year, the students in the Spanish IV class offered in their junior year have the opportunity to be enriched in many ways. I want the students to review and to advance in grammar through a variety of Spanish literature in short story form. From this genre, vocabulary knowledge broadens to encompass the range of themes found in the variety of famous short stories written by authors from the Spanish speaking world. An offering of two or three stories grouped according to theme lends itself to creative self-expression in writing as well as in oral communication. In addition, the use of film can be a delightful way to bring the cultural nuances, descriptions, and regional references of a piece of literature into a visual context. We also take a background look at the wealth of Spanish literature by reading the works of several authors. The writers' countries of origin and how they are witnesses to the events of their time often enhance a student's historical perspective. As a teacher, I become enthusiastic at this level, because I truly begin to see the students mature in their taste and appreciation for the Spanish language. I approach each story in a personal manner first, which is why I prefer the thematic approach to literature.

A typical Spanish IV class may have about twenty-five students of whom three to six are heritage language learners. I may assign several oral presentation tasks in group or as individual research projects throughout the school year, so as to enhance speaking skills. Writing assignments take on new meaning through journal entries, letters, dialogue skits, interviews, and award show role playing using themes from our stories. The writing assignments tend to be interesting and exciting for all of the students, but the assignment that remains the most memorable for me was the one that came from a Guatemalan student who had arrived in our school only seven months before the course started.

Deisy was a shy and humble seventeen-year-old tenth grader. Because her knowledge of English was extremely limited, Deisy was most comfortable in the Spanish IV class. As she tended to complete Spanish tests early, she would spend the remaining time jotting down simple poetic verses in her own words and in her lovely calligraphy. She wrote several *versitos en rima* in her journal as well. Some were original, and some were popular rhymes that children learn by heart in Guatemala.

I found them so enchanting that I asked Deisy if she would mind writing them over in her beautiful penmanship onto special paper that I would supply. I told her that I loved her short verses, because they treated everyday occurrences with a poetic sense of humor. Her *versitos* were absolutely *graciosos*! Besides, her handwriting was neat, so I told her that I would display them in the classroom. I recommended that her classmates listen to them and predicted that they would appreciate their cute messages. Within a week Deisy had her *versitos* written, drawn, and laminated.

Everyday that week, the motivation activity for the lesson was a *versito* read out loud by Deisy. The students pointed out the rhyme words, their meanings, and a translation in English. Each verse was easy to understand since they were short and fanciful, and the students looked forward to the next day's verse. After four days, the weekend assignment was to create a four-line *versito* on any topic. Some of the students thought this was going to be difficult because the verse had to rhyme, but the ones I received from them that Monday were very good. Love and nature were the most popular themes. Here are some *versitos* by the heritage language learners in the class:

Versitos en Rima

By Deisy from Guatemala

Al cortar una rosita
el dedito me espiné.
Con un besito de mi madre
el dedito me alivié.

Upon cutting a rose
I pricked my finger.
With my mother's gentle kiss
My finger felt all better.

****

¡Que bonitos ojos tienes
Son redondos como el sol.

Se parecen a los ceros
Que me pone el profesor!

What beautiful eyes you have!
They're as round as the sun.
They look like the zeros . . .
My teacher always gives me!

****

Llorando te pedí una pluma,
Llorando te escribí,
Llorando te pido que
No te olvides de mí.

Crying, I asked you for a pen,
Crying, I wrote to you,
Still crying, I ask that you
Never forget me.

****

De tu boca quiero un beso
De tu camisa un botón
De tu dedo ese anillo
Y de tu pecho el corazón.

From your mouth I'd like a kiss,
From your shirt a button,
From your finger that ring,
And from your chest … your heart!

———•·•———

By Stalyn from Ecuador

Yo tengo 20 amigos
Contigo 21.
A todos los quiero por igual
Pero a ti como ninguno.

No es amigo el que te mira
Ni novio el que te besa.
Es amigo el que te quiere
Y novio el que te aprecia.

I have 20 friends all together.
Including you makes 21.
I like them all equally
But I love you like no one else.

It's not a friend who's looking at you
Neither is it a boyfriend who's kissing you.
The friend is the one who loves you
And the boyfriend is the one who appreciates you.

———·—··—·——

By Mayra from Peru

Si tuviera una pluma de oro
Y la misma de cristal
Con la sangre de mis venas
Escribiría tu inicial.

If I only had a pen of gold
And another made of crystal
With the blood from my veins
I would write your initial.

*****

En el mar de la vida
Yo soy el capitán
Mi novia la sirena
Y mi suegra el huracán!

On the vast seas of life
I am the captain,
My girl is the mermaid,
And my mother-in-law … the hurricane!

———·—··—·——

By Olga from Colombia

Si no tienes a tu lado
Al que ahora tú amas
Ama al que ahora
Está a tu lado.

If you don't have beside you
The one you presently love
Love the one that is presently
By your side.

With this assignment Deisy was proud that her verses were validated. Her originality and artistic talents were highlighted as a teaching tool in Spanish from which others could learn. Her shyness and insecurity seemed to dissipate afterward and I noticed that she became more comfortable with her peers in this class. On several occasions later in the school year, Deisy became a valuable source when cultural references needed to be clarified, such as when we read a legend from Central America, or when we discussed dating practices in her country as related to a scene in a film that takes place in her native Guatemala. We learned so much from Deisy. The non-native students in our class had the opportunity to hear the Latino voices through the sharing of their cultural and linguistic knowledge. This activity helped us all to develop a more positive learning environment for the rest of the year.

Formidable Challenges, Strange Ironies, and Unanswered Questions

Emma Abreu-Perez

Meeting Sujeiry was a challenge.

In a multilevel class with many nationalities, trying to teach a language that is not appreciated, acknowledged or practiced results in a seemingly insurmountable obstacle for any teacher.

Everyday was a war zone, with the teacher trying to calm the students' tempers as they entered the classroom after their lunch period, already resistant to learning this language. They created every imaginable excuse in order to prevent the teacher from starting the lesson. All of the students seemed to be in "limbo." They were Hispanic, but resented being considered as such. Therefore, they resented being taught a language that made them feel alienated.

Still, their environment was permeated with the Spanish language and culture. The food, the television programs, and the community were Hispanic, but they resented it. Why? Finding an answer to that question was the goal that I tried to set for myself. Why were Sujeiry, Christine, José, Ingrid, Patrick, and the others so hard to handle, so hostile and resentful? What had happened to those students' heritage and language?

> "I hate Spanish? Why do I have to take this class? We are not going to use it, because in this country what we need is English. Anyway, how many credits do we need?"

> "I don't know," I said, "but I do know you need to be prepared in order to go to the university. And there you need credits for foreign language."

This explanation was not adequate. It didn't serve the purpose of fulfilling the excuse Sujeiry was looking for. During this quarreling and arguing, the other students took sides with her, saying, "Yeah, yeah, we don't need Spanish. Besides, we don't know Spanish."

"Don't worry, I'm here to help you learn the language," I said.

Every day at the beginning of the semester, ten or fifteen minutes were wasted in this manner. It seemed as if I was administering a medicine too painful to swallow. At the same time, I was giving myself the same medicine, trying to make the students understand the importance of the class.

What else was there to do? As always, I decided it was time to know my students better—their backgrounds and their academic skills. I realized that I had four different countries represented in my class and that, among them, I had some students who had been born in the United States. There were others, like Sujeiry, who had been brought to the country when they were little. Christine and Patrick, on the other had, had been born in the United States. Perhaps that was why Christine was "wild."

Sujeiry was both happy and resentful at the same time at being here. It was not her choice. She was living with her stepmother in an apartment crowded with half-brothers and half-sisters, that, according to her, she could not stand. The whole environment was not conducive to learning or supportive of good behavior.

This alienation gave me a clue to the reason for her hostility. Spanish was the language that Sujeiry's stepmother and half-brothers and half-sisters spoke. Therefore, for her, the language was synonymous with that environment. The rest of the group were in similar situations. Spanish had been a bad experience for them. The world that was depicted by the language was not a successful one. Why bother to learn it, then? For them, the language was the language of the losers, of the downtrodden.

How could I start to change the students' perception regarding the language? I didn't know. How as I going to prepare them for the New York State Spanish Regents Examination when they had never written a complete sentence in the language? I didn't have a clue. The class was supposed to take the Regents that semester, and here I was with a group that didn't want to learn to read or write in Spanish. Not an easy task, but I had to develop something.

Trying to find a commonality among the students became a real challenge for me. I knew that they all had been born in the United States, but aside from that, what else? I thought that being born or raised in the United States was the common bond, uniting them to a sole purpose. What a defeat it was to find out that there was no such unity. In addition to being from different social levels, different countries, and different nationalities, one student had an Englishman's spleen, another one had an American aloofness, and still another a Latin character! Therefore, there were wide differences among the students, and some even considered themselves more Americanized than the others.

Sujeiry made me aware of this one day when Christine arrived late. "Oh, too bad that she came, I can't stand her." This comment apparently was ignored by Christine, who was usually very quiet and almost always smiling.

"I can't stand her! She doesn't talk and is always smiling like an idiot. Besides she thinks that she is the best, because she was born here," Sujeiry continued. At this point, I had to intervene so Sujeiry would be quiet. As for Christine, she seemed completely unaware that Sujeiry's comments were addressed to her.

Through that assertion, I realized the big dichotomy between some of these students. Sujeiry was very critical of both the "hicks" from her country and the "Americans" born in the United States. I became aware that the ones who were not considered "full American" were the most belligerent in their reactions to the others. The irony of all this was that they themselves were the ones to make the distinction between the two groups and then get angry about it.

Copying, cutting, pasting, and deleting material in the preparation of my lessons became a daily routine for me. I tried to introduce them to the countries of their parents. It was not an easy task, because I had four countries represented in my class. At first, they did not seem to care or to be interested. But, with perseverance and care, I motivated them. I tried to be sure that the readings had more or less the same number of words, that the same topics or aspects were the same for each country, and that there were only positive aspects depicted in the readings. Otherwise, they would comment: "That country is underdeveloped"; "That country is backward"; or "What's good about that country?" "Oh, I don't want to live there"; or "Uhh, who wants to live in a country like that?"

Words like "below the poverty line," "illiteracy," "low infrastructure," "under-developed," and "third world country" had to be deleted in order to avoid hurtful comments or arguments and to prevent chaos in the classroom.

Teaching these students was taking a toll on me. I found myself having dreams about them. It bothered me to realize how much I was being affected by their idiosyncrasies. What bothered me most was to find out that, besides being their teacher, I was also their therapist. Every day, before the beginning of the class, I had to check their moods. By finding out "how they were doing," I got a clue as to what we could do or whether I needed to introduce something else instead of what I had planned or prepared.

With the passing of each month, I had the impression that I was still in the beginning of the semester. With each step taken or phase passed, there was a new discovery I made about them.

The last discovery I made about Sujeiry was the last time that I heard from her. It was when a colleague told me that she seemed to be distressed and was looking for me like crazy. "She has been here three times looking for you."

"I wonder what is happening to her. She passed the Spanish Regents, and she is graduating. So what else does she want from me?"

The last time I saw Sujeiry was that very same day when she finally found me. She entered my next period class, hugged me, crying. When she was finally able to talk, she told me about Christine's sudden and unexpected departure. Though Sujeiry's story was ending happily, her former "enemy," Christine, wouldn't be so lucky, at least not for now.

Chapter 6

Monitoring Your Students' Progress

Editors' Notes

Assessment has been a long-standing challenge for foreign language educators, one that became more pressing as the profession moved from an essentially grammar-based to a proficiency-based approach to teaching. Multiple choice, true-false, completion, question-answer, and even essays, among the once commonly accepted forms of assessment, had to be rethought, because they were designed, by and large, to determine students' mastery of target grammatical structures or their content-specific comprehension of listening and reading texts. In short, those forms of assessment were geared to find out what students knew rather than what they were actually able to do in the language being learned. Alternate forms of assessment, such as portfolios, contextualized individual performance tasks, peer- and self-assessments, and rubrics for evaluating student performance, all relative newcomers to the scene, were now deemed more appropriate representations of what students knew and what they could do, given this new proficiency-based orientation to language teaching and learning. Teachers found that their old reliable methods for testing students had to be redesigned in the face of the shifting paradigm.

Change has been slow in coming because of the still deeply ingrained feeling about the relationship between grammar and language learning. In spite of what has been written and said about proficiency, when the chips are down, knowledge of and ability to manipulate grammatical structures tend to be seen by many foreign language teachers as the most concrete and reliable evidence of language learning. This, in turn, is translated into continued use of the traditional forms of testing in many schools. Of course, part of this tendency stems from the profession's view of language learning as linear as opposed to recursive, as was pointed out in the Introduction to Part Two of this volume. Part of it also has to do simply with the comfort of habit and tradition. It is probably safe to say that the profession is currently in transition when it comes to assessment, as teachers strive to truly understand what the goals of instruction really are or should be and how to design and administer the alternate forms of assessment that will more accurately reflect their students' progress.

Against this backdrop, the complexity of assessing heritage language learners' proficiency in their own language becomes understandable. Heritage language learning, as we have seen, is in no way linear and, therefore, defies many of the standard approaches to teaching. In like manner, the most reliable way for teachers of heritage language learners to understand what their students know and can do in their language is through the very forms of assessment with which the profession as a whole is still somewhat uncomfortable. This is further complicated by the sense of urgency that seems to be prevalent in so many schools as they attempt to test their heritage language students for purposes of placement in language programs and for measuring and reporting student growth.

When the Project Development Team began to examine tests that were being used in schools for both placement and reporting, they were not surprised to discover that, in the wake of the urgency for some form of data, teachers were resorting to tests of grammatical structure to evaluate the proficiency of their students. In light of what you have read in this volume, it should be fairly evident that other modes of assessment are needed. This is the very challenge that the ACTFL-Hunter Team attempted to address.

In this chapter, Carmen Mercado, discusses the complexity of assessing heritage language learners as revealed in the research literature. She also describes the tripartite model for assessment that grew out of the ACTFL-Hunter College FIPSE Project. The tripartite model parallels the "Statement of Shared Goals and Fundamental Beliefs" and the "Framework for Learning about Your Students" that were presented earlier. Mercado points out that it offers a refreshingly comprehensive means by which teachers can learn about their students and, at the same time, provide them with valuable feedback that will enable and empower them to continue learning. It is evident that this model is still in its infancy and requires further refinement if it is to become workable within the constraints of time, staffing, and reporting procedures that are the norm in most schools.

That said, we present it here for teachers, administrators, and researchers to examine, discuss and revise. We hope, however, that in that process, the intent of the tripartite model to accurately reflect the richness of the learners' linguistic and cultural background, to encourage and empower learning, and to reassure or foster the learners' sense of self-respect will not be lost.

Monitoring the Progress of Heritage Language Learners: Assessment Trends and Emerging Practices

Carmen I. Mercado ✳

What must be monitored in order to understand the progress language learners are making in developing proficiency in their heritage languages? What research-based tools and practices exist that may be used for this purpose? What promising practices are emerging from local initiatives that inform our understanding of the assessment of proficiency in the heritage language? In this chapter, I begin by reviewing the existing knowledge base on assessment, in order to identify issues and trends that have implications for monitoring the progress of heritage language learners at the secondary level. There is a small but fertile body of literature on the assessment of language learners in bilingual contexts that inform assessment for students in heritage language programs.

I will then turn to describing practices that are emerging from the efforts of the ACTFL/Hunter College Project Development Team, who, motivated by a concern for equity and excellence, have developed a practice-based model that provides a framework for monitoring the progress of heritage language learners. Increasingly, scholars emphasize that teachers who are knowledgeable about particular groups of language learners should participate in the design of assessments (Mercado and Romero 1993; LaCelle-Peterson and Rivera 1994; Conference Proceedings 1996). It is, therefore, not surprising that the veteran classroom practitioners who are participants in the ACTFL/Hunter College partnership have much to say to the profession about teaching heritage languages, in general, and monitoring the progress of heritage language learners, in particular. There are tremendous gaps in what we know about heritage language learning at the high school level (Tse 1998), and, through their efforts, these practitioners are helping to fill in these gaps.

Two terms require clarification at the outset: "heritage language learners" and "assessment." As was pointed out by Barbara Miller in her introduction to this Part of the volume, heritage language learners are, first and foremost, language learners, so that much of what is said and known about language learners (i.e., English language learners, second language learners, bilingual learners) holds true for heritage language learners as well. Although "heritage language learners" include students who function primarily in their heritage language and who are studying English as a second language, most heritage language learners in foreign language classrooms are fluent speakers of English who have elected to retrieve and draw strength from the language of the home, despite the challenges that this may pose. Heritage languages are not spoken by the dominant culture, but are spoken in the family or associated with the heritage culture. Consequently, they often are not maintained and are rarely developed (Krashen 1998). Thus, heritage language learners are a very diverse group of students—experientially, academically, ethnically, and linguistically. They represent diverse speech communities, and, therefore, different varieties of the heritage language and different levels of proficiency in both the heritage language and English.

Because language and literacy are socially learned, the language and literacy knowledge that heritage learners construct is variable, reflecting the influence of the home and community culture and varying degrees of contact with the larger society (Altwerger and Ivener 1994, p. 68). However, what these learners share or have in common is that they have made a conscious effort to preserve their language heritage, and, hence, the bilinguality acquired by birth. Consequently, they bring distinct issues to the teaching-learning process that are unlike those of other language learners. These distinct issues, which go beyond language, must be taken into account in any assessments of their progress in heritage language programs.

Assessment, according to Chittenden (1991), is a process that is inclusive of, but more comprehensive than, testing. While testing tends to be a one-dimensional form of measurement, assessment is frequently described as multitrait-multimethod. As such, assessment focuses upon a number of variables judged to be more important and utilizes a number of techniques to assess them that are derived from multiple sources and multiple perspectives. Although these approaches are more common in elementary school settings, there is a growing trend toward their inclusion at the high school level, as this chapter will describe.

The Context of Assessment

Assessment is a general process that supports learning through ongoing monitoring of student progress and provides schools and teachers with a means for program improvement and accountability. It is also variable and context-specific, responding to the purposes and goals of particular instructional programs designed for specific learner populations (August and Hakuta 1997). Consequently, to understand what it means to monitor student progress in heritage language programs, it is also important to understand the goals that these programs seek to attain.

Programs for heritage language learners have been designed to provide those learners with the benefits derived from studying their language and, at the same time, preserve the nation's rich language heritage. Instruction in those programs is similar to, but distinct from, instruction in bilingual or dual language programs and, as has been pointed out previously, distinct from many aspects of traditional foreign language instruction as well. A focus on languages other than English is common to all, but the programs differ in their goals and purposes. As we already have seen in earlier chapters of this volume, the goals of instruction in a heritage language program are far more complex, reflecting the complexity of the learners themselves. In Emma Abreu-Perez's story of the preceding chapter, "Formidable Challenges, Strange Ironies, Unanswered Questions," we could see what it means to strive to preserve a heritage language within a public school system where heritage languages have been perceived as impediments to learning in school and an obstacle to social integration. In addition, the number of states that have adopted English-only amendments has increased over the past several years, and as a result of Proposition 224 in California, vital health and educational services are now denied to children of immigrants who do not speak English. How do these sociohistorical and sociopolitical realities shape the development and use of heritage languages in students' homes and communities, and how do they influence how heritage languages are taught, assessed, and learned in the classroom? Further, since language has deep affective roots and is a vital part of self-making, what emotional overtones are elicited by instructional approaches designed to preserve and safeguard resources in the face of those realities? A number of researchers are concerned about the impact of social and educational inequalities on human development, particularly for students from non-mainstream communities (Nieto 1992; C. and M. M. Suarez-Orozco 1995; Stanton-Salazar 1997; Tse 1998).

Depending on their length of time in the United States, many of these students may have endured long-term disparagement and denial of access to their mother tongue as a valued resource that is vital to learning and self-making (C. and M. M. Suarez-Orozco 1995). This denial, in turn, may have affected the self-esteem (Altwerger and Ivener 1994) of these students—their beliefs about who they are, where they come from, how they speak, and what they know. As Cummins (1994) expresses it, "When school personnel reject students' identities (by punishing them for using their native language, for example, as happens in many places), they force students to make an unnecessary and potentially traumatic choice between their two cultures, and the resulting conflict may actually interfere with language learning...." In short, as was evident in a number of the teachers' stories in the last chapter, students vary in the level of self-confidence they bring to the language learning situation (Cummins 1994, pp.46-47).

Other scholars, including the members of the ACTFL/Hunter Team, emphasize that the ridicule and correction that heritage language learners receive from more competent heritage language speakers (including teachers who have not been prepared to understand nonstandard varieties of the heritage language) also impacts on the self-esteem of these learners and interferes with their willingness to use the language to communicate (Zentella 1997; Krashen 1998; Tse 1998). Writing about the specific situation of Puerto Ricans, Zentella cautions that,

> The impact of such attitudes can be devastating; linguistic insecurity—intensified when the young are told they speak Spanish *matao* ("killed) or that their Spanglish is ruining both languages—often leads to the loss of the native language, with potentially severe repercussions for the successful development of their English. Ultimately, a stigmatized identity affects the students' entire career. [Zentella 1997, p. 269]

Participants in the ACTFL-Hunter College Project describe compellingly how they confront and address these socioemotional issues (they refer to them as "behavioral") head on in their day-to-day interactions in the classroom (Meeting with heritage language teachers, Hunter College, December 10, 1999):

"I find myself being a teacher, being a therapist. In order for students to learn you have to erase from their heads the damage that has been done to them."

"Students don't believe that they are good at learning Spanish."

What these teachers suggest is that even when the decision to study the heritage language has been made by the student (which is not always the case), there are attendant "behavioral" issues that must be addressed as part of the teaching and learning of language. A sampling of some of the behavioral issues identified by heritage language teachers are listed on Table 1.

Behavioral manifestations of emotions and attitudes that have a social basis frequently are interpreted by the uninformed as resistance to or lack of interest in learning or, even worse, sufficient cause for suspension. While acknowledging that these behaviors may be rooted in long-term social and educational inequalities, veteran classroom practitioners in the ACTFL-Hunter College Project concur that students need to learn that their emotions cannot get the better of them in institutional settings where other norms prevail and where so much is at stake. Teachers must play a critical role in supporting student learning by guiding them to regulate negative behaviors that may limit access to knowledge that students may value (for example, learning their heritage language). In the long run, such behaviors may undermine students' chances for successful participation in school. By protecting the students' "right to full participation in and ownership of [learning]" (Altwerger and Ivener 1994), these teachers are, in effect, building students' self-esteem.

It should be clear by now that issues of language, identity and motivation are inseparable within the context of heritage language instruction. Therefore, an important goal of such instruction always has been that of directly addressing affective-emotional issues through the integration of these issues in the study of the heritage language. Available research reinforces the importance of this

---

Table 1. Behavioral Issues Heritage Language Teachers Identify

Students:
- Deny or reject their native language and culture.
- Lack confidence in their abilities.
- Are sensitive to being corrected.
- May be unprepared for class.
- Occasionally are uncooperative.
- Sometimes are argumentative.
- Frequently are absent or late.

emphasis as part of supporting the development of heritage language proficiency (see, for example, Krashen 1998; Tse 1998). Teacher-participants in the ACTFL-Hunter College partnership describe how their practices focus on these concerns directly, as illustrated in Table 2. Socioemotional issues are also addressed indirectly, by assuring that students receive the support they need to experience success in learning the heritage language.

It is evident that assessing proficiency in heritage languages goes beyond "language." Through the knowledge and wisdom that come from practice (practice-generated theory) and from their lived experiences, teachers are identifying and addressing critical issues in heritage language learning and, as a result, are finding ways to enable heritage language learners to succeed.

Trends in Assessment

The assessment of student learning has undergone profound changes within the past decade (National Forum on Assessment October 1995). Efforts to experiment with alternative assessment approaches for language learners have been motivated by the challenge to minimize the risks associated with being a language learner in our society, which also includes the challenge of meeting rigorous learning standards measured through high stakes tests in English.

For a number of different reasons, standardized testing practices have been problematic for language learners, and language has been central to the difficulties. Although these test may assess students' grammatical competence, that is, students' knowledge of the structure of language, there is currently no standardized test capable of assessing students' sociolinguistic competence (Garcia 1994). Sociolinguistic competence refers to the extent to which students are able to use

---

Table 2. Addressing Socioemotional Issues in the Curriculum

- Teacher shares personal experience of rejection.
- Teacher discusses the economic power of knowing another language.
- Students do research on employment possibilities and salaries for bilinguals.
- Students and teachers discuss dialect varieties and their roles in society.
- Former students return and share with students the impact of knowing Spanish.
- Students read articles on the buying market for their communities.
- Teachers and students discuss the language requirement for college entry.
- Teachers create awareness of graduation requirements that promote language study.
- Students and teachers discuss the role of heritage languages in different jobs.

language appropriately for different purposes, in different contexts, and with different speakers. Cummins (1994) argues that to participate effectively in school, students need to learn to use language appropriately for social purposes, to interact with peers and teachers, and for academic purposes, especially for reading and writing literate prose. This aspect of language proficiency is different from the way students may use language for social and learning purposes in out-of-school contexts. Thus, focusing exclusively on grammatical knowledge runs the danger of overestimating the ability of students to use language for learning purposes in the classroom (Navarrete, et al. 1991). It also runs the danger of underestimating the strategies and resources heritage language learners use to communicate, most notably by making deviations from norms of standard usage more prominent than they really are, a phenomenon which Zentella (1997) refers to as the phenomenon of categorical perception.

Standardized tests are also incapable of gauging important influences on literacy development, specifically student attitudes affecting the will to learn, in general, and students' willingness to take risks, in particular. It is claimed that attitudes and dispositions, so fundamental to learning, are best revealed through ordinary interactions in the classroom (Altwerger and Iverner 1994).

Even so, test results have been used to justify subjecting students to instruction that is unchallenging, unstimulating, and unlikely to lead to high standards of performance. The devastating impact of these practices is well documented in the literature (see Mercado and Romero 1993; LaCelle-Peterson and Rivera 1994; Falk, MacMurdy, and Darling-Hammond October, 1995). As Mercado and Romero (1993) report:

> Because performance on standardized tests has been tied to promotional policies, many bilingual students have been retained, some as many as two and three times. Those who are not retained are typically subjected to the type of curriculum that mirrors the content of tests. Worse yet, many students are tested and placed inappropriately in special education programs on the basis of such measures. More specifically, as Ortiz and Maldonado-Colon argue, "behaviors directly or indirectly related to linguistic proficiency constitute the most frequent reason for referral of language minority students" [p.145].

Issues of validity, reliability, and equity aside, scores from standardized tests cannot provide teachers with the type of information they need to plan instruction. Authentic assessments, which "are not removed from the act of learning," (Ancess and Darling-Hammond September 1994) are designed to provide a more comprehensive profile of the language learner's strengths and weaknesses than can more formal assessments (García 1994). Valencia (1990) suggests that obtaining valid information on how heritage language learners are learning depends on obtaining products from authentic learning activities, that is, activities that students view as important for their learning. Otherwise, students' responses may not provide accurate evidence of what they know or of the progress they are making in developing proficiency in the heritage language. Zentella (1997) agrees that there are limitations to contrived exercises that are removed from meaningful and purposeful communication activities. She points out the effectiveness and efficiency of the following strategies for eliciting perceived and actual knowledge of the heritage language:

1. Personal narratives that encourage spontaneous and unreflective use of the heritage language.
2. Translation tasks focused on specific features of language known to be problematic to learners (e.g., verb tense).
3. Self-reports or student self-ratings, even though learners tend to underestimate their capabilities.

You will note that these strategies are not removed from the act of learning. However, the importance of these strategies notwithstanding, assessment is more than a series of strategies directed at eliciting information, which will become clear.

The National Forum on Assessment (October 1995), a coalition of education and civil rights organizations, has proposed several guiding principles for assessment that strengthen the connection between assessment and learning. Some of these are as follows:

1. Assessment is, first and foremost, about supporting student learning.
2. Even when assessment provides information for school improvement and accountability, it is about supporting student learning.
3. Assessments must also be fair to all students, and not limit their present and future opportunities.
4. Quality assessments are demanding and require the collaboration of knowledgeable educators.
5. Quality assessments also require the collaboration of students' homes and communities.
6. Assessment systems should be reviewed and improved to ensure that assessments are beneficial to students.

These principles are evident in assessment approaches used for more than a decade in alternative schools such as Central Park East Secondary School and International High School in New York City (Ancess and Darling-Hammond 1994). States and local districts also have moved to promote alternative assessment approaches even as they continue their support of high-stakes testing. For example, in New York City, the New York Assessment Network (NYAN), an umbrella organization that includes the Fund for New York City Public Education, the Office of Educational Research (OER) of the New York City Public Schools, the Center for Educational Options at City College, the Elementary Teachers Network of the Literacy Institute for Literacy Studies at Lehman College, and the Elementary School Assessment Project of the Center for Collaborative Education, introduced the Primary Learning Record (PLR) in New York City public schools.

The Primary Learning Record is a comprehensive framework for assessment that includes classroom observations, analysis of student work, and teacher conferences with students and parents to "take a different look" at students who bring different strengths, strategies, and styles to the learning setting. The goal is to obtain a well-rounded picture of their students, which includes learning about their families, their history, their cultures, and their languages through student and parent interviews. This comprehensive information will better position teachers to support student development, particularly in areas related to literacy, an aspect of language development (Falk, MacMurdy, and Darling-Hammond October 1995).

Although the Primary Learning Record was initially introduced at the elementary school level, the approach to assessment at International High School has some common features with it. International High School is a nationally recognized and highly successful alternative educational program with a small (under 500), but highly diverse student population comprised exclusively of English language learners who bring varying levels of proficiency in English and the primary language to the classroom. Thus, it represents a distinctive example of the possibilities inherent in quality assessment, which has important implications for the assessment of language learners in other program settings.

In describing the assessment process at International High school, Eric Nadelstern, its founding director and first principal, asserts that "the practices at International High School did not begin with assessment. They began with an instructional commitment to student diversity as a generative force for learning. It was this focus that inevitably led to authentic assessment" (Ancess and Darling-Hammond 1994, p. 6). Assessment, it is emphasized, needs to be based on a set of values and beliefs that give purpose and shape to all that is done to promote and support learning. At International High School, this includes promoting diversity as a goal of instruction, valuing collaborative learning, and encouraging the use of students' language resources (that is, speaking, reading, and writing in students' primary language) to learn challenging content in English. In effect, assessment practices at International High School form part of a coherent framework of values and beliefs guiding an instructional approach that has as its mission "fostering the linguistic, cognitive, and cultural skills necessary for success in high school, college, and beyond" (Ancess and Darling-Hammond September 1994, p. 3).

As Nadelstern cautions, this comprehensive approach to student assessment has evolved from traditional tests and quizzes to a continuous process of self-reflection, peer assessment, and teacher assessment organized around collaborative performance tasks and individual portfolio development (Ancess and Darling-Hammond September 1994). However, it must be emphasized that this type of assessment is not new. Perrone (1991) reports that it was common in most nineteenth-century schools and basic to practices in numerous early progressive schools influenced by the work of John Dewey, William Kilpatrick, Marietta Johnson, and Caroline Pratt, among others. These progressive schools sought to overcome the limitations of traditional tests through approaches likely to assess valued learning outcomes which were not suited to paper-and-pencil tests.

At International High School I (there are now three different schools/sites), the shift in thinking about assessment began by rethinking and transforming the way teachers were evaluated at the school. Teachers, it appears, go through a process similar to that of students, in which they maintain their own portfolios as part of an effort to promote accountability to the entire school community. At International High School, teacher evaluation is not a private act between teacher and supervisor, as it is in most schools.

In general, the school-wide assessment process for students at International High School has three major components:

1. Debriefings, which allow students to reflect on what they have learned in a particular class and to explain it orally to someone else.
2. Mid- and end-of-cycle reviews of student portfolios containing data summaries and samples of student work, a personal statement or self-assessment, a statement demonstrating mastery of concepts presented in the course, and self-, peer-, and faculty evaluations. Documents present-

ed as evidence for student progress and achievement are graded by the reviewers.

3. A final brief conference (five to eight minutes) between student and faculty evaluator to explain the grading system used in evaluating the student's work and to determine the final grade for the portfolio.

Although there are many distinctive aspects of this exceptional comprehensive approach to assessment, the most remarkable is the unique role that students play as they engage in "assessment for self-knowledge" about their capacity, potential, and effort, a process that is intended to promote student empowerment (Ancess and Darling Hammond September 1994).

The trends reviewed in this section are consistent with the recommendations of leading scholars working in the field of assessment for language learners. According to LaCelle-Peterson and Rivera (1994), assessment systems for second language learners should be:

(a) Comprehensive and attempt to assess all that students are learning;

(b) Flexible and allow students to show what they know in a variety of appropriate modes.

(c) Progress-oriented and track student progress from year to year.

(d) Student sensitive, bringing into the process the expertise of educators who know the needs and learning characteristics of particular groups of students.

The quality assessment approaches that have been described in this chapter are also demanding and require a great deal of support. Not surprisingly, their use is more the exception than the rule, although a number of schools have begun to work toward their use recognizing the possibilities that these approaches represent the best interest of students.

A Practice-Driven Tripartite Model for Monitoring Student Progress

The veteran teachers on the ACTFL-Hunter Project Development team are exploring ways to monitor the progress of their students, even as they navigate uncharted waters. They have generated an incipient tripartite model of student assessment that focuses on three important dimensions of language learning:

1. The *sociolinguistic dimension,* which focuses on students' use of the heritage language in their homes and communities.

2. The *usage analysis dimension,* which focuses on students' knowledge of the form, content, and function of written language.

3. The *behavioral dimension*, which focuses on students' social and academic behavior, specifically attitudes and dispositions that influence language learning.

In many ways, this incipient model of heritage language learning is analogous to several emerging models from the second language literature, in particular, the one proposed by Wong-Fillmore (1985). Wong-Fillmore's model also features three major interrelated processes in language learning: social processes, linguistic processes, and cognitive processes. Wong-Fillmore indicates that the social processes refer to the fact that target language learning requires contact with proficient speakers of that language to allow learners to observe how the language is used and to participate in exchanges with other target language speakers. Wong-Fillmore explains that target language learners "have to participate at some level since the quality of their participation plays a critical role in getting speakers to use the language in the special ways that make the speech samples from these contacts usable as data" (pp. 34-35).

Linguistic process refers to the important role that comprehensible input (Krashen 1998) has in the acquisition of language. According to Wong-Fillmore, target language speakers modify their speech to be comprehensible to the learner of that language based on what they assume the learners may find problematic or difficult to understand. Similarly, target language learners build interpretations and meanings in the language based on assumptions derived from their primary language about how language works. However, according to Wong-Fillmore, it is the cognitive processes that are central to target language learning. Cognitive processes "involve the analytical procedures and operations that take place in the heads of learners and ultimately result in the acquisition of language" (p. 36). Thus, cognitive processes allow target language learners to figure out the system of rules that are being followed, to synthesize this knowledge into a grammar, and to internalize it.

Wong-Fillmore suggests that this analytical framework, which is intended to explain variability in language learning, provides a useful tool to assess critical influences on language learning that are largely modifiable through the way learning environments are organized. All of these influences, with the exception of attitudinal/behavioral concerns, are captured in the tripartite model of heritage language learning and assessment emerging from the practice-driven theory of the members of the ACTFL-Hunter Team. Because English is the target language driving the Wong-Fillmore model, socioemotional issues do not usually play as dominant a role in the learning of high status majority languages as they do in the learning of lower-status heritage languages.

Although smaller in scale, the tripartite model has three distinctive features in common with the comprehensive approaches to assessment described previously. First, it seeks to go beyond examining students' grammatical competence to include other dimensions such as students' attitudes and learning strategies. Second, it acknowledges the important role that students and their homes and communities play in heritage language learning. Third, it reflects a system of values and beliefs premised on the view that the best way to support heritage language learners is by accepting socioemotional influences that impede successful learning as an integral part of the language learning experience and by attending to those influences in some significant way. These values and beliefs are best summed up by practitioners as a "tough love" approach to heritage language learning.

Four major strategies are used to gain insights on students' emerging competencies in the heritage language learning. These are (1) self-reports, (2) classroom observations, (3) analysis of student written work over time, and (4) contacts with the home.

Self-Reports

How do students use the heritage language outside of school?
What else do we need to know about students' exposure to the heritage language?

It is evident in this chapter that students are an important source of information on their own learning and on the type of support they may need to progress socially, linguistically, and academically. Upon entry into heritage language programs, teachers obtain an immediate reading on students' actual use of the heritage language and the frequency and purpose for which it is used in students' homes and communities. This information is used for purposes of student placement. Then, as students progress through the program, teachers also assess students' developing sociolinguistic competence through self-reports. Heritage language learners at the high school level are capable of tracking and reporting their use of language in out-of-school settings, thereby playing an essential role in their own assessment. As educators at International High School have found, the self-knowledge that comes from this type of engagement will facilitate the learning process, and ultimately empower the learners to become self-regulated and self-directed. Table 3, below, presents a sampling of the kinds of questions that can be asked of students as part of their initiation into their heritage language class or program, in this case Spanish.

Classroom Observations

What attitudes and perceptions do students bring that impact on their study of the heritage language?

What classroom behaviors should teachers attend to in teaching heritage languages?

Veteran teachers emphasize the importance of careful observation in the ongoing assessment of their heritage language learners. This allows them to structure and restructure the social environment to be responsive to students' changing socioemotional and academic needs. Ultimately, the purpose of ongoing assessment is to increase the likelihood that heritage language learners experience academic success. Teachers hold themselves accountable for supporting students' learning, but they also hold students accountable for actions and behaviors that are not in their best interest, nor in the interest of others who are members of the classroom community. Thus, for the members of the ACTFL-Hunter College Team, creating responsive learning environments is a negotiated process and a shared responsibility that is both the purpose and the outcome of assessment.

Intensive observation and careful listening during ordinary interactions in the classroom are the primary means to monitor how students are progressing in the learning of the heritage language. The teachers are especially sensitive to indicators of students' attitudes and dispositions toward learning the heritage language, and how those attitudes and dispositions fluctuate over time. Some of these indicators are listed in Table 4, on page 223.

Because of the significant role that social interactions play in the learning of

---

Table 3. Sample Questions

1. Is Spanish spoken in your home?
2. Do you speak Spanish to your parent(s)?
3. Can you hold a three-minute conversation in Spanish?
4. Could you function in a class that is conducted in Spanish?
5. Do you know how to write a letter in Spanish?
6. Can you read a newspaper in Spanish?
7. Would you like to begin to study a new language instead of Spanish?

language, and as the primary means of gaining access to comprehensible input in the heritage language (Krashen 1998), the first concern of teachers of heritage languages is organizational. As De Avila (1985) has also suggested, veteran teachers emphasize the importance of clearly establishing the rights, responsibilities, and roles of classroom participants as a way to minimize disruptions to social learning processes. It is both fair to and respectful of learners that criteria for appropriate behavior be established and that the students be held accountable for actions or interactions that violate expected norms.

Teachers of heritage language, in turn, play a key role in helping students to develop and adhere to rules for appropriate participation. Specifically, teachers devise or adapt checklists to help students to monitor (1) their knowledge of and respect for the rules of the classroom, and (2) their cooperativeness and respectful treatment of others. Teachers emphasize the importance of not overlooking transgressions. They insist that students must understand that there are consequences for violating agreed upon norms of appropriate conduct in a community of learners. This insistence may, in effect, serve to elevate the status of the classroom community as a place where serious learning takes place and where the respectful treatment of others is expected and safeguarded.

Teachers also look for evidence that students understand the meaning of quality participation and then guide them to develop these understandings, where and as needed. Students are responsible for being present, punctual, and prepared. They are also responsible for participating in classroom interaction in a way that contributes to their own learning and to the learning of others. That is, students are expected to contribute to the ongoing discussions and to make connections to and build upon the ideas of their peers and the teacher. The New

---

Table 4. Sources of Information on Student Attitudes

Attendance.
Actions in class.
Comments made in and out of class.
Body language.
Preparedness for lessons and tests.
Language use in class.
Attitudes toward grades and tests.
Denial and rejection of language and culture.
Off-task behavior in class.

York City Board of Education refers to this as "quality" or "accountable talk," an essential feature of quality instruction.

Finally, teachers of heritage languages look for and guide students to develop strategies for approaching the learning of the heritage language. Scholars of language learning agree that this is an especially important emphasis for the cognitively mature adolescent learner (Wong-Fillmore 1985; Cummins 1994). The challenge for heritage language learners is to make the familiar strange. Unlike typical second or foreign language learners who know relatively little about the language they are learning, heritage language learners come with some degree of previous exposure to their language from their homes and communities. It is precisely this familiarity that is often problematic. Teachers emphasize that students need to understand that learning the heritage language requires study even when the content appears familiar and intuitively known. They need to pay close attention to structural and functional details of the variety of the heritage language that is used in formal learning settings, such as schools, and be able to recognize its distinctive features in contrast to those of the spoken and written varieties that they use and understand. Students need to be aware, in the same way as adults, that there is a distinction between conversational proficiency and the type of language proficiency required for learning in academic settings. Further, students need to realize that a great deal of effort may be required when they first begin their formal study of the language, particularly for such challenging and less familiar activities as reading and writing for academic purposes, but that sustained practice over time will render these tasks less difficult.

Teachers of heritage languages also mediate the goal of learning the language by sequencing tasks so they are progressively more challenging and by drawing upon sociocultural knowledge from students' homes and communities to make challenging tasks and assignments manageable and attainable. Sociocultural adaptations include combining familiar elements from students' homes and communities with content that is less familiar or interesting to learners. For example, heritage language teachers report setting traditional forms of poetry to music, using choral recitation, and integrating poetry, geography, history, culture, and music into their lessons as ways to reduce anxiety and to increase interest in learning the formal or literate varieties of the heritage languages in school contexts.

In general, heritage language teachers help their learners by strategically mediating the challenges that these students face in the classroom. Their primary concern at virtually all times is building students' self-confidence by enabling them to experience success. Thus, assessment practices used by teachers of heritage languages are inseparable from teaching and reflect the view that the fundamental purpose of assessment is to support learners and learning. Although the scholarly literature acknowledges the importance of the social setting in the acquisition of language, little specific attention has been given to the concerns identified by teachers of heritage languages from large urban schools with high student-teacher ratios. This may be because much of the literature on language acquisition comes from settings with younger learners where these aspects may not be as salient as they are for adolescent learners.

Analysis of Oral and Written Language

How can we determine what students know about their heritage language? What do errors tell us about what students know and need to know about the heritage language?

As discussed previously, appropriate assessment is a big problem for all language learners. Specifically, it is the analyses of language usage, or the way students understand and use language to communicate/speak and to write in school contexts, that all too often results in inappropriate judgments about what students know or are capable of accomplishing in areas that extend well beyond language. We know that competence in academic language proficiency is usually conflated with intellectual abilities and capabilities (Cummins 1994). For this reason, the members of the ACTFL-Hunter College Team suggest a rather comprehensive and multifaceted approach to usage analysis that takes these concerns into account.

These teachers obtain both spontaneous and elicited, written and oral language samples to learn about the strengths and vulnerabilities that heritage language learners bring from their exposure to the heritage language in their homes and communities. In so doing, the teachers tap a wide range of language used in different contexts and for different purposes as the basis for their assessment. Zentella (1997) agrees with this procedure. She argues that analyses based solely on data elicited in constrained interactions can stereotype speakers as less competent than they are because of the phenomenon of categorical perception. Without samples of language use taken from a range of contexts, any deviations "from a norm may be seen as far more prominent than its negligible frequency would warrant" (Labov in Zentella 1997, p.184). Using examples of students' language taken from a wide range of samples enables the teacher to show their students that they are competent in some aspect of language use. This is particularly important for learners who exhibit some degree of linguistic insecurity, as many heritage language learners do. However, the process of obtaining valid and reliable indicators of communicative and grammatical competence and then engaging in the analyses of this information is complex and requires support from the school and its leadership.

The tasks and activities employed to gather these samples include observations of students' use of language during classroom interactions, discussions, and formal presentations. Opportunities to examine written language use come from the writing of personal narratives on topics that students or their teacher select (e.g., autobiographical writing) and from writing that responds to specific questions on highly familiar topics (e.g., writing about their day, their family, a favorite meal). The goal is to construct tasks and activities that invite heritage language learners to demonstrate their emerging competence in the language, rather than intimidate them. These tasks also elicit constructions, such as certain verb forms that are known to be problematic for heritage language learners. Zentella indicates that heritage language learners are adept at avoiding or talking around (circumlocution) challenging forms of language in situations that are more spontaneous and open, which explains why tasks need to be devised to elicit those constructions.

The members of the ACTFL-Hunter College Team have also devised and are experimenting with a framework for the analyses of language usage, which includes attention to form, content, and use of language. For these teachers, form includes (1) structure or knowledge of phonology, morphology, and syntax; (2) word use/choice/variety; (3) cohesion, paragraph development, topic sentence, and (4) punctuation. Tentative criteria for evaluating students' oral production have also been devised. These criteria have some distinct elements, appropriate to the oral modality, and give attention to fluency, information, use of target structures, choice of vocabulary, persuasiveness, and length of oral presentation. As evident, both criteria address an important concern—the need to establish standards of performance in the heritage language, which is essential to any assessment of heritage language development.

Because the knowledge students have about their heritage language is variable and may differ considerably from norms of standard usage, these teachers are examining how students' oral and written productions conceal (or reveal) what students know and what they have yet to learn. For example, *sabo* a nonstandard form of the verb *saber* (to know) in the first person singular in Spanish, is a common, predictable and highly stigmatized feature frequently found in the spoken and written language of heritage language learners. On closer examination, however, this patterned deviation reveals an attempt to regularize the verb system in Spanish, even as it reveals a lack of knowledge of this irregularity. Verbs, as Zentella suggests, are problematic for second and third generation Spanish speakers, as are spelling and word usage, and reflect the influence of competing language systems, including English. Although sociolinguists tell us that these constructions reflect processes of mutual influence that occur quite naturally in bilingual communities, they are often highly stigmatized features of language that are the basis for (inappropriate) judgments about students' language competence (Zentella 1997). Consequently, they warrant specific attention in assessment and instruction. At a minimum, interpreting students' writing requires a comparative knowledge of language variation.

In effect, "errors" or approximations in the use of language are explainable on the basis of students' emerging competence and on the influence of other language systems, including English (Cummins, 1994; Zentella 1997). We know that literacy-related skills interact with and impact on other language skills, such as speaking and listening, within and across languages (Cummins 1994). Thus, skills and competencies developed in one language variety will transfer to (or influence) other varieties of the same language as well as other languages. In treating errors as both a normal part of becoming proficient in the heritage language and as explainable on the basis of what students know, teachers are also making it safe for students to take risks, which is essential for learning and for helping to build students' self-confidence, which fuels the will to learn. Thus, the assessment of language usage has an impact beyond instruction. Assessment has the power to influence the lives of students' (Mercado and Romero 1993).

In addition, determining appropriate expectations for growth in the heritage language is also difficult. We are just beginning to understand the extraordinary variability that has been introduced into the classroom by adolescent heritage language learners who speak multiple varieties of the same language. It is by collaboration with colleagues and scholars in the examination of assessment procedures that teachers of heritage language learners will be able to continue to learn about, understand, and address this variability in ways that allow learners to succeed and learn.

Contacts with Caretakers

Phone conversations and, if necessary, home visits are also conducted to keep the lines of communication open between teachers and students' families. Through these contacts, teachers are able to probe and learn about out-of-school issues affecting students' participation and learning, such as students' home responsibilities. This information is essential if teachers are to provide students with the moral support and encouragement that are needed to deal with attendant stresses associated with learning, in general, and learning the heritage language, in particular. However, the success of these efforts is highly dependent on the relationships that teachers have with students and their families. The extent to which information is forthcoming and accurate is a function of the strength of this relationship (Mercado and Romero 1993). At the same time, individual outreach efforts by teachers also enable them to establish that they care about the student on a personal level, that they are willing to go out of their way to understand and respond to sudden changes in the conditions of students' lives that place their progress in school in jeopardy.

Conclusions

In this chapter I have sought to describe the character of assessment within the context of instruction for heritage language learners. Emerging assessment practices of teachers of heritage language learners give priority to monitoring changes in students' (1) attitudes and dispositions that may impede learning; (2) strategies that support language learning; (3) growth in knowledge of the written language through an analysis of language usage over time; and (4) monitoring the opportunity to practice and use the heritage language in nonschool contexts. These assessment practices focus on what scholars of language consider to be important influences on academic proficiency in tasks that are typical of the classroom and real-life settings. Thus, they go beyond giving attention to grammatical and structural control of a language within contrived exercises.

It is evident that quality assessments of this type pose a formidable challenge, even within the most supportive settings. For one thing, chronicling and analyzing heritage language learning is complex. It requires that the assessor have a sound theoretical base in language variation; it presupposes the development of academic language proficiency; it must take into account language interdependence in bilingual adolescent learners; and it must accommodate the complex nature of the relationship between language and identity. Because there are gaps in our knowledge base, specifically about the process of language restoration for adolescent learners from marginalized communities, teachers need to participate as members of a community of scholars dedicated to the examination of pedagogical questions and problems for which there are no definitive answers. They need to know that through ordinary interactions in the classroom they are, in effect, constructing this new knowledge.

One important goal of this chapter has been to highlight and document the contributions, from practice-based theory, that veteran heritage language teachers are making to our understanding and thinking about the learning of heritage languages and the monitoring of student progress as they engage in that learning. The knowledge gained from the ACTFL-Hunter College Project that is documented in this chapter validates, but also extends, our knowledge base and as such provides a powerful basis for improving the teaching and learning of heritage languages in school-based and university-based programs throughout the United States. The knowledge featured in this chapter also illustrates why it is so important to forge partnerships among educators in different communities of practice, specifically between school-based and university-based scholars. We need to learn from each other to serve our students well.

References

Altwerger, B. and B. L. Ivener. 1994. "Self- Esteem: Access to Literacy in Multicultural and Multilingual Classrooms." In K.Spangenberg-Urbschat and R. Pritchard (eds.), *Kids Come in All Languages*. Newark, DE: International Reading Association.

Ancess, J. and L. Darling-Hammond. September 1994. *Authentic Teaching, Learning, and Assessment with New English Language Learners at International High School.* The National Center for Restructuring Education, Education, Schools, and Teaching (NCREST). New York: Teachers College, Columbia University.

August, D. and K. Hakuta (eds.) 1997. *Improving Schooling for Language Minority Children.* Washington, DC: National Academy Press.

Chittenden, E. 1991. "Authentic Assessment, Evaluation, and Documentation." In Vito Perrone (ed.), *Expanding Student Assessment*, pp.22-31. Alexandria, VA: Association for Supervision and Curriculum Development.

Conference Proceedings. *The Invitational Roundtable on the Implications of the New Standards and High Stakes Assessments for Limited English Proficient Students.* December 3-4, 1996. A publication of the Northeast and Islands Regional Laboratory at Brown University Lab Consortium Site at Hunter College of the City University of New York.

Cummins, J. 1994. "The Acquisition of English as a Second Language." In K. Spangenberg-Urbschat and R. Pritchard (eds.), *Kids Come in All Languages*. Newark, DE: International Reading Association.

De Avila, E. 1985. *Motivation, Intelligence, and Access: A Theoretical Framework. In Issues in English Language Development.* An information exchange co-sponsored by the National Clearinghouse for Bilingual Education and the Georgetown University Bilingual Education Service Center. Rosslyn, VA: National Clearinghouse for Bilingual Education.

Falk, B., S. MacMurdy, and L. Darling-Hammond. October, 1995. *Taking a Different Look. How the Primary Language Record Supports Teaching for Diverse Learners.* The National Center for Restructuring Education, Education, Schools, and Teaching (NCREST). New York: Teachers College, Columbia University.

García, G.E. 1994. "Assessing the Literacy Development of Second Language Students: A Focus on Authentic Assessments." In K. Spangenberg-Urbschat and R. Pritchard (eds.), *Kids Come in All Languages.* Newark, DE: International Reading Association.

Krashen, S. D. 1998. "Heritage Language Development: Some Practical Arguments." In S.D.Krashen, L. Tse, and J. McQuillan (eds.). *Heritage Language Development*, pp. 3-13. Culver City, CA: Language Education Associates.

LaCelle-Peterson, M. and C. Rivera. 1994. "Is It Real for All Kids? A Framework for Equitable Assessment Policies for English Language Learners." *Harvard Educational Review*, Vol. 64, No. 1, pp.55-75.

Mercado, C. I. and M. Romero. 1993. "Assessment of Students in Bilingual Education." In M. B. Arias and U. Casanova (eds.), *Bilingual Education: Politics, Practice, and Research.* Chicago, IL: The National Society for the Study of Education.

National Forum on Assessment, October 1995.

Navarrete, C., J. Wilde, C. Nelson, R. Martinez, and G. Hargett. 1990. *Informal Assessment in Educational Evaluation: Implications for Bilingual Education.* Arlington, VA: National Clearinghouse for Bilingual Education.

Nieto, S. 1992. Affirming Diversity. *The Sociopolitical Context of Multicultural Education.* New York, NY: Longman

Perrone, V. 1991. Introduction. In V. Perrone (ed.), *Expanding Student Assessment*, pp. vii-xi. Alexandria, VA: Association for Supervision and Curriculum Development.

Stanton-Salazar, R. D. 1997. "A Social Capital Framework for Understanding the Socialization of Racial Minority Children and Youths." *Harvard Educational Review*, Vol. 67, No. 1, pp. 1-40.

Suarez-Orozco, C. and M. M. 1995. *Transformations. Immigration, Family Life, and Achievement Motivation among Latino Adolescents.* Stanford, CA: Stanford University Press.

Tse, L. 1998. "Ethnic Identity Formation and Its Implications for Heritage Language Development." In S. D. Krashen, L. Tse, and J. McQuillan (eds.), *Heritage Language Development*, pp. 15-29. Culver City, CA: Language Education Associates.

Valencia, Sheila. 1990. "A Portfolio Approach to Classroom Reading Assessment: The Whys, Whats, and Hows." *The Reading Teacher*, January 1990, pp. 338-340.

Wong-Fillmore, L. 1985. "Second Language Learning in Children: A Proposed Model." In Issues in English Language Development. An Information Exchange Co-Sponsored by the National Clearinghouse for Bilingual Education and the Georgetown University Bilingual Education Service Center, pp. 33-42. Rosslyn, VA: National Clearinghouse for Bilingual Education.

Zentella, A. C. 1997. *Growing Up Bilingual.* Malden, MA: Blackwell.

PART THREE

The National Perspective

Chapter 7

The ACTFL-Hunter College FIPSE Project and Its Contributions to the Profession

The ACTFL-Hunter College FIPSE Project and Its Contributions to the Profession

Guadalupe Valdés ✳

I am very honored to have been asked to provide a concluding piece to this special volume bringing together the work of the ACTFL-Hunter College FIPSE Project, "Collaborative Teacher Education Program: A Model for Second Language Instruction in Inner City Schools." It is a groundbreaking volume that I know will deeply influence the teaching of foreign languages in this country. It will be especially important for members of the profession who are concerned about the challenge of preparing foreign language teachers to address the needs of students who are raised in homes where non-English languages are spoken, who speak or merely understand the heritage language, and who are to some degree bilingual in English and the heritage language.

My assignment is to place the project in the national context of teaching heritage language learners and to identify the contributions that this volume and the work of the project make to the profession. I will begin by offering a brief overview of misunderstandings surrounding the discussion of bilingualism, of the place of bilingualism in education given our current policy context, and of the teaching of heritage languages. I will then discuss the contributions of the Project to the profession and the place of this volume in the existing literature on the teaching of heritage languages.

The Study of Bilingualism

The word "bilingualism" is a popular term that has been made to cover so many different phenomena that it has become virtually meaningless.

The above statement was made thirty years ago by Einar Haugen (1970, p.222), one of the first serious students of bilingualism in this country. Unfortunately, the terms "bilingual" and "bilingualism" continue to be used in various contradictory ways by members of the public as well as by both educators and researchers. Educators, for example, often use the term "bilingual" to refer to immigrant children entering school who have not yet begun to acquire English. "Bilingual" is considered the polite or even politically correct term with which to refer to children who are poor, disadvantaged, and newly arrived. One imagines that the use of the term also suggests the eventual reality of these children's residence in this country. They will acquire English and continue to use both English and a non-English language to some degree throughout most of their lifetimes.

Individuals who specialize in the training of conference interpreters make a very different use of the term. They consider that most interpreters will have two or three working languages. One of these two languages (referred to as language A) is the native language of the interpreter. Interpreters work *into* as well as *out of* their A language. The other language (referred to as language B) is a non-native language that, although not at the same level as language A, is very highly developed. Interpreters work *into* as well as *out of* their B language. C languages are passive languages from which interpreters interpret into their A or B languages. They do not interpret into C languages. In the case of conference interpreters, the term *bilingual* is reserved for those very few individuals who are said to have acquired or developed two A languages.

Students of bilingualism (e.g., Haugen 1956; Mackey 1962; Fishman 1965, 1966; Weinreich 1974; Baetens-Beardsmore 1982; Grosjean 1982; Hakuta 1986; Hamers and Blanc 1989) have either presented their own definitions of bilingualism and/or have reflected the range of definitions proposed by others. A numbers of scholars (e.g., Bloomfield 1935, p. 56) subscribed to very narrow definitions of the phenomenon: "the native-like control of two languages." Others (e.g., Macnamara 1967) have favored much broader definitions and define bilingualism as minimal competence in reading, writing, speaking or listening in a language other than the first. Haugen (1956), on the other hand, defined bilingualism as the condition of "knowing" *two* languages rather than one. For Haugen, the key element in the expression "knowing two languages" is the word two. What is of interest is not the degree of proficiency developed in each of the two languages, but rather the fact that proficiency has been developed (to whatever degree) in *more than one* language.

The Problem of the Monolingual Perspective

A number of researchers (e.g., Romaine 1995; Cook 1997; Mohanty and Perregaux 1997; Woolard 1999) have pointed out that bilingualism has unfortunately been seen as anomalous, marginal and in need of explanation. In spite of the fact that the majority of the populations of the world is bilingual or multilingual,[1] the position that has been taken by many researchers is that the norm for human beings is to know a single language. As Cook notes (1997, p. 280), "A person who has two languages is strange in some sense, obviously different from the *normal* person. Hence, the questioner looks for the differences caused by this unnatural condition of knowing two or more languages...." As Woolard points out, until very recently, multiplicity and simultaneity were not part of sociolinguistic theory, and notions of unitary language, bounded, and discrete codes were never problematized. The tendency among many researchers, therefore, was to propose that "true" or "real" bilinguals were the sum of *two native-speaking monolinguals*. According to this perspective, a true bilingual is two native speakers in one person.

The native speaker norm, even as a popular concept, however, is difficult to apply to most bilinguals. As Haugen (1970, p. 225) pointed out:

> To be natively competent in two languages would then mean to have had two childhoods, so that all the joys and frustrations of the fundamental period of life could penetrate one's emotional response to the simple words of the language. It would mean to have acquired the skills of reading and writing that go with two separate educational systems such as all literate societies now impose on their adolescents, or the corresponding rigorous forms of initiation and skill development that formed part of all nonliterate societies. It would mean to have two different identities, one looking at the world from one point of view, the other from another: it would mean sharing in the social forms, prejudices, and insights of two cultures. In short, it would mean being two entirely different people.

While absolutely equivalent abilities in two languages are theoretically possible, except for rare geographical and familial accidents, individuals seldom have access to two languages in exactly the same contexts in every domain of interaction. They do not have the opportunity of using two languages to carry out the exact same functions with all individuals with whom they interact or to use their languages intellectually to the same degree. They thus do not develop identical strengths in both languages.

The heritage language students with whom the ACTFL-Hunter College FIPSE Project is concerned are young American bilinguals who are not two monolinguals in one; they have not lived two lives, and they have not been educated in two languages. They are, by and large, English speakers who have grown up in this country as members of families or communities where non-English languages are spoken. The speakers of Spanish and the speakers of Haitian Créole with whom teachers in the project worked, face the same challenges that confront youngsters of similar backgrounds all over the country. Most Americans reject the idea that the maintenance of either immigrant or indigenous languages is intrinsically, socially, or economically valuable. Negative attitudes toward bilingualism are deeply embedded in what Schiffman (1998) has termed American "linguistic culture."

Bilingualism and Education: The Current Policy Context

For educators who are concerned about non-English languages in the United States, these are ambivalent times. On the one hand, there is a growing internationalist perspective that emphasizes global interconnectedness as well as the need for this nation to become, what Tucker (1984) has termed, a "language-competent" society. Proponents of this view (e.g., R. Lambert 1986; Tucker 1990 1994) see language competence as a crucial national priority. They (especially R. Lambert 1986, p.7) have argued for a coherent strategy that will (1) augment the capacity of American businesses to be competitive in global markets; (2) increase the effectiveness of our foreign affairs specialists, and (3) expand "international communication and the gathering, management, and analysis of information from abroad."

Along with this internationalist perspective, there is another view that can be characterized as protective and perhaps insular and that regards the presence of non-English languages in this country with suspicion. Proponents of this view (U.S. English, English only) are less concerned with developing language competence for international participation than with defending the status of the English language in a country that they view as increasingly non-English speaking.

Taking into account these two very different perspectives, the question facing American educators today is: How does the United States produce a citizenry that is prepared to function in a multicultural and multilingual world while at the same time remain sensitive to the anxieties and fears of those groups that are concerned about the status of English in this country? There are, obviously, no simple answers to this question. Moreover, the issue evokes numerous additional questions. For example: What does it mean to produce a citizenry that is language competent? What languages does this include? Are languages to be valued according to their traditional status in academic study, or will they be valued according to their function in the broader world? What will our policies be toward the "new" immigrant languages? Shall we continue to allow immigrant and other heritage languages to die before we teach them again to monolingual speakers of English? Shall we make it a condition that English be learned at a certain level of fluency before we undertake to teach new languages or to retrieve or maintain heritage languages? The questions are many and the issues complex. Yet, a meaningful exploration of the role of educational institutions in developing non-English language resources in this country must address these questions and issues. If these institutions can perform more effectively, they may enable this country to preserve a precious national resource and to do so in an environment governed by professional expertise rather than political conflict.

To date, the response of American society has been to ignore the language resources of our immigrant groups and to take the position that the loss of ethnic languages is part of the price to be paid for becoming American. As Ricento (1998) has argued, "deep values" within our society reject the idea that the maintenance of immigrant and indigenous languages is intrinsically, socially or economically valuable. Until recently, the educational establishment had worked very much within this tradition. Following language-related controversies in the early part of the century (e.g., Meyer v. Nebraska in 1923), public schools have played a minimal role in maintaining heritage languages in immigrant communities. Educational involvement in language issues was limited to the teaching of "foreign" (i.e., non-English and not personally linked) languages to students who were monolingual speakers of English.

During the past thirty years, however, the passage and implementation of the Bilingual Education Act of 1968 provided a forum for language policy in this country and directly involved educational institutions in a debate focusing on the obligations of school districts to meet the needs of linguistic minority students. Even though the primary focus of bilingual education policy was in large part compensatory and transitional, it nevertheless offered access to instruction in immigrant languages to a minority of newly arrived immigrant youngsters.[2] Given increased political opposition to bilingual education (e.g., Proposition 227 in California), there is little optimism about future opportunities for the development of bilingualism and biliteracy among non-English–background children in regular elementary school programs. Furthermore, the only hope left for advocates of early non-English–language teaching for young mainstream children are two-way bilingual or dual immersion programs which bring majority Anglophone children into the same classrooms with non-English-speaking minority children.[3]

Interestingly, as debates rage on about the use of non-English languages in education for young children, there is continued support for the teaching of foreign languages. For example, standards for foreign language teaching were developed as part of the Goals 2000 initiative, and the first NAEP examination is currently being developed for administration in the year 2004. More important, perhaps, the Standards were specifically written to take into consideration not only the needs of traditional foreign language learners, but also the special strengths of home-background or heritage learners.

The Teaching of Ethnic/Heritage or Minority Languages As Academic Subjects

In contrast to bilingual education or mother-tongue teaching programs in which the primary focus is subject-matter instruction in children's ethnic language as well as the acquisition of the societal language, instruction in languages as academic subjects has involved teaching these languages as part of the regular middle-school, high school, and university curriculum. Languages taught as *academic subjects* are known as "foreign" languages and include languages labeled by the United States Office of Education and by the Modern Language Association (MLA) as "commonly taught" such as French, German, and Spanish and those labeled "less commonly taught" languages such as Russian, Chinese, Korean and Arabic. As Brod and Huber (1997) point out, however, the line between commonly and less commonly taught languages is arbitrary. Until 1986, the MLA survey listed seven most commonly taught languages. Currently, the survey lists twelve languages as commonly taught and 124 other languages in which enrollment has increased threefold between 1968 and 1985 and grown by 84 percent since 1986.

Within the last decades, the increasing population of non-English–background students in this country has had a significant impact on foreign language instruction—especially on the types of language classes that must be developed for students who already have some proficiency in such languages. To date, Spanish is the language with the strongest current enrollments at both the secondary and post-secondary levels. According to Brod and Huber (1997), at the college level, Spanish enrollments account for 53 percent of all registrations, with 22.2 percent of all programs offering courses for bilingual speakers. At the secondary level, according to Draper and Hicks (1996), Spanish accounts for 64.5 percent of all enrollments. Courses in Spanish for bilingual speakers account for a small but rapidly growing segment of these enrollments. What this means is that instructors trained to teach Spanish as a foreign language have had to open their doors to bilingual students who, in some cases, are more fluent in the language than the teachers are but who often cannot read or write in Spanish. Schooled exclusively in English since elementary school, these students have had no experience in reading and writing in Spanish. To make matters worse from the perspective of many teachers, such students are often speakers of stigmatized varieties of Spanish (e.g., rural Mexican Spanish; rural Puerto Rican Spanish) or contact varieties of Spanish that are severely "contaminated" by English.

The Role of Pedagogical Theory in the Teaching of Heritage Languages

Efforts to develop pedagogies suitable for teaching "foreign" languages to heritage speakers date from the early seventies, a time in which the increasing enrollment of Mexican-origin students was felt strongly at the university level in the Southwest. Until recently, efforts to develop both theories and policies that might guide the teaching of heritage languages, however, had been carried out by isolated individuals at different institutions reacting to problems faced by students in very different programs. As a result, the multiple practices and pedagogies currently being used to teach heritage speakers are not directly supported by a set of coherent theories about the role of instruction in the development of language proficiencies in bilingual language learners. Even within the current climate of support and interest in such instruction provided by the American Association of Teachers of Spanish and Portuguese (AATSP), the American Council on the Teaching of Foreign Languages (ACTFL), and the National Foreign Language Center as well as the models provided by the work carried out in Australia in implementing instruction for home-background speakers (Scarino 1988; Ingram 1994; Valdés 1995), discussions among practitioners at all levels are characterized by disagreements about appropriate outcomes and goals of instruction.[4]

There is no clear educational policy that can guide the goals of language instruction for heritage-language-speaking students in the light of current and future economic and social goals. Korean and Chinese parents, for example, are exerting much effort so that their children can earn high school credits for the study of these languages. At the urging of these parents, the College Board has recently developed subject-matter examinations in these two languages. Growing interest in what were previously considered "minor" languages by students is confirmed by the work recently carried out by Krashen and others (1998). Focusing on both language attitudes and language pedagogies, this work concludes that heritage-background youngsters have increasingly positive attitudes toward their ancestral language. If appropriate teaching methods are used, further language study (after English has been well acquired) yields particularly good results after early adolescent rebellion has ended.

What is needed in order to support this growing interest in developing heritage/immigrant language resources is a coherent body of pedagogical theories about what can be accomplished in a classroom setting relative to out-of-school acquisition, functions and rewards. Very little empirical research is available about the outcomes of different kinds of instruction. There have been no policy discussions at the national or state levels that focus on language education for both monolingual-English speaking and heritage background students. Foreign language instruction at the high school level generally is still aimed primarily at monolingual-English-speaking college-bound students; and college and university language instruction is still largely defined by the literature-focused upper-level courses in which students are eventually expected to enroll. Specific goals have not been established for the teaching of languages as heritage languages, and no policies directly guide the implementation of programs, the training of teachers, and the measurement of outcomes.

The ACTFL-Hunter College FIPSE Project

From its inception, the ACTFL-Hunter College Project sought to address one of the most difficult challenges facing the broadening of foreign language teaching to include the teaching of heritage learners: the challenge of teacher preparation. It is true that other projects have addressed the same problem. There have been numerous summer workshops, for example, which have brought together foreign language teachers for several weeks and have offered them an intensive course encompassing both methods and theory. What was different about the ACTFL-

Hunter College Project is that it sought to establish a model for teacher preparation that was collaborative and deeply grounded in practice. It did not assume that teachers who agreed to teach heritage language learners could simply be "taught" about the issues under girding such instruction in a series of lectures over a number of Saturday mornings. The Project very rightly took the position that teachers involved in the project had to collaboratively construct an understanding of the challenges, the questions, and the theories that could inform their practice. Project leaders also understood the importance of practice itself and the wisdom that particular tales from the field would bring to the group of practitioners grappling with the same problems.

This volume as a compendium of what was learned by a group of teachers over the course of a three-year period, is also an invaluable guide for other teachers, for teacher educators, and for members of the profession who are desperately in need of concrete examples of classroom practice. The voices in this volume are strong and clear. The teachers in the project had not been trained to work with students who already speak or understand the target language and/or who have a strong connection with that language. Their challenge involved understanding the needs of minority language communities, getting to know a new group of students, and adapting or developing pedagogical approaches that could address the special needs of these learners. What they have given us in this volume is a fine-grained depiction of their questions, their doubts, and their new discoveries, as well as their triumphs and successes both large and small.

What is particularly important about the volume is that it fills an enormous gap in the existing literature on the teaching of heritage languages. It offers us, for the first time, a text that can be used in teacher education courses, in teacher inservice training, and in informing others about the issues that surround heritage language instruction. Up to this point, most of us have used a variety of materials in methods courses designed to prepare both secondary and post-secondary teachers to work with heritage learners. I suspect, however, that all of us have found it difficult to bridge the discontinuity between theory and practice. We could not bring into our classes the reality of classrooms, the dilemmas, the challenges, and the rewards to prospective teachers of heritage students. We had difficulty explaining what one must do differently with heritage speakers and how one fills up class time. In this volume, we see the answers to these questions clearly.

Teaching Heritage Language Learners: Voices from the Classroom contains a well-selected combination of elements that can be utilized, for example, to build the main core of a one-semester course on the teaching of heritage languages. The review of the literature in Chapter One, "Where We've Been; What We've Learned" (Draper and Hicks), for instance, covers the key questions surrounding the teaching of heritage languages and contains an excellent list of references. The review can serve as an excellent introduction to the topic from which students can be asked to branch out and read further.

Chapter Two of the volume, "Getting to Know the Heritage Language Learner," can provide a very important anchoring in reality for prospective teachers. The profiles of five actual heritage language learners (Jason, Manny, Pierre and Abdoulaye, and José,) in combination with the retrospectives of adult heritage learners in "Heritage Language Learners Look Back" offer a very comprehensive view of the difficulties and challenges that face youngsters who grow up in homes where non-English languages are spoken. Through the lives of teachers, readers are helped to understand what it means to lose and try to recover a heritage language (Giangreco), the sense of loss that remains even when bilingualism in English and another language has been acquired (Rizk), and the distances that emerge between parents and children when children cannot speak to their parents in the heritage language (Parker). These descriptions will be most effective in helping prospective teachers visualize heritage language learners. I anticipate that these profiles will serve as points of departure for class discussion, for personal retrospective essays, and for classroom observation in heritage language classes.

Chapter Two also includes a framework designed to assist teachers in acquiring essential information about their heritage language students. I found the "Framework for Learning About Your Students" to be extraordinarily thorough in focusing on the issues and questions that must inform practice. I could imagine using this framework in a methods class and asking prospective teachers to answer questions for their particular groups of heritage learners. What is especially valuable about the Framework is that it immediately makes evident to trained foreign language teachers the difference between learners and heritage speakers. It covers learners' attitudes toward their heritage language, use of language in the school and community, types of proficiency, motivation, academic preparedness, cultural connectedness, emotional factors, and societal factors. Each of the sets of questions on the topics contained in the Framework could be expanded upon by key background readings on language variation, language use, bilingualism, language attitudes, etc.

Chapter Three, in many ways addresses some of the most important issues that teachers will face in teaching heritage language learners. Scalera's piece on teacher beliefs, her openness and frankness about her doubts and challenges, allows us to talk about the many anxieties that non-native speakers have about teaching heritage speakers. It also reminds us that, as teachers—whether native or non-native—we must constantly re-examine our practices, our assumptions, and our attitudes toward our students.

From my perspective, the "Statement of Goals and Fundamental Beliefs" included in this section, will guide us in thinking about what must come together in the teaching of heritage languages. This summary makes evident that we must consider teachers, students, the learning environment, and curriculum, and that we must be clear about our goals and fundamental beliefs about such instruction. The goals and beliefs that the members of the ACTFL-Hunter College Project share with readers in this volume are a very special gift from the teachers and collaborators of the project to the profession. They offer us a template against which we can examine our own beliefs and our own practices.

Chapter Four, "Standards and Heritage Language Learners," raises central and key questions about standards and moves us much beyond the existing standards documents. It also offers us a vision of language arts instruction that few teachers of foreign language have experienced. McCallister's piece on the teaching of reading and writing is an extended scenario within which both prospective teachers and trained foreign language teachers might begin to imagine their own classrooms and the kinds of activities that might support the development of literacy in heritage languages.

The reality of the classroom becomes even more vivid in Chapter Five. Through the pieces in this chapter, a prospective teacher can develop a sense of exemplary practice from the perspective of researchers and yet hear the clear voices of the teachers themselves. I am struck by the teachers' strength, by their honesty, and by their willingness to help us learn from their often-painful journeys. The belief systems identified by Sylvan are clearly in evidence in the teachers' descriptions of their classrooms and their students. Teachers respect students' prior knowledge; they assume and work with heterogeneity in their classrooms; they establish a sense of family in their classrooms; they select culturally relevant content; they play multiple roles as teachers, mentors, advisors, and guidance counselors; and they continually reflect on their teaching. I cannot think of a more effective way to help prospective teachers to engage in a discussion of reflective practice than to have them read this chapter.

Finally, Chapter Six includes an excellent discussion of assessment that puts into perspective the challenges to be faced by researchers and practitioners in developing the kinds of measurement procedures that can give us information about the special competencies of heritage language learners. This section raises very important issues that must be addressed by the entire foreign language teaching profession in serving the needs of heritage learners.

A Model for the Profession

The ACTFL-Hunter College Project set out to develop a model of collaborative teacher preparation for the profession. It sought to address the challenges faced by new teachers of heritage learners by creating a mechanism within which practicing teachers of foreign languages might be able to collectively identify what they should know and be able to do in order to work more effectively with these special language learners. Project leaders rejected top-down, banking approaches to inservice education and established instead a context in which talented teachers who were engaged in the practice of heritage language teaching could come together to explore, discuss, and grapple with the many issues that touched upon their practice.

I see the work presented in this volume as clear evidence of the success of the ACTFL-Hunter College Project model. It is clear that teachers carefully examined complex theoretical issues. They came to an understanding of language variation, of bilingualism, and of policies surrounding the education of heritage language students. Their contributions to this volume reveal their impatience with conceptions of balanced bilingualism, with policies that view all speakers of non-English language as candidates for ESL classes, and with textbooks and materials that do not speak to students' need to connect with their culture.

What is exciting about this volume is that it does much more than simply rephrase what others have said about heritage learners. This suggests that the teacher preparation context allowed them to come to their own understanding of issues identified by others and to problematize the assumptions underlying such identification. By allowing participants to reframe questions, to offer new definitions, and to produce a set of guiding principles and goals to guide their practice, project leaders invited teachers to "own" both the challenges and the solutions. I am convinced that as a professional development model, the ACTFL-Hunter College Project will offer much to all of us. I look forward to the companion to this volume that will guide us in establishing similar collaborative projects with other teachers in other settings. There is much that we must learn from the Project Development Team about the specifics of implementing the model. In the meantime, I know that this volume will serve many roles. It will be used as a point of departure for a national conversation on teacher preparation, and it will fill an enormous gap in the teacher preparation literature. I especially look forward to using this volume in my classes.

Notes

1. Contrary to what is generally believed by monolingual individuals, most of the world's population is bilingual. Monolingualism is characteristic of a *minority* of the world's peoples. According to figures cited in Stavenhagen (1990), for example, 5,000 to 8,000 different ethnic groups reside in approximately 160 nation states. Moreover, a number of scholars, for example, Grimes (1992), estimate that there are over 6,000 distinct languages spoken in that same small number of nation states. What is evident from these figures is that few nations are either monolingual or monoethnic. Each of the world's nations has groups of individuals living within its borders who do not speak the societal language or who may speak it with limitations, and who use other languages in addition to or instead of the national language to function in their everyday lives. Moreover, from the work conducted by researchers especially in non-Western societies (e.g., Mohanty 1982a, 1982b, 1990), we also know that many societies are multilingual and that individuals normally acquire and use two or three languages in addition to their mother tongue in response to the multiethnic nature of everyday interactions.

2. In California, for example, during the 1997-1998 school year, of 1, 406,166 students identified as limited English proficient, only 29 percent were enrolled in bilingual education programs.(Rumberger 1998)

3. Dual immersion programs provide instruction in *primary* language for minority students who can begin their academic work in a language they already speak and understand. They bring together mainstream and minority children. Early results of the measurement of achievement levels of both minority and majority children in dual immersion programs (e.g., the work carried out by Lindholm and Gavlik 1994) have been most encouraging. Test scores, while not as high as some educators would wish, appear to suggest that low achievement is not concentrated among students of lower socio-economic levels. In spite of these encouraging results, because of mainstream parents' apprehensions about bilingualism and its long-term effects on their children's achievement, it is unlikely that the country will move to a wholesale implementation of such programs.

4. There has been much debate on issues such as the following: the difference between foreign language and heritage language instruction (Valdés 1981), the implications of the study of linguistic differences for the teaching of Spanish to bilingual students (Floyd 1981; Guitart 1981; Solé 1981); the teaching of the prestige or standard variety (Valdés-Fallis 1976, 1978; Valdés 1981, 1982; Hidalgo 1987, 1993, 1997; Politzer 1993; Colombi 1997; García and Otheguy 1997; Porras 1997; Torreblanca 1997); the teaching of grammar (Alonso de Lozano 1981), the teaching of spelling (Valdés-Fallis 1975; Stazeck and Aid 1981), the teaching of reading and writing (Faltis 1981, 1984; Teschner 1981; Villarreal 1981); testing and assessment (Barkin 1981; Ziegler 1981; Valdés 1989); the relationship between theory and practice (Merino and Samaniego 1993); the role of the FL teaching profession in maintaining minority languages (Valdés 1992); and the development of academic language abilities at both the graduate and the undergraduate levels (Faltis 1981, 1984; Valdés, Lozano, and García-Moya 1981; Roca 1990; D'Ambruoso 1993; Faltis and DeVillar 1993; Gorman 1993; Hocker 1993; Merino, Samaniego, and Trueba 1993; Quintanar-Sarellana, Huebner, and Jensen 1993; Valdés 1995, 1998; Colombi and Alarcon 1997).

References

Alonso de Lozano, L. 1981. "Enseñanza del subjuntivo a hispanohablantes." In G. Valdés, A. G. Lozano, and R. García-Moya (eds.), *Teaching Spanish to the Hispanic Bilingual: Issues, Aims, and Methods*, pp. 140-145. New York: Teachers College Press.

Baetens-Beardsmore, H. 1982. *Bilingualism Basic Principles*. Clevedon, Avon: Tieto Ltd.

Barkin, F. 1981. "Evaluating Linguistic Proficiency: The Case of Teachers in Bilingual Programs." In G. Valdés, A. G. Lozano, and R. García-Moya (eds.), *Teaching Spanish to the Hispanic Bilingual: Issues, Aims, and Methods*, pp. 215-234. New York: Teachers College Press.

Bloomfield, L. 1935. *Language*. London: Allen and Unwin.

Brod, R., and B. J. Huber. 1997. "Foreign Language Enrollments in United States Institutions of Higher Education." *ADFL Bulletin*, Vol. 28, No. 2, pp. 55-61.

Colombi, M. C. 1997. "Perfil del discurso escrito en textos de hispanohablantes: teoría y práctica." In M. C. Colombi and F. X. Alarcon (eds.), *La enseñanza del español a hispanohablantes: Praxis y teoría*, pp. 175-189. Boston: Houghton Mifflin.

Cook, V. 1997. "The Consequences of Bilingualism and Cognitive Processing." In A. M. B. de Groot and J. F. Kroll (eds.), *Tutorials in Bilingualism : Psycholinguistic Perspectives*, pp. 279-299. Mahwah NJ: Earlbaum.

D'Ambruoso, L. 1993. "Spanish for Spanish Speakers: A Curriculum." In B. J. Merino, H. T. Trueba, and F. A. Samaniego (eds.), *Language and Culture in Learning: Teaching Spanish to Native Speakers of Spanish*, pp. 203-207. London: Falmer Press.

Draper, J. B., and J. H. Hicks. 1996. "Foreign Language Enrollments in Public Secondary Schools," Fall 1994. *Foreign Language Annals*, Vol. 29, No.3, pp. 303-306.

Faltis, C. J. 1981. "Teaching Spanish Writing to Bilingual College Students." *NABE Journal*, Vol.6, pp. 93-106.

Faltis, C. J. 1984. "Reading and Writing in Spanish for Bilingual College Students: What's Taught at School and What's Used in the Community." *The Bilingual Review/ La Revista Bilingüe*, Vol. 11, pp. 21-32.

Faltis, C. J., and R. A. DeVillar. 1993. "Effective Computer Uses for Teaching Spanish to Bilingual Native Speakers: A Socioacademic Perspective." In B. J. Merino, H. T. Trueba, and F. A. Samaniego (eds.), *Language and Culture in Learning: Teaching Spanish to Native Speakers of Spanish*, pp. 160-169. London: Falmer Press.

Fishman, J. A. 1965. *Who Speaks What Language to Whom and When?* Vol. 2, 67-68.

Floyd, M. B. 1981. "Language Variation in Southwest Spanish and Its Relation to Pedagogical Issues." In G. Valdés, A. G. Lozano, and R. García-Moya (eds.), *Teaching Spanish to the Hispanic Bilingual: Issues, Aims, and Methods*, pp. 30-45. New York: Teachers College Press.

García, O., and R. Otheguy, R. 1997. "No sólo de estándar se vive el aula: lo que nos enseñó la educación bilingüe sobre el español de Nueva York." In M. C. Colombi and F. X. Alarcon (eds.), *La enseñanza del español a hispanohablantes: Praxis y teoría*, pp. 156-174. Boston: Houghton Mifflin.

Gorman, S. 1993. "Using Elements of Cooperative Learning in the Communicative Foreign Language Classroom." In B. J. Merino, H. T. Trueba, and F. A. Samaniego (eds.), *Language and Culture in Learning: Teaching Spanish to Native Speakers of Spanish*, pp. 144-152. London: Falmer Press.

Grimes, B. F. 1992. *Ethnologue: Languages of the World*. (12th edition) Dallas: Summer Institute of Linguistics.

Grosjean, F. 1982. *Life with Two Languages.* Cambridge, MA: Harvard University Press.

Guitart, J. 1981. "The Pronunciation of Puerto Rican Spanish in the Mainland: Theoretical and Pedagogical Considerations." In G. Valdés, A. G. Lozano, and R. García-Moya (eds.), *Teaching Spanish to the Hispanic Bilingual: Issues, Aims, and Methods*, pp. 46-58. New York: Teachers College Press.

Hakuta, K. 1986. Mirror of Language: *The Debate on Bilingualism.* New York: Basic Books.

Hamers, J. F., and M. H. A. Blanc. 1989. *Bilinguality and Bilingualism.* Cambridge: Cambridge University Press.

Haugen, E. 1956. *Bilingualism in the Americas: A Bibliography and Research Guide.* Vol. 26. University, Alabama: University of Alabama Press.

Haugen, E. 1970. "On the Meaning of Bilingual Competence." In R. Jakobson, and others (eds.), *Studies in General and Oriental Linguistics*, pp. 222-229. Tokyo: TEC Company Limited.

Hidalgo, M. 1987. "On the Question of 'Standard' v. 'Dialect': Implications for Teaching Hispanic College Students." *Hispanic Journal of the Behavioral Sciences*, Vol. 9, No. 4, pp. 375-395.

Hidalgo, M. 1993. "The Teaching of Spanish to Bilingual Spanish-Speakers: A 'Problem' of Inequality." In B. J. Merino, H. T. Trueba, and F. A. Samaniego (eds.), *Language and Culture in Learning: Teaching Spanish to Native Speakers of Spanish*, pp. 82-93. London: Falmer Press.

Hidalgo, M. 1997. "Criterios normativos e ideología lingüística: aceptación y rechazo del español de los Estados Unidos." In M. C. Colombi and F. X. Alarcon (eds.), *La enseñanza del español a hispanohablantes: Praxis y teoría*, pp. 109-120. Boston: Houghton Mifflin.

Hocker, B. C. 1993. "Folk Art in the Classroom." In B. J. Merino, H. T. Trueba, and F. A. Samaniego (eds.), *Language and Culture in Learning: Teaching Spanish to Native Speakers of Spanish*, pp. 153-159. London: Falmer Press.

Ingram, D. E. 1994. "Language Policy in Australia in the 1990's." In R. D. Lambert (ed.), *Language Planning Around the World: Contexts and Systemic Change*, pp. 69-109. Washington, D.C.: National Foreign Language Center.

Krashen, S., L. Tse, and J. McQuillan. 1998. *Heritage Language Development.* Culver City: Language Education Associates.

Lambert, R. D. 1986. *Points of Leverage: An Agenda for a National Foundation for International Studies.* New York: Social Science Research Council.

Lozano, A. G. 1981. "A Modern View of Teaching Grammar." In G. Valdés, A. G. Lozano, and R. García-Moya (eds.), *Teaching Spanish to the Hispanic Bilingual: Issues, Aims, and Methods*, pp. 81-90. New York: Teachers College Press.

Mackey, W. F. 1962. "The Description of Bilingualism." *Canadian Journal of Linguistics*, Vol.7, pp., 51-85.

Macnamara, J. 1967. *The Linguistic Independence of Bilinguals.* Vol. 6, 729-736.

Merino, B. J., and F. A. Samaniego. 1993. "Language Acquisition Theory and Classroom Practices in the Teaching of Spanish to the Native Spanish Speaker." In B. J. Merino, H. T. Trueba, and F. A. Samaniego (eds.), *Language and Culture in Learning: Teaching Spanish to Native Speakers of Spanish.* London: Falmer Press.

Merino, B. J., H. T. Trueba, and F. A. Samaniego (eds.). 1993. *Language and Culture in Learning: Teaching Spanish to Native Speakers of Spanish.* London: The Falmer Press.

Mohanty, A. K. 1982a. Cognitive and Linguistic Development of Tribal Children from Unilingual and Bilingual Environment. In R. Rath, H. S. Asthana, D. Sinha, and J. B. P. Sinha (eds.), *Diversity and Unity in Cross-Cultural Psychology*, pp. 78-87. Lisse: Swets and Zeitlinger.

249

Mohanty, A. K. 1982b. "Bilingualism among Kond Tribals in Orissa [India]: Consequences of Mother Tongue Maintenance and Multilingualism in India." *Indian Psychologist*, Vol. 1, No. 33-44.

Mohanty, A. K. 1990. "Psychological Consequences of Mother Tongue Maintenance and Multilingualism in India." *Psychology in Developing Societies*, Vol. 2, PP. 31-51.

Mohanty, A. K., and C. Perregaux. 1997. "Language Acquisition and Bilingualism." In J. W. Berry, P. R. Dasen, and T. S. Saraswathi (eds.), *Handbook of Cross-Cultural Psychology: Basic Processes and Human Development*, Vol. 2, pp. 217-253. Boston: Allyn and Bacon.

Politzer, R. L. 1993. "A Researcher's Reflections on Bridging Dialect and Second Language Learning: Discussion of Problems and Solutions." In B. J. Merino, H. T. Trueba, and F. A. Samaniego (eds.), *Language and Culture in Learning: Teaching Spanish to Native Speakers of Spanish*, pp. 45-57. London: Falmer Press.

Porras, J. E. 1997. "Uso local y uso estándar: un enfoque bidialectal a la enseñanza del español para nativos." In M. C. Colombi and F. X. Alarcon (eds.), *La enseñanza del español a hispanohablantes: Praxis y teoría*, pp. 190-197. Boston: Houghton Mifflin.

Quintanar-Sarellana, R., Huebner, T., and Jensen, A. 1993. "Tapping a Natural Resource: Language Minority Students as Foreign Language Tutors." In B. J. Merino, H. T. Trueba, and F. A. Samaniego (eds.), *Language and Culture in Learning: Teaching Spanish to Native Speakers of Spanish*, pp. 208-221. London: Falmer Press.

Ricento, T. 1998. "National Language Policy in the United States." In T. Ricento and B. Burnaby (eds.), *Language and Politics in the United States and Canada*, pp. 85-115. Mahwah NJ: Lawrence Erlbaum.

Roca, A. 1990. "Teaching Spanish to the Bilingual College Student in Miami." In J. J. Bergen (ed.), *Spanish in the United States: Sociolinguistic Issues*, pp. 127-136. Georgetown: Georgetown University Press.

Romaine, S. 1995. *Bilingualism.* (2nd edition) Oxford: Blackwell.

Rumberger, R. W. 1998. "California LEP Enrollment Growth Rate Falls." *UC Linguistic Minority Research Institute Newsletter*, Vol. 8, No. 1, pp. 1-2.

Scarino, A., D. Vale, P. McKay, and J. Clark. 1988. *Australian Language Levels Guidelines: Book 1:Language Learning in Australia; Book 2: Syllabus Development and Programming; Book 3: Method, Resources, and Assessment*: Curriculum Development Center.

Schiffman, H. F. 1996. *Linguistic Culture and Language Policy.* London: Routledge.

Solé, Y. 1981. "Consideraciones pedagógicas en la enseñanza del español a estudiantes bilingües." In G. Valdés, A. G. Lozano, and R. García-Moya (eds.), *Teaching Spanish to the Hispanic Bilingual: Issues, Aims, and Methods*, pp. 21-29. New York: Teachers College Press.

Staczek, J. J., and F. M. Aid. 1981. "Hortografía Himortal: Spelling Problems among Bilingual Students." In G. Valdés, A. G. Lozano, and R. García-Moya (eds.), *Teaching Spanish to the Hispanic Bilingual: Issues, Aims, and Methods*, pp. 146-156. New York: Teachers College Press.

Teschner, R. V. 1981. "Spanish for Native Speakers: Evaluating Twenty- Five Chicano Compositions in a First-Year Course." In G. Valdés, A. G. Lozano, and R. García-Moya (eds.), *Teaching Spanish to the Hispanic Bilingual: Issues, Aims, and Methods*, pp. 115-139. New York: Teachers College Press.

Torreblanco, M. 1997. "El español hablado en el Suroeste de los Estados Unidos y las normas lingüísticas españolas." In M. C. Colombi and F. X. Alarcon (eds.), *La enseñanza del español a hispanohablantes: Praxis y teoría*, pp. 133-139. Boston: Houghton Mifflin.

Tucker, G. R. 1984. "Toward the Development of a Language-Competent American Society." *The*

International Journal of the Sociology of Language, Vol. 45, pp. 153-160.

Tucker, G. R. 1990. "Second-Language Education: Issues and Perspectives." In A. M. Padilla, H. H. Fairchild, and C. M. Valadez (eds.), *Foreign Language Education: Issues and Strategies*, pp. 13-21. Newbury Park, CA.: Sage Publications.

Tucker, G. R. 1991. "Developing a Language-Competent American Society: the Role of Language Planning." In A. G. Reynolds (ed.), *Bilingualism, Multiculturalism, and Second Language Learning*. Hillsdale, N.J.: Lawrence Erlbaum.

Valdés, G. 1989. "Testing Bilingual Proficiency for Specialized Occupations: Issues and Implications." In B. R. Gifford (ed.), *Test Policy and Test Performance: Education, Language and Culture*, pp. 207-229. Boston: Kluwer Academic Publishers.

Valdés, G. 1992. "The Role of the Foreign Language Teaching Profession in Maintaining Non-English Languages in the United States." In H. Byrnes (ed.), *Languages for a Multicultural World in Transition: 1993 Northeast Conference Reports*, pp. 29-71. Skokie, IL: National Textbook Company.

Valdés, G. 1995. "The Teaching of Minority Languages as 'Foreign' Languages: Pedagogical and Theoretical Challenges." *Modern Language Journal*, Vol. 79, No. 3, pp. 299-328.

Valdés, G., and M. Geoffrion-Vinci. 1998. "Chicano Spanish: The Problem of the 'Underdeveloped' Code in Bilingual Repertoires." *Modern Language Journal*, Vol. 82, No. 4, pp. 473-501.

Valdés, G., T. P. Hannum, and R. V. Teschner. 1982. *Cómo se escribe: curso de secundaria para estudiantes bilingües*. New York: Scribner's.

Valdés, G., A. G. Lozano, and R. García-Moya (eds.). 1981. *Teaching Spanish to the Hispanic Bilingual: Issues, Aims, and Methods*. New York: Teachers College Press.

Valdés-Fallis, G. 1976. "Language Development Versus the Teaching of the Standard Language." *Lektos*, December, pp. 20-32.

Valdés-Fallis, Guadalupe. 1975. "Teaching Spanish to the Spanish-speaking: Classroom Strategies." *System*, Vol. 3, No. 5, pp. 54-62.

Villarreal, H. 1981. "Reading and Spanish for Native Speakers." In G. Valdés, A. G. Lozano, and R. García-Moya (eds.), *Teaching Spanish to the Hispanic Bilingual: Issues, Aims, and Methods*, pp. 157-168. New York: Teachers College Press.

Weinreich, U. 1974. *Languages in Contact*. The Hague: Mouton.

Woolard, K. A. 1999. "Simultaneity and Bivalency as Strategies in Bilingualism." *Journal of Linguistic Anthropology*, Vol. 8, No. 1, pp. 3-29.

Ziegler, J. 1981. "Guidelines for the Construction of a Spanish Placement Examination for the Spanish-Dominant Spanish-English Bilingual." In G. Valdés, A. G. Lozano, and R. García-Moya (eds.), *Teaching Spanish to the Hispanic Bilingual: Issues, Aims, and Methods*, pp. 211-214. New York: Teachers College Press.

The Authors

Emma Abreu-Perez (M.A. Binghamton University) is a teacher of Native Language Arts at Louis B. Brandeis High School of the New York City Board of Education. She truly enjoys working with young people.

Jocelyne Daniel (M.A. City College of the City University of New York) is a teacher of bilingual/Haitian Créole Social Studies in Spring Valley High School of the East Ramapo Central School District, Spring Valley, New York. She believes that language goes with the rhythm of one's heart and one's identity, and she is dedicated to the teaching of languages.

Jamie B. Draper (M.S. Georgetown University) is a consultant to the American Council on the Teaching of Foreign Languages.

John Figueroa (M.A. Hunter College of the City University of New York) is a teacher of Spanish at Roslyn High School in Roslyn, New York. He is also a doctoral degree candidate at the Graduate Center of the City University of New York. John has always worked to get to know all of his students well and to make his classroom a place where his students can feel at home.

Maria C. Giacone (M.A. Queens College) is Director of Professional Development for the New York City Board of Education. She also holds a Professional Diploma in Administration and Supervision from Hunter College.

Vincent Giangreco (M.A. Hunter College of the City University of New York) is Adjunct Professor in the English Department of the John Jay College of Criminal Justice of the City University of New York and an instructor in the International English Language Institute at Hunter College of the City University of New York. Vinnie is also a jazz guitarist who has lived and worked as a musician in Europe.

Maria Hahn-Thomson (B.A. Baruch College of the City University of New York) is a teacher of Spanish at the Bayard Rustin High School for the Humanities of the New York City Board of Education. Maria is also preparing a Masters Degree as a reading specialist at Brooklyn College. She is happy to always have the opportunity to learn from her students.

June H. Hicks (B.A. Manhattanville College) is Member Liaison at the American Council on the Teaching of Foreign Languages.

Adriana L. Macera-Aloia (M.S.Ed. Iona College) is a teacher of Spanish and Italian at West Lake High School in Thornwood, New York. She has traveled many times to Spanish-speaking countries with her students.

Cynthia McCallister (Ed.D. University of Maine) is Assistant Professor in the Department of Teaching and Learning at New York University. She teaches courses in language and literacy education, supervises student teachers, and is active in staff development projects.

Carmen Mercado (Ph.D. Fordham University) is Associate Professor in the Department of Curriculum and Teaching of Hunter College of the City University of New York. Carmen has been engaged in collaborative action research with teachers, students, and families locating and applying sociocultural resources within Latino communities to create educational equity and excellence for all learners.

Barbara L. Miller (Ph.D. New York University) is Chairperson of the English and Communication and Theater Department at Hunter College High School and Adjunct Associate Professor in the Department of Curriculum and Teaching at Hunter College of the City University of New York. Throughout her thirty-year career in education, her students have taught her what it means to be a teacher who learns and a learner who teaches.

Jean Mirvil (M.Ed. Bank Street College, M.A. Queens College) is Principal of P.S. 116 of the New York City Board of Education. He hopes that because of his many years as a classroom teacher and his work as an administrator, he will be able to help others to a better job with future learners.

Andrew Parker (M.A. Hunter College, M.A. State University of New York at Buffalo) teaches English as a Second Language in the Adult Learning Center of the Queens Borough Library System in New York City.

Migdalia Romero (Ph.D. New York University) is Professor of applied linguistics in the Department of Curriculum and Teaching at Hunter College of the City University of New York. Her thirty-year career has been dedicated to bilingual education.

Jacqueline Rizk (B.A. State University of New York at Brockport) is a Human Resources Generalist with Citigroup in New York City. She is deeply appreciative of everything that her parents have given her to enrich her life culturally.

Diana Scalera (M.S. New York Institute of Technology) is a teacher of Spanish and video production at the High School for Environmental Studies of the New York City Board of Education. She is also a foreign language methods instructor at Hunter College of the City University of New York. Diana is the daughter of heritage language learners of Italian and dedicates her contributions to this book to her parents.

Claire E. Sylvan (Ed.D. Teachers College) is a teacher of humanities and a member of the School Leadership Team at International High School: A Charter School at LaGuardia Community College in Long Island City, New York. She has developed programs of native language instruction and taught a wide range of courses to heritage language learners.

Guadalupe Valdés (Ph.D. Florida State University) is Professor of Education and Professor of Spanish and Portuguese at Stanford University. She works in the area of applied linguistics. Her research is focused on the English-Spanish bilingualism of Latinos in the United States.

Dora Villani (M.A. Hunter College of the City University of New York) is a teacher of Spanish and Curriculum Leader at Ardsley High School in Ardsley, New York. She loves to teach and always has.

John B. Webb (Ed.D. New York University) is Director of the Program in Teacher Preparation at Princeton University. While working on the FIPSE Grant Project, he was chairperson of the Foreign Language Department of Hunter College High School and Adjunct Associate Professor in the Department of Curriculum and Teaching at Hunter College of the City University of New York.

The Cover:
True Energy
Oil on wood relief
48" by 42" by 14"
Artist: Carlo Thertus

―――•-•―――

Statement by the Artist

True Energy was created through an experimentation of translation of sound and communication.

In September 1998, during an opening for the children of C.A.S.K. (Creative Art Space for Kids, Inc.), Ms. McGlorin was playing the cello, and her father was playing the violin. They were speaking to each other with their instruments. Their combination of sound, harmony, and the children's positive energy filled the gallery.

I personally felt so good that I said to myself, "This is true energy!" Right there, I wanted to translate Ms. McGlorin's and her father's artistic expression of this beautiful sound of music to a different language of visual art.

Through this experimentation, I have learned one of the greatest lessons in life— that every human being has much good to offer one another. If one can cultivate positively from one another, it doesn't matter what part of the world he or she may come from. Just imagine what makes America a great country.

I was born and raised in Haiti, and my culture is very different from that of Ms. McGlorin and her father. Since I was a little boy, my passion for music has always been of hard beats: bongos, congas, and such.

My point is that by allowing ourselves to cultivate from one another, the benefits will be tremendous. I experienced this myself in the creation of *True Energy*. I translated the language of sound to a visual language.

Language is the most important human gift: Hebrew, Chinese, Japanese, Italian, Spanish, Créole, French, English, Russian, Hindi, drawing, painting, sculpting, dancing, acting, singing, sign language. It doesn't matter which one we use, because each one allows us to express ourselves. Self-expression is the greatest of human gifts.

– Carlo Thertus, August 2000
www.cask.org
www.gofindart.com

Index